ALCOOLS

ALCOOLS

Guillaume Apollinaire

Translated by ANNE HYDE GREET

With a Foreword by WARREN RAMSEY

UNIVERSITY OF CALIFORNIA PRESS · BERKELEY
AND LOS ANGELES

To my parents

University of California Press
Berkeley and Los Angeles

© 1965 by The Regents of the University of California

Second Printing, 1974
ISBN: 0-520-00029-3

Library of Congress Catalog Card Number: 65-20148

Printed in the United States
of America

Foreword

Un soir de demi-brume à Londres
Un voyou qui ressemblait à
Mon amour vint à ma rencontre
Et le regard qu'il me jeta
Me fit baisser les yeux de honte

More than a half-century has passed since the manuscript beginning with these lines was fished out of limbo, read and read again, and a dazzled magazine editor called across the room that here, at last, was a first-rate poem. A reader of the sixties might find other terms in which to express his approval, though some of Paul Léautaud's are still serviceable: "I read, read twice, three times, was carried away, dazed, delighted, deeply moved. Such melancholy, such evocative tone, such bohemianism, such rangings of the mind, and that faintly gypsy air and the total absence of that abomination of ordinary verse, *la rime riche* . . ."[1] Whatever the language of criticism, the unchanging fact is that "La Chanson du Mal-Aimé," like others of Apollinaire's poems translated with distinction in this book, still has all its power to stir enthusiasm.

Guillaume Apollinaire, as Wilhelm-Apollinaris de Kostrowitski called himself by 1909, when Léautaud forced a long-postponed decision concerning "La Chanson du Mal-Aimé" at the *Mercure de France*, was already well known to fellow-craftsmen of the little magazines and to avant-garde painters. He was also familiar to artistic gatherings where he was regarded primarily as a character, to publishing houses for which he did

[1] Paul Léautaud, "La Chanson du Mal-Aimé," *Le Flâneur des Deux Rives* (March, 1954), p. 7.

hackwork of various kinds, as well as to a number of European capitals and gambling resorts whose ambiguous offspring he seemed to be. Born twenty-nine years before in Rome, he was not the son of an eminent prelate, though both "Kostro" and Picasso were fond of intimating as much, but of an Italian army officer who never officially acknowledged his existence, and a Polish lady of many passions, the most enduring of which drove her tirelessly from casino to casino. Wilhelm, the elder of her two sons, had attended religious schools in Monaco and Cannes, and public high school in Nice. He had sought to integrate the scattered strands of unsettling experience by bouts of schoolboy piety, by huge doses of unsystematic reading, by febrile love affairs in Paris, in the Ardennes, in the Rhineland and London, and by much writing of verse. Partly because it was composed in acquired French by a young man who obviously knew the German Romantics well, partly because the author would have had a good deal of sheer verbalizing capacity in any language, that verse had attracted attention. But the French literary mind is capable of granting generous recognition on some levels, while withholding it on others. In the earliest years of the century it was probably impossible to tell whether young Kostrowitski was just another promising literary man with several languages and a gift for pastiche, or—in an age which requires a fresh vision of the world from its artists (as Guillaume Apollinaire was to declare with some insistence)—an authentic poet.

Even as first published in that distant spring of 1909 (when it lacked two stanzas of the Zaparogian Cossacks' horrendous letter and, unlike the more characteristic final version, was punctuated), "La Chanson du Mal-Aimé" has the authority of the more mature Apollinaire, the vibrancy of a modern poet speaking in his own voice. It was another four years before he published his first real collection of poems, *Alcools*, for *Le Bestiaire ou Cortège d'Orphée* (1911), graceful badinage and woodcuts by Dufy notwithstanding, is insubstantial. The poet engaged himself in such activities as critic of literature, critic of

art, and polemist and theorist for Cubism, all with such zeal that he was sometimes lost sight of in the *animateur*. The First World War and a head wound may have been the only possible catalyzers of a second major collection, *Calligrammes* (1918). Behind the picturesque comings and goings of Apollinaire the man, however, lay sure accomplishment. The critical conscience of a time had recognized a poet.

Before coming to what was new in Apollinaire, it is well to recall what was delicately old, and what was indicative, too, of a verbal power without which experimentation would have been futile. Since Anne Greet included a version of "Nuit rhénane" in her own book of poems, *Spring Eclogue* (1961), one may suppose that this was a growing-point in her development, as in Apollinaire's. The poem is a skillful dislocation, akin to Heine's, of folk song mood and material.[2] Farther on in this volume "Nuit rhénane" can be read both in final form and in English. Here it is as first published, complete with periods, commas, and date line from the Rhineland where Apollinaire met Annie Playden:

Mon verre est plein d'un vin trembleur comme une flamme.
Écoutez la chanson lente d'un batelier
Qui raconte avoir vu, sous la lune, sept femmes
Tordre leurs cheveux verts et longs jusqu'à leurs pieds.

Debout, chantez plus haut en dansant une ronde,
Que je n'entende plus le chant du batelier,
Et mettez près de moi toutes les filles blondes
Au regard immobile, aux nattes repliées.

Le Rhin, le Rhin est ivre, où les vignes se mirent.
Tout l'or des nuits tombe, en tremblant, s'y refléter.

[2] See Pierre Orecchioni, *Le Thème du Rhin dans l'Inspiration de Guillaume Apollinaire* (Paris: Lettres Modernes, 1956), esp. Chapter II, "Le Volkslied Rhénan et son influence sur Apollinaire."

La voix chante toujours, à en râle-mourir,
Ces fées aux cheveux verts qui incantent l'été.

Mon verre s'est brisé comme un éclat de rire.

Honnef, mai 1902[3]

If the nasalized vowels of the opening lines do not "crackle," as Apollinaire thought they should,[4] at least they have their effect of lingering out the line, and "flamme" makes them all but flare and flicker. The first line of the second quatrain is sufficiently dancelike, nasals again providing the emphases. With its attenuating subjunctive leading into the negative "plus," the next verse virtually confronts presence with absence. It is easy to imagine an echo reverberating down the valley with the emphatic first syllable of "batelier."

As in many a ballade, witches emerging from water suggest depths of the psyche. And since this is Apollinaire, with his penchant for the magical, they are seven. As with Heine and other Romantic ironists, the ending jars with a "tone of voice" dominant till then. River mists dissolve, undines vanish, and the reader is hauled ashore by the mention of laughter, on whose human connections Bergson had recently insisted. Incidentally, it should be noted that the ending comes off every bit as well in Anne Greet's English:

My glass has shattered like a burst of laughter

Here, as throughout, these translations attest an indispensable quality: a certain reluctance to swing on the ancient iambic seesaw of English, an easiness on the downbeat. It would be hard to say how the translator arrives at

[3] Michel Décaudin, *Le Dossier d' "Alcools"* (Geneva: Droz, 1960), p. 178.
[4] "Laissez pétiller un son nasal et continu" from "Victoire," quoted by LeRoy C. Breunig, "The Chronology of Apollinaire's *Alcools*," *PMLA*, LXVII (December, 1952), 907.

Up dancers form a ring sing louder
Drown out the boatman's song

French has a living subjunctive to trail away with

Que je n'entende plus le chant du batelier

But anything half as involved in English would have been wrong. Toned-down imperatives and retarding monosyllables let the sound fade in an English way.

The Rhineland poems, which Apollinaire thought of publishing separately before finally incorporating them into *Alcools*, are not all manipulated folk songs. The performing animals shown jogging along the bank in one are more meaningful than those of *Le Bestiaire*, which had been fanciful creatures or mere transposed human beings, objects of wit and irony. Charged with a deeper symbolism, the gypsies' bear, monkey, dog, and donkey in "Mai" add another dimension to the carnival theme as an analogy for the human predicament. They offer glimmers of awareness different from the human, more "open," as Rilke would have said, and D. H. Lawrence would have thought.

There is another kind of poem in *Alcools*, less finished than "Nuit rhénane," and more promising, prophetic of the direction Apollinaire's poetry was to take. Such is "La Dame," where an allegorical image is wrested from experience no longer literary. Such is "La Porte," where a symbol of a modern kind acquires that *lacune*, that marked-out circumambient space an object often has in a Braque painting of the Cubist period. "La Porte" had begun with some conversational fumbling. Most of that was left out, and the completed poem stands cleanly and strongly outlined, a work of art existing in space as well as in time:

La porte de l'hôtel sourit terriblement
Qu'est-ce que cela peut me faire ô ma maman
D'être cet employé pour qui seul rien n'existe
Pi-mus couples allant dans la profonde eau triste

Anges frais débarqués à Marseille hier matin
J'entends mourir et remourir un chant lointain
Humble comme je suis qui ne suis rien qui vaille

Enfant je t'ai donné ce que j'avais travaille

The hotel door smiles its terrible smile
What can it mean to me my mother
To be that clerk for whom alone nothing exists
Pi-mus fish coupled in the deep sad water
Fresh angels disembarked at Marseille yesterday morning
I hear a distant song that dies over and over
Humble as I am who am nothing worthwhile

Child I gave you what I had now labor

More than once, over these pages, the American reader will
find himself thinking of Hart Crane, who also read Apollinaire,
even though Crane said that, being a resident of Cleveland,
Ohio, he did not feel obliged to take the modern machinery of
Paris quite as seriously as Apollinaire did.[5] Here, as in Crane's
poetry, one will find doors, black swollen gates, bridges, mar-
riages of Faustus and Helen, and all the perils of strong emotion.

[5] "All this talk from Matty on Apollinaire," he wrote Munson, "about
being gay and *so* distressingly and painfully delighted about the tele-
graph, the locomotive, the automat, the wireless, the street cars and elec-
tric lamp posts, annoys me. There is no reason for *not* using them—but
why is it so important to stick them in. I am interested in possibilities.
Apollinaire lived in Paris, I live in Cleveland, Ohio. These quotidian
conveniences so dear to him are not of especial pleasure to me here. I am
not going to pity myself—but, on the other hand, why should I stretch
my face continually into a kind of 'glad' expression. Besides,—sadness
(you will shrink in horror at this) has a real and lasting appeal to me."
Philip Horton, *Hart Crane* (Compass edition, 1957), p. 104.

Thus, in the above poem, "sad, deep water" and one meaning of
anges ("angelfish") effectively suggest the viscous, as they were
meant to do. They could also have swamped the poem. Distanc-
ing is achieved by one of those scraps of curious lore with which
Apollinaire's verse is crammed. The pi-mus fish of Chinese leg-
end swim in couples so closely joined that the same pair of eyes
serves both creatures. The lines devoted to the pi-mus fish re-
main exactly central to the poem as it exists in time, when read
aloud. Meanwhile in the process of revision, the word *tout* was
replaced by *rien*, poetically more sophisticated, etymologically
suggesting "something" as well as "nothing." The last line is
dropped well below the others typographically: the poet is al-
ready concerned with the problems of arrangement in space
that he was to pursue further in the ideographic word-pictures
of *Calligrammes*. Clipped emphasis in this second poetic voice
signifies rejection, as the preceding lines suggest some obcure
search for the opposite. The door, a characteristic image, is ordi-
narily closed, here, as at the beginning of "Le Voyageur," and
elsewhere. But the poet's main problem, that of isolating an
episode from immediate experience and lending it objectivity,
has been solved.[6]

Alcools is a remarkably ambitious book. Like the title itself,
the longer and later poems show how much the author wanted
to get into it: nothing less than the whole burden of poetic en-
thusiasm as expressed by Plato in the *Ion*. Apollinaire is inviting
his readers to be drunken—on the spiritual air of Nietzschean
high places. Better prepared and more resilient than Crane, if
somewhat less intensely imaginative, Apollinaire came equally
close to voicing the affirmations of a time. The mode is the
psychological notation of the Rimbaldian Symbolists:

Actions belles journées sommeils terribles

[6] See Marie-Jeanne Durry, *Guillaume Apollinaire: Alcools*, Tome
I (Paris: Société d'édition d'enseignement supérieur, 1956).

Végétation Accouplements musiques éternelles
Mouvements Adorations douleur divine
Mondes qui vous ressemblez et qui nous ressemblez
Je vous ai bus et ne fus pas désaltéré

Mais je connus dès lors quelle saveur a l'univers

Je suis ivre d'avoir bu tout l'univers
Sur le quai d'où je voyais l'onde couler et dormir les bélandres

 Deeds fine days uneasy sleep
 Vegetation Couplings eternal music
 Motion Worship divine sorrow
 Worlds that resemble us and yourselves
 Though I have drained you I am thirsty still

 But I know the savor of the universe

 I reel on universe
 Along the quai where I saw waves flow and barges rock

Apollinaire cannot be said to have realized some revolutionary or Futurist dream of *pensers nouveaux* in verse. Such a task lay beyond even his capacities, and it was open to his misgivings. There is something heroically outsize about "Vendémiaire," with its debt to Whitman and the poetic mode that was being called Hegelian at about this time. Parts of the poem are a trifle too praiseful and all-encompassing to be quite convincing, except as a bold rhetorical conclusion to an important book. They suggest a kind of poetry Apollinaire might have written had he been a complete Cubo-Futurist. He was not, and we have the brief masterpieces, rather lower pitched.

A number of these are to be found in *Alcools*. Among the Romantic lyrics are "Cors de Chasse" and "Automne malade."

"La Tzigane" and "Saltimbanques" renew late nineteenth-century themes in a way endlessly stimulating to twentieth-century readers and writers. "Marizibill" is another of the brief episodic poems finding the symmetries of a dramatic lyric. Its title, a sort of inspired exercise in phonetic spelling, brings the poem closer to the time and place of its conception by the change of a few letters (from "Marie-Sybille"). Here too, growing out of prison desolation, the end of the love affair with Marie Laurencin, and a medieval *chanson de toile*, is "Le Pont Mirabeau."

Equally to the poetic point are longer episodic poems. An early one, "Le Larron," with its Chorus, Thief, Old Man, and Actor, is an incipient parable play. Apollinaire is best remembered, however, for two other lines of development. Episodes are sometimes connected by a conceit, as in "Le Brasier"[7] or "Les Fiançailles." The poet elaborates on the theme of casting previous selves into the crucible, toward discovery of an authentic self. Or he loafs and invites his soul to reconciliation with fully apprehended objects:

> J'observe le repos du dimanche
> Et je loue la paresse
> Comment comment réduire
> L'infiniment petite science
> Que m'imposent mes sens

("Les Fiançailles")

> I observe the Sunday calm
> And praise indolence
> How how to reduce
> The infinitely little knowledge
> That my senses impose upon me

[7] On the thematic content of the poem see Robert Champigny, "Le Temps chez Apollinaire," *PMLA*, LXVII (March, 1952), esp. pp. 9, 10.

The less concerted development of this poem permits anticipations of "Zone." We find:

> J'ai eu le courage de regarder en arrière
> Les cadavres de mes jours
> Marquent ma route et je les pleure
> Les uns pourrissent dans les églises italiennes
> Ou bien dans de petits bois de citronniers
> Qui fleurissent et fructifient

> I have been brave enough to look back
> The corpses of my days
> Dot my journey and I mourn them
> Some rot in Italian churches
> Or in little lemon groves
> That flower and bear fruit

Within the segments of "Les Fiançailles," more freely associated than those of "Le Brasier," within the loose grouping of verses and the single line, there is characteristic contrast between fresh imagery and familiar rhythm. There are moments when the alexandrine seems to have been discovered all over again:

> Une Madone à l'aube a pris les églantines
> Elle viendra demain cueillir les giroflées

Amid such near *bel canto* comes the image like "eyelids":

> Au petit bois de citronniers s'énamourèrent
> D'amour que nous aimons les dernières venues
> Les villages lointains sont comme leurs paupières
> Et parmi les citrons leurs cœurs sont suspendus

In the little lemon grove there fell in love
With love that we love the latest dove comers
Like their eyelids are towns in the distance
And among the lemons their hearts are swaying

This is the Apollinaire who haunted Léon-Paul Fargue:

En face du tunnel où se cache la fée
De l'aube qui demain vendra ses madeleines
Sur un quai somnolent tout mouillé de rosée
Dans le bruit du tambour, dans le bruit de la mer

("La Gare")

Not the least of Apollinaire's functions was that of reminding other poets of the traditional resources of French verse. His poetry has its "Vergers," a little like those of Rilke's French verse, reflecting devotion to past periods and styles. Into those green hereditary precincts he introduced objects sometimes rich and strange, almost invariably curious and interesting. "Paupières," above, is compact with the poetic future. It is not the inevitable word within its pattern; but it anticipates the Surrealist reshuffling to come.

"Zone," the rather hurriedly prefixed poetic preface to Apollinaire's book, caused excitement from Prague to San Francisco and can still do so. This is all the more remarkable because it is compounded of several well-known poetic styles, not even excluding a few lines in the manner of Charles Péguy. The second verse signals the paradoxical clash of tone and imagery:

Bergère ô tour Eiffel le troupeau des ponts bêle ce matin

Mallarmé, the conscience of two or three poetic generations, had observed mildly that the Eiffel Tower surpassed his expectations. In the manner of his followers, the leser Symbolists, Apollinaire had written, among other poems, "Merlin et la vieille Femme."

His predecessors would not, in short, have acknowledged the existence of the modern technological clutter. That might be a fit subject for the spiritual offspring of M. Homais, or perhaps for a strident school of painters who had already provoked the discriminating protest of James Joyce. But to take Marinetti and his crew seriously, to turn a World's Fair monument into a symbol helping to shepherd the significant experiences of a life-time—that was definitely a brave act of Futurist faith.

"Zone" and other late poems grapple determinedly with features of the modern landscape, however remote and magical the world preceding the Great War may now appear. Here the poetic result is achieved by letting objects hang suspended in the blue distance of a pastoral. Baudelaire, whose modern reputation Apollinaire the critic would do much to establish,[8] had shown the way. But Apollinaire's *églogues de la cité* go much further. And it is chiefly in its paradoxically pastoral tone that "Zone" differs from a work which it resembles and possibly owes to, Blaise Cendrars' "Pâques à New-York."[9] The modern malaise of the latter poem is without letup. "Zone" is less insistent.

Further on, the flocks return, as "troupeaux d'autobus" this time. And the "I" of the poem surveys a line of previous selves fixed in idealized attitudes. There is the pious infant in blue and white, the figure of idealized friendship, the devout adolescent. There is the young man on the Riviera, under blossoming lemon trees:

> Sous les citronniers qui sont en fleur toute l'année
> Avec tes amis tu te promènes en barque

> Under lemon trees that flower the year long
> You take ship with friends

[8] See Apollinaire, *Introduction à l'œuvre poétique de Baudelaire,* 1917.

[9] See Durry, *op. cit.,* pp. 234-258.

His situation in Prague is hardly less idyllic:

Tu te sens tout heureux une rose est sur la table

and he climbs the Hradchen at night to listen to folk songs in
the cabarets. In Marseilles he is surrounded by stacks of water-
melons, in Coblenz he stays at a larger-than-life hotel, in Rome
he is installed under an exotic tree, in Amsterdam he is accom-
panied by a young woman less beautiful than he imagines her.
Such scenes alternate with moments of pathetic immediacy,
among them the glimpse of the refugees—a bit uncannily pro-
phetic, as passages in Apollinaire have a way of being—clutch-
ing the red coverlet, the homely relic of no value and great con-
sequence.

Forms of the comic familiar to pastoral are here: wit in the
likening of Christ to an aviator, humor in the following lines
bringing in fabled magicians, sardonic comment behind

Tu te moques de toi et comme le feu de l'Enfer ton rire
pétille[10]

and satire in the sketches of the derelicts. Meanwhile

La cétoine qui dort dans le cœur de la rose

offers the irony of death and decay characteristically undercutting
the pastoral situation.

The fetishes from Africa and the Pacific islands appearing
toward the end of the poem have considerable aesthetic interest,
because Apollinaire's enthusiasm for such works helped shape
twentieth-century taste. But they have none of the disquieting

[10] Breunig, in "The Laughter of Apollinaire," *Yale French Studies*,
No. 31 (1964), would associate this and other passages with the Sur-
realist conception of "dark humor," and with the absurdist theater.

power of the religious symbols in Baudelaire's poetry: the su-
perego, to use a term of that Freudian day, is neither looming
nor censorious. Like Milton before him, Baudelaire tested the
limits of pastoral even as he gave it unusual flexibility. Urgently
felt contrast between the everyday and the ideal, the actually
perceived and the imagined, are usually absent from this check-
ered shade. The nostalgic, on the other hand, the stylized pa-
thetic, the wittily and even the grotesquely comic—these are
marks of pastoral as they are of "Zone" and long stretches of
verse in Apollinaire's lesser collections.

This is not to explain away or even necessarily to touch the
profounder characteristics of Apollinaire the man. If the reader
has not already done so he is likely, after reading *Alcools*, to go
on exploring this poetic mind, one of the richest and most re-
sponsive of our century, through several collections of verse and
highly organized prose. The "I" of "Zone," the first person
colloquizing there with two forms of the second person, must
bear some relation to the poet's ego. The "je" of "Zone," how-
ever, is curiously abstract, poetically unformed, unlike the "tu"
and "vous" cast in their recognizable aesthetic molds. Perhaps
the poet most nearly did justice to the depth and complexity of
the "je" in brief episodes where he felt under no constraint to
establish connections. But that is merely an opinion, and the
reader must look for his own Apollinaire, as divided and mys-
terious as the times he wrote for, beginning with the collection
that gives him the amplest perspectives.

Meanwhile it seems fitting to note that *Alcools* or a work re-
sembling it might conceivably have been written in English in
the first place. If circumstances had been only a little different,
if Wilhelm Apollinaris de Kostrowitski had found Annie Play-
den less unrelenting, if, in short, she had consented to marry
him instead of going off to Texas to escape. . . . Then this
record of the fluctuations of the modern mind might have been
composed in the language elected by another Pole, Jozef Kon-
rad Korzeniowski. Kostrowitski was pursuing Annie furiously
in 1901 and 1902. A Pole not much over twenty, *connaissant*

plusieurs langages, as he would confess in "La Jolie Rousse," with embarrassing Slavic ease, would have made the transition readily. It is a question whether Annie would ever have made a gentleman of him, but she would pretty certainly have got him to speaking English.

Even as things stand there is real resemblance between an image of London appearing in certain of Conrad's works— which, under slightly different circumstances, might have been written in French—and certain poems and parts of poems by Apollinaire. Almost as aptly as others are called "Rhénanes," these might be entitled, say, "Inscriptions Anglaises." And they have a direct, lived-out immediacy from which Apollinaire's verse always benefits.

It may be objected that a rather gloomy view of London shines through "L'Émigrant de Landor Road" and "La Chanson du Mal-Aimé." But the same might be said of *The Secret Agent* and other examples of Conrad's English realism. For both Apollinaire and Conrad, grimy bricks and blood-drenched fog (*brouillard sanguinolent*) suggest the wild side of *any* city. They evoke even as they screen what Henry James, another expatriate who never really fitted in, sensed as going on beneath the vast smug surface of things. London is required to provide concrete images from which the mysterious, and even the sinister, may develop. This is a little unfair to London, but it is only one side of a penny, the whole coin standing for that fascination with things English that did so much to shape French literary expression during the early years of the century.

The fluid octosyllabics of Apollinaire's first really notable poem, "La Chanson du Mal-Aimé," cover bewildering variety, yet the theme is the well-tried one of striving after the absolute. This finds its statement in imagery having the drained-white hue familiar from Melville and other American writers, as well as the poets whom Apollinaire knew:

> *Voie lactée ô sœur lumineuse*
> *Des blancs ruisseaux de Chanaan*

Et des corps blancs des amoureuses
Nageurs morts suivrons-nous d'ahan
Ton cours vers d'autres nébuleuses

Milky way luminous sister
Of Canaan's white streams
And white flesh of loving women
Shall we dead swimmers follow gasping
Your course toward other nebulae

This stanza thirteen, repeated as stanza twenty-seven after the Cossacks' song and as stanza forty-nine after the episode of the seven swords, becomes the triple pier of an Apollinairean bridge. Imagery of whiteness is persistent. In stanza thirty-two it appears as

Ma colombe ma blanche rade

My dove my white harbor

Lest we dissociate the Absolute from evil, either in *Moby Dick* or here, there is

Malheur dieu pâle aux yeux d'ivoire

Unhappiness pale god with ivory eyes

of stanza thirty-five. Three stanzas further on:

L'hiver est mort tout enneigé
On a brulé les ruches blanches

Winter is dead all hidden with snow
They have burned the white bee-hives

and in the following stanza:

> Mort d'immortels argyraspides
> La neige aux boucliers d'argent

> Death of deathless argyraspids
> The snow with silver shields

The first of the swords is silver-white:

> La première est toute d'argent
> Et son nom tremblant c'est Pâline
> Sa lame un ciel d'hiver neigeant

> The first is all of silver
> And its trembling name is Pensive
> Its blade is a snowy sky of winter

And perhaps most of all like a thawed-out Mallarmé:

> Sur un lac blanc et sous l'haleine
> Des vents qui tremblent au printemps
> Voguait cygne mourant sirène

> Across a white lake breathed on
> By winds trembling in springtime
> Sailed a swan a dying siren

of stanza fifty-three.

The Romantic and Symbolist theme of quest thus intensely presented is relieved by the three-stanza pastoral interlude beginning "C'est le printemps vient-t'en Pâquette" and by comic passages in the vein of Alfred Jarry, especially the three stanzas of Cossack invective. This theme receives its resolution, anticlimactic in the classical and technical sense, in the final stanzas

telling of returning to a Paris rattling with streetcars and fiery with those new flowers, "les roses de l'électricité"[11] (as they are called in "Les Fiançailles").

"La Chanson du Mal-Aimé" is a far-ranging poem, but nothing contributes more to its vitality than the bold beginning in a murky London. Just as "those grimy brick houses which existed in large quantities before the era of reconstruction dawned upon London" and the meanness of Mr. Verloc's little shop open out toward violent drama to follow in *The Secret Agent*, giving it footing in everyday reality, so do early stanzas of this poem lend density to what might otherwise have been thin and rarefied. To recall only a few lines more beyond the ones placed at the beginning of this Introduction:

> *Je suivis ce mauvais garçon*
> *Qui sifflotait mains dans les poches*
> *Nous semblions entre les maisons*
> *Onde ouverte de la mer Rouge*
> *Lui les Hébreux moi Pharaon*

> *Que tombent ces vagues de briques*
> *Si tu ne fus pas bien aimée*
> *Je suis le souverain d'Égypte*
> *Sa sœur-épouse son armée*
> *Si tu n'es pas l'amour unique*

> *Au tournant d'une rue brûlant*
> *De tous les feux de ses façades*
> *Plaies du brouillard sanguinolent*
> *Où se lamentaient les façades*
> *Une femme lui ressemblant*

[11] For the poet's appreciation of modern technology, see Anna Balakian, "Apollinaire and the Modern Mind," *Yale French Studies*, Vol. II, No. 2 (1949), 79-90.

C'était son regard d'inhumaine
La cicatrice à son cou nu
Sortit saoule d'une taverne
Au moment où je reconnus
La fausseté de l'amour même

I followed that lawless boy
Whistling his hands thrust in his pockets
Between the houses
Gaping Red Sea waters
I was Pharaoh he the Hebrews

May these brick waves clatter down
If I did not love you well
I am Egypt's sovereign lord
His sister-queen his army
If you are not my only love

At a street corner burning
With all the lamps of its windows
Wounds in the bloody fog
There where windows lamented
A woman resembling her

She had the self-same cruel stare
And scar upon her bare neck
Staggered out from a tavern
Just then I perceived
Love's duplicity

London street urchin, fleeing Israelites, drunken woman reeling from the pub—all these are likened to Annie, as she is identified with *l'amour unique* and, finally, with the unattainable Absolute. The pursuer is at once Pharaoh, his sister-wife, and

his army. So many analogous figures for hunter and quarry, swiftly and freely associated, bring us well along the way toward the "everything always present," the multidimensional time of modern art. Apollinaire was to discuss this in his own terms as the *simultanéisme* of the Cubo-Futurists, holding the artist responsible for more facets of an object, presented in a single aesthetic perception, than could be grasped in an instant of chronological time.[12]

The closeness of the bond between the Egyptian monarch and his queen recalls the "mon enfant, ma sœur" and similar images of the beloved in the poetry of Baudelaire, as of Poe and the Pre-Raphaelites. The same close bond looks forward toward the mystical reconciliation, the resolved antinomies, of Surrealism. Passage and poem are further strengthened by the hint of the arcane, the element of strangeness called for by several modern poetics having little else in common.

Of fundamental importance, too, is the *coloring* of the passage. In the first place, the pervasive color imagery sets it off sharply from later passages relating to the Absolute, where whiteness is the rule. Secondly, the color red, named or suggested by a red object in many stanzas, stands for human vitality and movement, as in the poetry of Wallace Stevens. Finally, the whole exploration of orders of reality is grounded on vividly noted particularities of a modern city.

Mr. Verloc of *The Secret Agent* walks off toward Chesham Square in the morning sun "against which nothing could be said except that it looked bloodshot." Apollinaire being to a rare degree the poet of both sides of the penny, of two roads traveled at once, of multidimensional time, it is possible to think of him writing in English the celebrated metaphor for the bloodshot morning sun at the end of "Zone." He was also the theorist of the two ways supposedly hardest to navigate: that of "poetry"

[12] On the temporal dimensions of Cubist art, see Roger Shattuck, *Guillaume Apollinaire, Selected Writings* (New York: New Directions, 1950), esp. sections V-VII of the Introduction.

and that of "truth," the imaginary and the real, the invented and the raw residue of fact. "The plastic virtues: purity, unity and truth," he wrote, apropos of the Cubists. The Symbolists before him had paid due heed to the cathartic and unitive values of the creative process. For them, too, purity and unity were plastic virtues. They had, however, and here Paul Valéry was to follow them, minimized the mimetic function of art. Apollinaire is still the poet who has stated most forcefully the twentieth-century view that art is also a search for truth, a lever of discovery, adding like other cognitive acts to the sum of what is known.

The "false windows," as Valéry called them, remain—the lines and masses added or adding themselves, for balance, helping to order experience in the work of art. But they exist only by virtue of their opposition to the real windows, as heresies, we are told, have only the life they borrow from a parent faith. Without real windows the simulated ones do not exist.

Thus we can never forget that Apollinaire was in fact, as well as in poetic fiction, the "ill-loved"[13]—less, it is true, by an English girl who chanced to be in the Rhineland one summer, or by some archetypal figure that failed to stand forward in the rose garden, than, at all the decisive points, by society in the persons of its immediate representatives. Unacknowledged son, following the wanderings of his mother and "uncle"; over-polite tutor in a polite household; bank clerk and author of potboilers on a variety of subjects, acquiring in no other way the literary competence that made him useful to the painters, enabling him to transcend what his friends called the strain of weakness in his character—the wonder is that he did nothing more drastic than

[13] See Marcel Adéma, *Guillaume Apollinaire, le mal-aimé*, 1952, esp. pp. 69 ff., 141, 142; André Rouveyre, *Apollinaire* (Paris: Gallimard, 1945), esp. pp. 263-268; Francis Steegmuller, *Apollinaire, Poet among the Painters* (New York: Farrar, Strauss, 1963); Roger Shattuck, *The Banquet Years: The Arts in France* (New York: Harcourt, Brace, 1958).

run off from Stavelot without paying the hotel bill or become inconclusively involved in the removal of art objects from the Louvre.

"Zone," that well-rounded work developing between two morning suns, favoring the *recorso* form as the title suggests, also refers through its title to an area beyond the city limits of Paris given over, in Apollinaire's day, to derelicts and their hovels. Apollinaire had good reason to be acquainted with the "zone," the outer margin of society. He was not one of us Dostoevsky readers who can mutter with a pleasant shiver, "There but for the grace of God go I." Born and brought up outside the conventions, he was easily compromised. After his brief imprisonment in La Santé, which shook him seriously, he might readily have drifted beyond the limits of conventional society. Instead, a little like Dostoevsky after the Siberian exile, he took to identifying somewhat uncritically, enthusiastically, with contradictory manifestations and values of the society in which he found himself. We may call this his Futurism. Or we may call it a quest for identity culminating in his war service—as cavalryman, then, by his own wish, as infantryman—his head wound and his death from Spanish influenza. It makes, in any case, for one of the meaningful personal histories in the tangled, dark-brown-spotted web of twentieth-century events. It makes for poetry representing, if not quite the highest pitch of artistic accomplishment, something close to it, and for the triumph of a temperament.

WARREN RAMSEY

Berkeley, California
September, 1964

Acknowledgments

I owe a special debt of gratitude to Professor Judd Hubert of the University of Illinois, who read the entire manuscript, for his tactful and illuminating suggestions and constant encouragement. This same debt I owe Professor Warren Ramsey of Berkeley who gave me the benefit of his knowledge and imaginative insights and who encouraged me to write the notes to the poems.

Other acknowledgments go to those who read and criticized some of these translations at various times in the past eight years: Louise Bogan, LeRoy C. Breunig, Pierre Delattre, William Maxwell, and my parents; to Robert Y. Zachary, of the University of California Press, who kept me working; to three French scholars whom I know only through their invaluable books on Apollinaire: Michel Décaudin, Madame Marie-Jeanne Durry, and Marcel Adéma.

A. H. G.

1964

This new printing contains a number of emendations to the translations, many of them inspired by the generous criticism of Professor Scott Bates of the University of Sewanee and Professor S. I. Lockerbie of the University of Stirling.

A. H. G.

1973

Table des Matières Contents

TABLE DES MATIÈRES CONTENTS

R JAUDON.

Zone

A la fin tu es las de ce monde ancien

Bergère ô tour Eiffel le troupeau des ponts bêle ce matin

Tu en as assez de vivre dans l'antiquité grecque et romaine

Ici même les automobiles ont l'air d'être anciennes
La religion seule est restée toute neuve la religion
Est restée simple comme les hangars de Port-Aviation

Seul en Europe tu n'es pas antique ô Christianisme
L'Européen le plus moderne c'est vous Pape Pie X
Et toi que les fenêtres observent la honte te retient
D'entrer dans une église et de t'y confesser ce matin
Tu lis les prospectus les catalogues les affiches qui chantent tout
 haut
Voilà la poésie ce matin et pour la prose il y a les journaux
Il y a les livraisons à 25 centimes pleins d'aventures policières
Portraits des grands hommes et mille titres divers

J'ai vu ce matin une jolie rue dont j'ai oublié le nom
Neuve et propre du soleil elle était le clairon
Les directeurs les ouvriers et les belles sténo-dactylographes
Du lundi matin au samedi soir quatre fois par jour y passent
Le matin par trois fois la sirène y gémit
Une cloche rageuse y aboie vers midi
Les inscriptions des enseignes et des murailles
Les plaques les avis à la façon des perroquets criaillent

Zone

You are weary at last of this ancient world

Shepherdess O Eiffel tower whose flock of bridges bleats at the
 morning

You have lived long enough with Greek and Roman antiquity

Here even automobiles look old
Only religion stays new religion
As simple as hangars at the airfield

Alone in Europe you Christianity are not antique
The one modern European is you Pope Pius X
And you whom windows watch what shame keeps you
From entering a church and confessing your sins this morning
Handbills catalogues advertisements that sing aloud
Furnish your morning's poetry and for prose there are news-
 papers
Dime detective novels packed with adventure
Biographies of great men a thousand and one titles

This morning I saw a fine street whose name slips my mind
New and bright the sun's clarion
Where executives and workers sweet stenographers
Hurry every weekday dawn and dusk
Three times a morning sirens groan
A choleric bell barks at noon
Lettering on billboards and walls
Doorplates and posters twitter like parakeets

3

J'aime la grâce de cette rue industrielle
Située à Paris entre la rue Aumont-Thiéville et l'avenue des
 Ternes

Voilà la jeune rue et tu n'es encore qu'un petit enfant
Ta mère ne t'habille que de bleu et de blanc
Tu es très pieux et avec le plus ancien de tes camarades René
 Dalize
Vous n'aimez rien tant que les pompes de l'Église
Il est neuf heures le gaz est baissé tout bleu vous sortez du dortoir
 en cachette
Vous priez toute la nuit dans la chapelle du collège
Tandis qu'éternelle et adorable profondeur améthyste
Tourne à jamais la flamboyante gloire du Christ
C'est le beau lys que tous nous cultivons
C'est la torche aux cheveux roux que n'éteint pas le vent
C'est le fils pâle et vermeil de la douloureuse mère
C'est l'arbre toujours touffu de toutes les prières
C'est la double potence de l'honneur et de l'éternité
C'est l'étoile à six branches
C'est Dieu qui meurt le vendredi et ressuscite le dimanche
C'est le Christ qui monte au ciel mieux que les aviateurs
Il détient le record du monde pour la hauteur

Pupille Christ de l'œil
Vingtième pupille des siècles il sait y faire
Et changé en oiseau ce siècle comme Jésus monte dans l'air
Les diables dans les abîmes lèvent la tête pour le regarder
Ils disent qu'il imite Simon Mage en Judée
Ils crient s'il sait voler qu'on l'appelle voleur
Les anges voltigent autour du joli voltigeur
Icare Énoch Élie Apollonius de Thyane
Flottent autour du premier aéroplane
Ils s'écartent parfois pour laisser passer ceux que transporte la
 Sainte-Eucharistie
Ces prêtres qui montent éternellement élevant l'hostie

There is charm to this Paris factory street
Between rue Aumont-Thiéville and the avenue des Ternes

Here is the young street and you still a baby
Dressed by your mother only in blue and white
A pious child and with your oldest friend René Dalize
You like nothing so much as church ceremonies
Nine o'clock the gas turns blue you slip out of bed
To pray all night in the school chapel
While an eternal adorable amethyst depth
Christ's flaming halo revolves forever
He is the lovely lily we all worship
He is the red-haired torch no wind may blow out
Pale and scarlet son of the sorrowful mother
Tree hung with prayer
Twofold gallows of honor and eternity
Six-pointed star
God who dies Friday and rises on Sunday
Christ who flies higher than the aviators
And holds the world's record

Christ pupil of the eye
Twentieth pupil of the centuries he knows his business
And changed to a bird this century ascends like Jesus
Devils in hell raise their heads to stare
They say it imitates Simon Magus in Judea
They say if it lifts to call it a lifter
Angels fly past the graceful trapeze artist
Icarus Enoch Elijah Apollonius of Tyana
Hover near the original airplane
Or give place to those whom the Eucharist elevates
Priests rising continuously as they raise the Host

L'avion se pose enfin sans refermer les ailes
Le ciel s'emplit alors de millions d'hirondelles
A tire-d'aile viennent les corbeaux les faucons les hiboux
D'Afrique arrivent les ibis les flamants les marabouts
L'oiseau Roc célébré par les conteurs et les poètes
Plane tenant dans les serres le crâne d'Adam la première tête
L'aigle fond de l'horizon en poussant un grand cri
Et d'Amérique vient le petit colibri
De Chine sont venus les pihis longs et souples
Qui n'ont qu'une seule aile et qui volent par couples
Puis voici la colombe esprit immaculé
Qu'escortent l'oiseau-lyre et le paon ocellé
Le phénix ce bucher qui soi-même s'engendre
Un instant voile tout de son ardente cendre
Les sirènes laissant les périlleux détroits
Arrivent en chantant bellement toutes trois
Et tous aigle phénix et pihis de la Chine
Fraternisent avec la volante machine

Maintenant tu marches dans Paris tout seul parmi la foule
Des troupeaux d'autobus mugissants près de toi roulent
L'angoisse de l'amour te serre le gosier
Comme si tu ne devais jamais plus être aimé
Si tu vivais dans l'ancien temps tu entrerais dans un monastère
Vous avez honte quand vous vous surprenez à dire une prière
Tu te moques de toi et comme le feu de l'Enfer ton rire pétille
Les étincelles de ton rire dorent le fond de ta vie
C'est un tableau pendu dans un sombre musée
Et quelquefois tu vas le regarder de près

Aujourd'hui tu marches dans Paris les femmes sont ensanglantées
C'était et je voudrais ne pas m'en souvenir c'était au déclin de la
 beauté

Entourée de flammes ferventes Notre-Dame m'a regardé à
 Chartres

At last the plane lands with wings outspread
Through heaven come flying a million swallows
At full speed crows owls falcons
Ibises flamingoes storks from Africa
Roc so celebrated in song and story
Clutching Adam's skull the original head
Eagle from the horizon pounces screaming
Hummingbird arrives from America
From China long supple pihis
Who have only one wing and fly in couples
Here comes the dove immaculate spirit
Escorted by lyrebird and ocellated peacock
That funeral pyre the phoenix engendering himself
Momentarily veils all with his ardent ash
Sirens quit their perilous perches
And arrive each singing beautifully
Everyone eagle phoenix pihis
Fraternizes with the flying machine

Now you stride alone through the Paris crowds
Busses in bellowing herds roll by
Anguish clutches your throat
As if you would never again be loved
In the old days you would have turned monk
With shame you catch yourself praying
Or jeer and your laughter crackles like hellfire
Its sparks gild the depths of your life
Which like a painting in a dark museum
You approach sometimes to peer at closely

Today you stroll through Paris the women are bloodstained
It was as I would rather forget it was during beauty's decline

From fervent flames Our Lady gazed down on me in Chartres

Le sang de votre Sacré-Cœur m'a inondé à Montmartre
Je suis malade d'ouïr les paroles bienheureuses
L'amour dont je souffre est une maladie honteuse
Et l'image qui te possède te fait survivre dans l'insomnie et dans
 l'angoisse
C'est toujours près de toi cette image qui passe

Maintenant tu es au bord de la Méditerranée
Sous les citronniers qui sont en fleur toute l'année
Avec tes amis tu te promènes en barque
L'un est Nissard il y a un Mentonasque et deux Turbiasques
Nous regardons avec effroi les poulpes des profondeurs
Et parmi les algues nagent les poissons images du Sauveur

Tu es dans le jardin d'une auberge aux environs de Prague
Tu te sens tout heureux une rose est sur la table
Et tu observes au lieu d'écrire ton conte en prose
La cétoine qui dort dans le cœur de la rose

Épouvanté tu te vois dessiné dans les agates de Saint-Vit
Tu étais triste à mourir le jour où tu t'y vis
Tu ressembles au Lazare affolé par le jour
Les aiguilles de l'horloge du quartier juif vont à rebours
Et tu recules aussi dans ta vie lentement
En montant au Hradchin et le soir en écoutant
Dans les tavernes chanter des chansons tchèques

Te voici à Marseille au milieu des pastèques

Te voici à Coblence a l'hotel du Géant

Te voici à Rome assis sous un néflier du Japon

Te voici à Amsterdam avec une jeune fille que tu trouves belle et
 qui est laide
Elle doit se marier avec un étudiant de Leyde

Your Sacred Heart's blood drowned me in Montmartre
I am sick of hearing blessed words
My love is a shameful disease
You are sleepless anguished but possessed by an image
Which hovers never distant

Now you are by the Mediterranean
Under lemon trees that flower the year long
You take ship with friends
One from Nice one from Menton two from La Turbie
Terrified we see in the depths giant squid
And fish the Saviour's symbols gliding through seaweed

You are in a tavern garden near Prague
You feel happy instead of writing your stories in prose
To stare at a rose on the table and
A rosebug alseep in the rose's heart

Aghast you trace your likeness in the agates at Saint Vitus
And that day almost died of grief to see yourself portrayed
As Lazarus distracted by daylight
The hands of the ghetto clock run backward
You also creep slowly backward through life
Climbing to the Hradchen listening at twilight
To Czech songs from the taverns

You in Marseilles among piles of watermelons

You in Coblenz at the Giant's hotel

In Rome sitting under a Japanese medlar tree

In Amsterdam with a girl you find pretty but who is ugly
And engaged to a student from Leyden

On y loue des chambres en latin Cubicula locanda
Je m'en souviens j'y ai passé trois jours et autant à Gouda

Tu es à Paris chez le juge d'instruction
Comme un criminel on te met en état d'arrestation

Tu as fait de douloureux et de joyeux voyages
Avant de t'apercevoir du mensonge et de l'âge
Tu as souffert de l'amour à vingt et à trente ans
J'ai vécu comme un fou et j'ai perdu mon temps
Tu n'oses plus regarder tes mains et à tous moments je voudrais
 sangloter
Sur toi sur celle que j'aime sur tout ce qui t'a épouvanté

Tu regardes les yeux pleins de larmes ces pauvres émigrants
Ils croient en Dieu ils prient les femmes allaitent des enfants
Ils emplissent de leur odeur le hall de la gare Saint-Lazare
Ils ont foi dans leur étoile comme les rois-mages
Ils espèrent gagner de l'argent dans l'Argentine
Et revenir dans leur pays après avoir fait fortune
Une famille transporte un édredon rouge comme vous trans-
 portez votre cœur
Cet édredon et nos rêves sont aussi irréels
Quelques-uns de ces émigrants restent ici et se logent
Rue des Rosiers ou rue des Écouffes dans des bouges
Je les ai vus souvent le soir ils prennent l'air dans la rue
Et se déplacent rarement comme les pièces aux échecs
Il y a surtout des Juifs leurs femmes portent perruque
Elles restent assises exsangues au fond des boutiques

Tu es debout devant le zinc d'un bar crapuleux
Tu prends un café à deux sous parmi les malheureux

Tu es la nuit dans un grand restaurant

One can rent rooms there in Latin Cubicula locanda
I remember three days there and three at Gouda

You are in Paris arraigned before the judge
Arrested like a criminal

You went on sad and merry journeys
Before growing aware of lies and old age
Love made you unhappy at twenty again at thirty
I have lived like a fool and wasted my youth
You no longer dare examine your hands and at any moment I
 could weep
Over you over her whom I love over all that has fright-
 ened you

With tears in your eyes you see the shabby refugees
Who have faith in God and pray the mothers nurse their
 children
Their smell fills the waiting room at the *gare* St. Lazare
Like the three kings they believe in a star
Hoping to strike it rich in Argentina
And return home wealthy
One family carries a crimson quilt as you your heart
Quilt and our dreams are equally unreal
Some of these refugees stay on and lodge
In slums on the rue des Rosiers or the rue des Écouffes
I have seen them often out walking at dusk
They keep close to home like chessmen
And are mostly Jewish their wives wear wigs
Pallid they sit at the back of little shops

You stand at the counter of a dirty bar
Taking a café for two *sous* among the wretched

You are in a huge restaurant at night

Ces femmes ne sont pas méchantes elles ont des soucis cependant
Toutes même la plus laide a fait souffrir son amant

Elle est la fille d'un sergent de ville de Jersey

Ses mains que je n'avais pas vues sont dures et gercées

J'ai une pitié immense pour les coutures de son ventre

J'humilie maintenant à une pauvre fille au rire horrible ma
 bouche

Tu es seul le matin va venir
Les laitiers font tinter leurs bidons dans les rues

La nuit s'éloigne ainsi qu'une belle Métive
C'est Ferdine la fausse ou Léa l'attentive

Et tu bois cet alcool brûlant comme ta vie
Ta vie que tu bois comme une eau-de-vie

Tu marches vers Auteuil tu veux aller chez toi à pied
Dormir parmi tes fétiches d'Océanie et de Guinée
Ils sont des Christ d'une autre forme et d'une autre croyance
Ce sont les Christ inférieurs des obscures espérances

Adieu Adieu

Soleil cou coupé

These women are not evil only careworn
Each has tortured her lover even the ugliest

Who is the daughter of a policeman on the Isle of Jersey

Her hands which I had not noticed are calloused and cracked

Pity fills me for the scars on her belly

Now I humble my mouth to a poor creature with a horrible laugh

You are alone morning comes
Milkmen clink bottles along the street

Night leaves like a lovely Métive
Ferdine the false or watchful Lea

You sip a liquor as burning as your life
Your life you drain like an *eau-de-vie*

And stride home to Auteuil
To sleep among your fetishes from Oceania or Guinea
Other forms of Christ and other faiths
Lesser Christs of dim aspirations

Farewell Farewell

Sun slit throat

Le Pont Mirabeau

Sous le pont Mirabeau coule la Seine
 Et nos amours
 Faut-il qu'il m'en souvienne
La joie venait toujours après la peine

 Vienne la nuit sonne l'heure
 Les jours s'en vont je demeure

Les mains dans les mains restons face à face
 Tandis que sous
 Le pont de nos bras passe
Des éternels regards l'onde si lasse

 Vienne la nuit sonne l'heure
 Les jours s'en vont je demeure

L'amour s'en va comme cette eau courante
 L'amour s'en va
 Comme la vie est lente
Et comme l'Espérance est violente

 Vienne la nuit sonne l'heure
 Les jours s'en vont je demeure

Passent les jours et passent les semaines
 Ni temps passé
 Ni les amours reviennent
Sous le pont Mirabeau coule la Seine

 Vienne la nuit sonne l'heure
 Les jours s'en vont je demeure

Mirabeau Bridge

Past Mirabeau bridge flows the Seine
 And our love
 Must I remember
Joy followed always after pain

 Let night come sound the hour
 Time draws in I remain

Hand in hand let us stay face to face
 While past the
 Bridge of our embrace
Flows one long look's weary wave

 Let night come sound the hour
 Time draws in I remain

Love creeps by like the flowing tide
 Love slips by
 How slow is life and
Expectation how violent

 Let night come sound the hour
 Time draws in I remain

Days creep by and the weeks creep by
 Neither past
 Time nor loves return
Past Mirabeau bridge flows the Seine

 Let night come sound the hour
 Time draws in I remain

La Chanson du Mal-Aimé

à Paul Léautaud

Et je chantais cette romance
En 1903 sans savoir
Que mon amour à la semblance
Du beau Phénix s'il meurt un soir
Le matin voit sa renaissance.

Un soir de demi-brume à Londres
Un voyou qui ressemblait à
Mon amour vint à ma rencontre
Et le regard qu'il me jeta
Me fit baisser les yeux de honte

Je suivis ce mauvais garçon
Qui sifflotait mains dans les poches
Nous semblions entre les maisons
Onde ouverte de la mer Rouge
Lui les Hébreux moi Pharaon

Que tombent ces vagues de briques
Si tu ne fus pas bien aimée
Je suis le souverain d'Égypte
Sa sœur-épouse son armée
Si tu n'es pas l'amour unique

Au tournant d'une rue brûlant
De tous les feux de ses façades
Plaies du brouillard sanguinolent
Où se lamentaient les façades
Une femme lui ressemblant

The Song of the Poorly Loved

to Paul Léautaud

And I sang this air
In 1903 unaware
That if my love resembling
The fair Phoenix dies one evening
Morning sees it born anew

One misty dusk in London
A hoodlum resembling
My love came to meet me
And the look that he flung me
Made me lower my eyes in shame

I followed that lawless boy
Whistling his hands thrust in his pockets
Between the houses
Gaping Red Sea waters
I was Pharaoh he the Hebrews

May these brick waves clatter down
If I did not love you well
I am Egypt's sovereign lord
His sister-queen his army
If you are not my only love

At a street corner burning
With all the lamps of its windows
Wounds in the bloody fog
There where windows lamented
A woman resembling her

C'était son regard d'inhumaine
La cicatrice à son cou nu
Sortit saoule d'une taverne
Au moment où je reconnus
La fausseté de l'amour même

Lorsqu'il fut de retour enfin
Dans sa patrie le sage Ulysse
Son vieux chien de lui se souvint
Près d'un tapis de haute lisse
Sa femme attendait qu'il revînt

L'époux royal de Sacontale
Las de vaincre se réjouit
Quand il la retrouva plus pâle
D'attente et d'amour yeux pâlis
Caressant sa gazelle mâle

J'ai pensé à ces rois heureux
Lorsque le faux amour et celle
Dont je suis encore amoureux
Heurtant leurs ombres infidèles
Me rendirent si malheureux

Regrets sur quoi l'enfer se fonde
Qu'un ciel d'oubli s'ouvre à mes vœux
Pour son baiser les rois du monde
Seraient morts les pauvres fameux
Pour elle eussent vendu leur ombre

J'ai hiverné dans mon passé
Revienne le soleil de Pâques
Pour chauffer un cœur plus glacé
Que les quarante de Sébaste
Moins que ma vie martyrisés

She had the self-same cruel stare
And scar upon her bare neck
Staggered out from a tavern
Just then I perceived
Love's duplicity

When at last good Ulysses
Returned to his own land
His ancient hound remembered him
Near a tapestry thick and fine
His wife waited his coming

Shakuntala's royal husband
Tired of victories rejoiced
To find she had grown pale
With waiting her eyes dim with love
As she fondled her male gazelle

I thought of those happy kings
When love's counterfeit and she
I still am enamored of
Clashed their faithless shadows
And made me so unhappy

Regrets hell builds upon
Let lethean skies engulf my vows
For one kiss the kings of earth
Had died those renowned poor
For her had sold their shadows

I have been wintering in my past
Return again Easter sun
And warm a heart more frozen
Than the forty of Sebaste
Who were less tortured than my life

Mon beau navire ô ma mémoire
Avons-nous assez navigué
Dans une onde mauvaise à boire
Avons-nous assez divagué
De la belle aube au triste soir

Adieu faux amour confondu
Avec la femme qui s'éloigne
Avec celle que j'ai perdue
L'année dernière en Allemagne
Et que je ne reverrai plus

Voie lactée ô sœur lumineuse
Des blancs ruisseaux de Chanaan
Et des corps blancs des amoureuses
Nageurs morts suivrons-nous d'ahan
Ton cours vers d'autres nébuleuses

Je me souviens d'une autre année
C'était l'aube d'un jour d'avril
J'ai chanté ma joie bien-aimée
Chanté l'amour à voix virile
Au moment d'amour de l'année

AUBADE
CHANTÉE A LÆTARE UN AN PASSÉ

C'est le printemps viens-t'en Pâquette
Te promener au bois joli
Les poules dans la cour caquètent
L'aube au ciel fait de roses plis
L'amour chemine à ta conquête

Mars et Vénus sont revenus

My fair ship my memory
Have we sailed long enough
Seas too bitter for drinking
Have we rambled far enough
From fair dawn to sad twilight

Farewell false love whom I mistook
For the woman who is leaving me
The woman whom I lost
Last year in Germany
And shall not see again

Milky way luminous sister
Of Canaan's white streams
And white flesh of loving women
Shall we dead swimmers follow gasping
Your course toward other nebulae

I remember a different year
The dawn of an April day
I sang my darling joy
Sang love with a manly voice
Just at the year's hour of love

AUBADE

SUNG AT LÆTARE A YEAR AGO

Spring is here come away Pâquette
And wander in the charming groves
Hens cackle in the courtyard
Dawn in the sky makes rosy folds
Love moves toward your undoing

Mars and Venus have returned

Ils s'embrassent à bouches folles
Devant des sites ingénus
Où sous les roses qui feuillolent
De beaux dieux roses dansent nus

Viens ma tendresse est la régente
De la floraison qui paraît
La nature est belle et touchante
Pan sifflote dans la forêt
Les grenouilles humides chantent

Beaucoup de ces dieux ont péri
C'est sur eux que pleurent les saules
Le grand Pan l'amour Jésus-Christ
Sont bien morts et les chats miaulent
Dans la cour je pleure à Paris

Moi qui sais des lais pour les reines
Les complaintes de mes années
Des hymnes d'esclave aux murènes
La romance du mal aimé
Et des chansons pour les sirènes

L'amour est mort j'en suis tremblant
J'adore de belles idoles
Les souvenirs lui ressemblant
Comme la femme de Mausole
Je reste fidèle et dolent

To embrace with maddened lips
Before ingenuous landscapes
Where beneath leafy roses
Fair rosy gods dance naked

Come for my tenderness is queen
Of the present flowering
Nature is fair and touching
Pan whistles in the forest
The moist frogs sing

Many of those gods have died
It is for them the willows weep
Great Pan Love Jesus Christ
Are all quite dead and tomcats howl
In the alley I weep in Paris

I who know praises for queens
The laments of my youth
Hymns of slaves to the moray
The ballad of the unhappy lover
And songs for sirens

Love is dead yet I tremble
And dote upon fair images
Memories that resemble her
Like the wife of King Mausolus
I remain true and grieving

Je suis fidèle comme un dogue
Au maître le lierre au tronc
Et les Cosaques Zaporogues
Ivrognes pieux et larrons
Aux steppes et au décalogue

Portez comme un joug le Croissant
Qu'interrogent les astrologues
Je suis le Sultan tout-puissant
O mes Cosaques Zaporogues
Votre Seigneur éblouissant

Devenez mes sujets fidèles
Leur avait écrit le Sultan
Ils rirent à cette nouvelle
Et répondirent à l'instant
A la lueur d'une chandelle

RÉPONSE DES COSAQUES ZAPOROGUES
AU SULTAN DE CONSTANTINOPLE

Plus criminel que Barrabas
Cornu comme les mauvais anges
Quel Belzébuth es-tu là-bas
Nourri d'immondice et de fange
Nous n'irons pas à tes sabbats

Poisson pourri de Salonique
Long collier des sommeils affreux
D'yeux arrachés à coup de pique

THE SONG OF THE POORLY LOVED

True as a mastiff
To his master ivy to the tree
And as the Zaporogian Cossacks
Devout drunkards and thieves
To the steppes and decalogue

Carry like a yoke that Crescent
Which astrologers consult
I am sultan omnipotent
O my Zaporogian Cossacks
I am your dazzling lord

Become my faithful subjects
The Sultan had written them
They laughed when they read the news
And answered on the spot
By candlelight

REPLY OF THE ZAPOROGIAN COSSACKS
TO THE SULTAN OF CONSTANTINOPLE

More villainous than Barabbas
Horned like the wicked angels
What Beelzebub are you yonder
Nourished on refuse and on mire
We'll not attend your revels

Rotten fish of Salonika
Long necklace of awful nightmares
Of eyes bunged out and spitted

Ta mère fit un pet foireux
Et tu naquis de sa colique

Bourreau de Podolie Amant
Des plaies des ulcères des croûtes
Groin de cochon cul de jument
Tes richesses garde-les toutes
Pour payer tes médicaments

Voie lactée ô sœur lumineuse
Des blancs ruisseaux de Chanaan
Et des corps blancs des amoureuses
Nageurs morts suivrons-nous d'ahan
Ton cours vers d'autres nébuleuses

Regret des yeux de la putain
Et belle comme une panthère
Amour vos baisers florentins
Avaient une saveur amère
Qui a rebuté nos destins

Ses regards laissaient une traîne
D'étoiles dans les soirs tremblants
Dans ses yeux nageaient les sirènes
Et nos baisers mordus sanglants
Faisaient pleurer nos fées marraines

Mais en vérité je l'attends
Avec mon cœur avec mon âme
Et sur le pont des Reviens-t'en
Si jamais revient cette femme
Je lui dirai Je suis content

THE SONG OF THE POORLY LOVED

Your mother let a leaky fart
And you were son of her colic

Hangman of Podolia Lover
Of wounds of scabs and ulcers
Pig snout mare's ass
Keep your riches you'll need them all
To pay the pharmacist

Milky way luminous sister
Of Canaan's white streams
And white flesh of loving women
Shall we dead swimmers follow gasping
Your course toward other nebulae

Sorrowful as a whore's eyes
And gorgeous as a panther
Your Florentine kisses my love
Had a sour savor
Disheartening to our fates

Her glances left a train of
Stars across the trembling eves
In her eyes the sirens swam
And our kisses that raged and bled
Grieved our fairy godmothers

Yet verily I wait for her
In my heart in my soul
And on the bridge of Turn again
If ever that woman turns again
I shall tell her I am content

Mon cœur et ma tête se vident
Tout le ciel s'écoule par eux
O mes tonneaux des Danaïdes
Comment faire pour être heureux
Comme un petit enfant candide

Je ne veux jamais l'oublier
Ma colombe ma blanche rade
O marguerite exfoliée
Mon île au loin ma Désirade
Ma rose mon giroflier

Les satyres et les pyraustes
Les égypans les feux follets
Et les destins damnés ou faustes
La corde au cou comme à Calais
Sur ma douleur quel holocauste

Douleur qui doubles les destins
La licorne et le capricorne
Mon âme et mon corps incertain
Te fuient ô bûcher divin qu'ornent
Des astres des fleurs du matin

Malheur dieu pâle aux yeux d'ivoire
Tes prêtres fous t'ont-ils paré
Tes victimes en robe noire
Ont-elles vainement pleuré
Malheur dieu qu'il ne faut pas croire

Et toi qui me suis en rampant
Dieu de mes dieux morts en automne
Tu mesures combien d'empans
J'ai droit que la terre me donne
O mon ombre ô mon vieux serpent

My heart and head grow empty
All heaven is flowing out through them
O my casks of the Danaïdes
How may I find happiness
Like a small guileless child

Never shall I forget her
My dove my white harbor
O daisy stripped of leaves
My far isle my Désirade
My rose my tree of cloves

Satyrs and Pyraustas
Aegipans will-o'-the-wisps
Damned or faustes destinies
Neck in a noose as at Calais
Upon my grief what holocaust

Grief that doubles destinies
The unicorn the capricorn
My soul and my uncertain flesh
Flee from you divine funeral pyre
Adorned with stars with morning's flowers

Unhappiness pale god with ivory eyes
Have your mad priests adorned you
Have your victims in black robes
Vainly mourned
Unhappiness whom none should take on trust

And you who trail after me
God of my gods all dead in autumn
You measure how much dust
Is rightly mine
My shadow my ancient snake

Au soleil parce que tu l'aimes
Je t'ai menée souviens-t'en bien
Ténébreuse épouse que j'aime
Tu es à moi en n'étant rien
O mon ombre en deuil de moi-même

L'hiver est mort tout enneigé
On a brûlé les ruches blanches
Dans les jardins et les vergers
Les oiseaux chantent sur les branches
Le printemps clair l'avril léger

Mort d'immortels argyraspides
La neige aux boucliers d'argent
Fuit les dendrophores livides
Du printemps cher aux pauvres gens
Qui resourient les yeux humides

Et moi j'ai le cœur aussi gros
Qu'un cul de dame damascène
O mon amour je t'aimais trop
Et maintenant j'ai trop de peine
Les sept épées hors du fourreau

Sept épées de mélancolie
Sans morfil ô claires douleurs
Sont dans mon cœur et la folie
Veut raisonner pour mon malheur
Comment voulez-vous que j'oublie

LES SEPT ÉPÉES

La première est toute d'argent
Et son nom tremblant c'est Pâline

Into the sunlight which you crave
I led you remember well
Shadowy wife that I love
You are mine and you are nil
My shadow that mourns for me

Winter is dead all hidden with snow
They have burned the white bee-hives
In gardens and in orchards
Birds sing from every bough
Bright springtime light April

Death of deathless argyraspids
The snow with silver shields
Flees those pallid dendrophori
Of springtime dear to poor folk
Who smile once more with brimming eyes

And me I have a heart as heavy
As a Damascus lady's arse
I loved you O my love too well
And now I suffer too much pain
The seven swords are out of their sheaths

Seven swords of melancholy
Needing no edge O bright griefs
Stick in my heart while folly
Would harp on my unhappiness
How can you bid me forget

THE SEVEN SWORDS

The first is all of silver
And its trembling name is Pensive

Sa lame un ciel d'hiver neigeant
Son destin sanglant gibeline
Vulcain mourut en la forgeant

La seconde nommée Noubosse
Est un bel arc-en-ciel joyeux
Les dieux s'en servent à leurs noces
Elle a tué trente Bé-Rieux
Et fut douée par Carabosse

La troisième bleu féminin
N'en est pas moins un chibriape
Appelé Lul de Faltenin
Et que porte sur une nappe
L'Hermès Ernest devenu nain

La quatrième Malourène
Est un fleuve vert et doré
C'est le soir quand les riveraines
Y baignent leurs corps adorés
Et des chants de rameurs s'y traînent

La cinquième Sainte-Fabeau
C'est la plus belle des quenouilles
C'est un cyprès sur un tombeau
Où les quatre vents s'agenouillent
Et chaque nuit c'est un flambeau

La sixième métal de gloire
C'est l'ami aux si douces mains
Dont chaque matin nous sépare
Adieu voilà votre chemin
Les coqs s'épuisaient en fanfares

Et la septième s'exténue
Une femme une rose morte

Its blade is a snowy sky of winter
Its bloody fate is Ghibelline
Vulcan died while forging it

The second named Gay Blade
Is a fair joyous rainbow
Gods wield it at their weddings
It has killed thirty musketeers
And was dowered by Carabosse

The third of womanish blue
Is not the less a cypriape
Named Puck of Faltenin
And carried on a cloth
By Ernest Hermes become a dwarf

The fourth Milady
Is a green and gold river
Where shore-dwelling girls at twilight
Bathe their loved bodies
And songs of oarsmen hover

The fifth Saint-Faggot
Is the fairest of distaffs
A cypress upon a tomb
Where the four winds kneel
And a torch by night

The sixth Excalibur
Is the friend with such sweet hands
From whom each morning parts us
Farewell yonder lies your road
Now cocks weary on their fanfares

And the seventh languishes
A woman a dead rose

Merci que le dernier venu
Sur mon amour ferme la porte
Je ne vous ai jamais connue

Voie lactée ô sœur lumineuse
Des blancs ruisseaux de Chanaan
Et des corps blancs des amoureuses
Nageurs morts suivrons-nous d'ahan
Ton cours vers d'autres nébuleuses

Les démons du hasard selon
Le chant du firmament nous mènent
A sons perdus leurs violons
Font danser notre race humaine
Sur la descente à reculons

Destins destins impénétrables
Rois secoués par la folie
Et ces grelottantes étoiles
De fausses femmes dans vos lits
Aux déserts que l'histoire accable

Luitpold le vieux prince régent
Tuteur de deux royautés folles
Sanglote-t-il en y songeant
Quand vacillent les lucioles
Mouches dorées de la Saint-Jean

Près d'un château sans châtelaine
La barque aux barcarols chantants
Sur un lac blanc et sous l'haleine
Des vents qui tremblent au printemps
Voguait cygne mourant sirène

Thank heaven that the latest comer
Shuts the door upon my love
Nay I have never known you

Milky way luminous sister
Of Canaan's white streams
And white flesh of loving women
Shall we dead swimmers follow gasping
Your course toward other nebulae

The heavens declare
That devils of gambling guide us
To lost music their violins
Make mortals dance
Backwards down the hill

Fates unfathomable fates
Kings shaken by folly
And those shivering stars
False women sharing your beds
Among deserts leveled by history

Luitpold the old prince regent
Tutor of two mad kings
Does he weep remembering them
When glowworms waver
Gilt flies of Midsummer Eve

Near a manor without a lady
The barque with tuneful barcaroles
Across a white lake breathed on
By winds trembling in springtime
Sailed a swan a dying siren

Un jour le roi dans l'eau d'argent
Se noya puis la bouche ouverte
Il s'en revint en surnageant
Sur la rive dormir inerte
Face tournée au ciel changeant

Juin ton soleil ardente lyre
Brûle mes doigts endoloris
Triste et mélodieux délire
J'erre à travers mon beau Paris
Sans avoir le cœur d'y mourir

Les dimanches s'y éternisent
Et les orgues de Barbarie
Y sanglotent dans les cours grises
Les fleurs aux balcons de Paris
Penchent comme la tour de Pise

Soirs de Paris ivres du gin
Flambant de l'électricité
Les tramways feux verts sur l'échine
Musiquent au long des portées
De rails leur folie de machines

Les cafés gonflés de fumée
Crient tout l'amour de leurs tziganes
De tous leurs siphons enrhumés
De leurs garçons vêtus d'un pagne
Vers toi toi que j'ai tant aimée

Moi qui sais des lais pour les reines
Les complaintes de mes années
Des hymnes d'esclave aux murènes
La romance du mal aimé
Et des chansons pour les sirènes

THE SONG OF THE POORLY LOVED

One day the king drowned himself
In the silver pool then floated upward
With gaping mouth and reached once more
The shore to slumber there quietly
His face turned toward a changing sky

June your sun's flaming lyre
Burns my aching fingers
Sad melodious madness
Through my fair Paris I wander
Without the heart to die

Here Sundays last forever
Organs of Barbary
Sob in gray courtyards
Flowers on Paris balconies
Lean like Pisa's tower

Paris nights are drunk with gin
And blaze with electricity
Green fires flashing along their spines
Tramways up and down their rails
Shed tunes of mechanical folly

Cafés swollen with smoke
Cry their gypsy loves
From syphons with dripping noses
Waiters with loincloth aprons
Toward you you whom I adored

I who know praises for queens
The laments of my youth
Hymns of slaves to the moray
The ballad of the poorly loved
And songs for sirens

Les Colchiques

Le pré est vénéneux mais joli en automne
Les vaches y paissant
Lentement s'empoisonnent
Le colchique couleur de cerne et de lilas
Y fleurit tes yeux sont comme cette fleur-là
Violâtres comme leur cerne et comme cet automne
Et ma vie pour tes yeux lentement s'empoisonne

Les enfants de l'école viennent avec fracas
Vêtus de hoquetons et jouant de l'harmonica
Ils cueillent les colchiques qui sont comme des mères
Filles de leurs filles et sont couleur de tes paupières
Qui battent comme les fleurs battent au vent dément

Le gardien du troupeau chante tout doucement
Tandis que lentes et meuglant les vaches abandonnent
Pour toujours ce grand pré mal fleuri par l'automne

The Crocuses

The meadow is deadly though fair in autumn
Cows grazing there
Slowly are poisoned
There crocuses color of eye-ring color of lilac
Bloom your eyes like these flowers
Like their rings and like autumn are violet
My life from your eyes slowly takes poison

School children noisily come
Wearing jackets playing harmonicas
To pick crocuses that are like mothers
Daughters of their daughters they are color of your eyelids
Fluttering like flowers in a crazy wind

Softly the cowherd sings
While cows slow and lowing abandon
Forever meadows so evilly flowered by autumn

Palais

à Max Jacob

Vers le palais de Rosemonde au fond du Rêve
Mes rêveuses pensées pieds nus vont en soirée
Le palais don du roi comme un roi nu s'élève
Des chairs fouettées des roses de la roseraie

On voit venir au fond du jardin mes pensées
Qui sourient du concert joué par les grenouilles
Elles ont envie des cyprès grandes quenouilles
Et le soleil miroir des roses s'est brisé

Le stigmate sanglant des mains contre les vitres
Quel archer mal blessé du couchant le troua
La résine qui rend amer le vin de Chypre
Ma bouche aux agapes d'agneau blanc l'éprouva

Sur les genoux pointus du monarque adultère
Sur le mai de son âge et sur son trente et un
Madame Rosemonde roule avec mystère
Ses petits yeux tout ronds pareils aux yeux des Huns

Dame de mes pensées au cul de perle fine
Dont ni perle ni cul n'égale l'orient
Qui donc attendez-vous
De rêveuses pensées en marche à l'Orient
Mes plus belles voisines

Toc toc Entrez dans l'antichambre le jour baisse
La veilleuse dans l'ombre est un bijou d'or cuit
Pendez vos têtes aux patères par les tresses
Le ciel presque nocturne a des lueurs d'aiguilles

Palace

to Max Jacob

Toward Rosemonde's palace in the depth of Dream
My reveries go barefoot to spend the evening
A king's gift the palace like a naked king rises
Flogged flesh or roses from the rose garden

See my thoughts advancing in the depth of the garden
They smile at the concert performed by frogs
They fancy the cypresses tall distaffs
And the sun mirror of roses is broken

What archer sore wounded by sunset has pierced
The bleeding stigmata of hands against the windows
My mouth at the love-feasts of white lamb has tasted
The resin embittering Cyprian wine

Perched on the adulterous king's pointed knees
In the May of her age and in her best finery
Madame Rosemonde with an air of mystery
Rolls little round eyes like the eyes of Huns

Lady of my thoughts with ass of fine pearl
Neither pearl nor ass can the Orient rival
For whom then are you waiting
Reveries walking toward the Orient
Loveliest of my neighbors

Tap tap Come into the hallway day draws in
The night-light in the shadows is a gem of baked gold
Hang your heads on the hatpegs by their tresses
The sky nearly nocturnal glimmers with needles

On entra dans la salle à manger les narines
Reniflaient une odeur de graisse et de graillon
On eut vingt potages dont trois couleurs d'urine
Et le roi prit deux œufs pochés dans du bouillon

Puis les marmitons apportèrent les viandes
Des rôtis de pensées mortes dans mon cerveau
Mes beaux rêves mort-nés en tranches bien saignantes
Et mes souvenirs faisandés en godiveaux

Or ces pensées mortes depuis des millénaires
Avaient le fade goût des grands mammouths gelés
Les os ou songe-creux venaient des ossuaires
En danse macabre aux plis de mon cervelet

Et tous ces mets criaient des choses nonpareilles
 Mais nom de Dieu!
 Ventre affamé n'a pas d'oreilles
Et les convives mastiquaient à qui mieux mieux

Ah! nom de Dieu! qu'ont donc crié ces entrecôtes
Ces grands pâtés ces os à moelle et mirotons
Langues de feu où sont-elles mes pentecôtes
Pour mes pensées de tous pays de tous les temps

PALACE

We entered the dining room our nostrils
Sniffed an odor of grease and burnt fat phlegm
We had twenty soups three were color of urine
And the king had two poached eggs in bouillon

Then the cook's boys brought in the meats
Roasts of thoughts deceased in my brain
My beautiful stillborn dreams in underdone slices
And my gamy memories served in meat pasties

Now those thoughts dead for millenia
Had the flat flavor of huge frozen mammoths
Bones or dreamers came from charnel-houses
In a dance of death to the folds of my brain

And all those meats cried out peerless things
 But in God's name!
 Starved stomach hath no ears
And the guests all munched their hardest

In God's name! then cried out those cuts of meat
Those huge pasties marrowbones and stews
Tongues of fire where are they now my pentecosts
For my thoughts of all countries of all times

Chantre

Et l'unique cordeau des trompettes marines

Singer

And the solitary cord of sea lutes

Crépuscule

à Mademoiselle Marie Laurencin

Frôlée par les ombres des morts
Sur l'herbe où le jour s'exténue
L'arlequine s'est mise nue
Et dans l'étang mire son corps

Un charlatan crépusculaire
Vante les tours que l'on va faire
Le ciel sans teinte est constellé
D'astres pâles comme du lait

Sur les tréteaux l'arlequin blême
Salue d'abord les spectateurs
Des sorciers venus de Bohême
Quelques fées et les enchanteurs

Ayant décroché une étoile
Il la manie à bras tendu
Tandis que des pieds un pendu
Sonne en mesure les cymbales

L'aveugle berce un bel enfant
La biche passe avec ses faons
Le nain regarde d'un air triste
Grandir l'arlequin trismégiste

Twilight

to Mademoiselle Marie Laurencin

Ghosts brush by her
Day droops in the grass
Columbine disrobes and
Admires her reflection in the pool

A charlatan of twilight
Praises the feats to be performed
Stars color of milk
Spangle pale heaven

Wan harlequin mounts the boards
Bows to his audience
Wizards from Bohemia
Fairies and sorcerers

Then he unhooks a star
Then twirls it in his palm
While a hanged man with his toes
Clashes cymbals

The blind man rocks a fine baby
A doe goes by with her fawns
The dwarf stares sadly
As harlequin grows
 And grows
 And grows

Annie

Sur la côte du Texas
Entre Mobile et Galveston il y a
Un grand jardin tout plein de roses
Il contient aussi une villa
Qui est une grande rose

Une femme se promène souvent
Dans le jardin toute seule
Et quand je passe sur la route bordée de tilleuls
Nous nous regardons

Comme cette femme est mennonite
Ses rosiers et ses vêtements n'ont pas de boutons
Il en manque deux à mon veston
La dame et moi suivons presque le même rite

Annie

On the shores of Texas
Between Mobile and Galveston there is
A great garden filled with roses
There is also a villa
Which is one huge rose

A woman passes often
In the garden alone
And when I pace the road edged with lime trees
Our eyes meet

As she is a Mennonite
Her rose trees and her garments have no buttons
My jacket's missing two
That lady and I observe almost the same rite

La Maison des Morts

à *Maurice Raynal*

S'étendant sur les côtés du cimetière
La maison des morts l'encadrait comme un cloître
A l'intérieur de ses vitrines
Pareilles à celles des boutiques de modes
Au lieu de sourire debout
Les mannequins grimaçaient pour l'éternité

Arrivé à Munich depuis quinze ou vingt jours
J'étais entré pour la première fois et par hasard
Dans ce cimetière presque désert
Et je claquais des dents
Devant toute cette bourgeoisie
Exposée et vêtue le mieux possible
En attendant la sépulture

Soudain
Rapide comme ma mémoire
Les yeux se rallumèrent
De cellule vitrée en cellule vitrée
Le ciel se peupla d'une apocalypse
Vivace
Et la terre plate à l'infini
Comme avant Galilée
Se couvrit de mille mythologies immobiles
Un ange en diamant brisa toutes les vitrines
Et les morts m'accostèrent
Avec des mines de l'autre monde
Mais leur visage et leurs attitudes
Devinrent bientôt moins funèbres

The House of the Dead

to Maurice Raynal

The house of the dead
Bordered the graveyard and enclosed it like a cloister
In windows
Like dress-shop windows
Dummies instead of standing and smiling
Lay grinning for eternity

I had been two or three weeks in Munich
When first I entered by chance
That unfrequented graveyard
And my teeth chattered
Before all the bourgeoisie
Who were laid out so beautifully dressed
Awaiting burial

Suddenly
Swift as memory
Their eyes caught fire once more
From glassy cell to glassy cell
The sky was peopled with a thriving
Apocalypse
And the earth boundlessly flat
As before Galileo
Was covered with a thousand steadfast mythologies
A diamond angel shattered all the windows
And the dead accosted me
With unearthly looks
But their faces and gestures
Soon grew less funereal

Le ciel et la terre perdirent
Leur aspect fantasmagorique

Les morts se réjouissaient
De voir leurs corps trépassés entre eux et la lumière
Ils riaient de leur ombre et l'observaient
Comme si véritablement
C'eût été leur vie passée

Alors je les dénombrai
Ils étaient quarante-neuf hommes
Femmes et enfants
Qui embellissaient à vue d'œil
Et me regardaient maintenant
Avec tant de cordialité
Tant de tendresse même
Que les prenant en amitié
Tout à coup
Je les invitai à une promenade
Loin des arcades de leur maison

Et tous bras dessus bras dessous
Fredonnant des airs militaires
Oui tous vos péchés sont absous
Nous quittâmes le cimetière

Nous traversâmes la ville
Et rencontrions souvent
Des parents des amis qui se joignaient
A la petite troupe des morts récents
Tous étaient si gais
Si charmants si bien portants
Que bien malin qui aurait pu
Distinguer les morts des vivants

Puis dans la campagne
On s'éparpilla

Sky and earth lost
Their fantastic appearance

The dead rejoiced
To see their dead bodies between them and the sun
Each laughed at his shadow and observed it
As if it were
Really his past life

Then I counted them
There were forty-nine men
Women and children
Who visibly improved in looks
And glanced at me now
With so much heartiness
So much tenderness even
That taking a liking for them
Then and there
I invited them to go walking
Far from the archways of their house

And all arm in arm
Humming martial tunes
Yea all your sins are forgiven
We left the graveyard

We crossed the city
And kept on meeting
Relatives friends who joined
The little troupe of newly dead
All were so gay
So charming so healthy
It would have taken a shrewd man
To distinguish the dead from the living

Then in the country
We scattered

Deux chevau-légers nous joignirent
On leur fit fête
Ils coupèrent du bois de viorne
Et de sureau
Dont ils firent des sifflets
Qu'ils distribuèrent aux enfants

Plus tard dans un bal champêtre
Les couples mains sur les épaules
Dansèrent au son aigre des cithares

Ils n'avaient pas oublié la danse
Ces morts et ces mortes
On buvait aussi
Et de temps à autre une cloche
Annonçait qu'un nouveau tonneau
Allait être mis en perce

Une morte assise sur un banc
Près d'un buisson d'épine-vinette
Laissait un étudiant
Agenouillé à ses pieds
Lui parler de fiançailles

Je vous attendrai
Dix ans vingt ans s'il le faut
Votre volonté sera la mienne

Je vous attendrai
Toute votre vie
Répondait la morte

Des enfants
De ce monde ou bien de l'autre
Chantaient de ces rondes
Aux paroles absurdes et lyriques
Qui sans doute sont les restes

Two cavalrymen joined us
We welcomed them warmly
They cut viburnum twigs
And elderberry
Which they whittled into whistles
And gave the children

Later in a rustic ball
The couples their hands on each other's shoulders
Whirled to the shrill sound of zithers

They hadn't forgotten dancing
Those dead men and women
We drank too
And from time to time a bell
Announced the broaching
Of a new barrel

A dead woman who sat on a bench
Near a barberry bush
Allowed a student
Kneeling at her feet
To speak to her of betrothal

I shall wait for you
Ten years twenty if I must
Your will shall be mine

I shall wait for you
All your life
She answered

Children
Of this world or of the other
Sang those rounds
With absurd lyric verses
That doubtlessly are relics

Des plus anciens monuments poétiques
De l'humanité

L'étudiant passa une bague
A l'annulaire de la jeune morte
Voici le gage de mon amour
De nos fiançailles
Ni le temps ni l'absence
Ne nous feront oublier nos promesses
Et un jour nous aurons une belle noce
Des touffes de myrte
A nos vêtements et dans vos cheveux
Un beau sermon à l'église
De longs discours après le banquet
Et de la musique
De la musique

Nos enfants
Dit la fiancée
Seront plus beaux plus beaux encore
Hélas! la bague était brisée
Que s'ils étaient d'argent ou d'or
D'émeraude ou de diamant
Seront plus clairs plus clairs encore
Que les astres du firmament
Que la lumière de l'aurore
Que vos regards mon fiancé
Auront meilleure odeur encore
Hélas! la bague était brisée
Que le lilas qui vient d'éclore
Que le thym la rose ou qu'un brin
De lavande ou de romarin

Les musiciens s'en étant allés
Nous continuâmes la promenade

Au bord d'un lac

Of man's
Oldest poetic monuments

The student slipped a ring
On the dead girl's third finger
Here is the pledge of my love
Of our betrothal
Neither time nor absence
Can make us forget our vows
And one day we shall have a splendid wedding
Myrtle tufts
In our clothes and in your hair
A fine sermon at the church
Long speeches after dinner
And music
Music

Our children
Said the fiancée
Will be lovelier lovelier still
Alas! the ring was broken
Than if they were of silver or of gold
Of emerald or diamond
More brilliant brilliant still
Than heaven's stars
Than the first light of morning
Than your eyes my fiancé
More fragrant still
Alas! the ring was broken
Than lilac newly flowered
Than roses thyme or sprig
Of lavender or rosemary

The musicians had departed
We continued our stroll

By a lake

On s'amusa à faire des ricochets
Avec des cailloux plats
Sur l'eau qui dansait à peine

Des barques étaient amarrées
Dans un havre
On les détacha
Après que toute la troupe se fut embarquée
Et quelques morts ramaient
Avec autant de vigueur que les vivants

A l'avant du bateau que je gouvernais
Un mort parlait avec une jeune femme
Vêtue d'une robe jaune
D'un corsage noir
Avec des rubans bleus et d'un chapeau gris
Orné d'une seule petite plume défrisée

Je vous aime
Disait-il
Comme le pigeon aime la colombe
Comme l'insecte nocturne
Aime la lumière

Trop tard
Répondait la vivante
Repoussez repoussez cet amour défendu
Je suis mariée
Voyez l'anneau qui brille
Mes mains tremblent
Je pleure et je voudrais mourir

Les barques étaient arrivées
A un endroit ou les chevau-légers
Savaient qu'un écho répondait de la rive
On ne se lassait point de l'interroger

We played ducks and drakes
Skimming flat pebbles
Across water that hardly stirred

Boats were moored
In a harbor
When everyone was on board
We untied them
And some of the dead rowed
In as lively a fashion as the living

In the prow of the boat that I was steering
A dead man spoke with a young woman
Who wore a yellow dress
A black blouse
With blue ribbons and a grey hat
Adorned with one small uncurling feather

I love you
He said
As the pigeon loves the dove
As the nocturnal insect
Loves the light

Too late
Answered the living woman
Deny deny that forbidden love
I am a wife
See how my ring glitters
My hands tremble
I weep and I want to die

The boats had landed
At a spot where the soldiers
Knew of an echo answering from the shore
We asked and asked it

Il y eut des questions si extravagantes
Et des réponses tellement pleines d'à-propos
Que c'était à mourir de rire
Et le mort disait à la vivante

Nous serions si heureux ensemble
Sur nous l'eau se refermera
Mais vous pleurez et vos mains tremblent
Aucun de nous ne reviendra

On reprit terre et ce fut le retour
Les amoureux s'entr'aimaient
Et par couples aux belles bouches
Marchaient à distances inégales
Les morts avaient choisi les vivantes
Et les vivants
Des mortes
Un genévrier parfois
Faisait l'effet d'un fantôme
Les enfants déchiraient l'air
En soufflant les joues creuses
Dans leurs sifflets de viorne
Ou de sureau
Tandis que les militaires
Chantaient des tyroliennes
En se répondant comme on le fait
Dans la montagne

Dans la ville
Notre troupe diminua peu à peu
On se disait
Au revoir
A demain
A bientôt
Beaucoup entraient dans les brasseries
Quelques-uns nous quittèrent

There were questions so extravagant
And answers so to the point
We could have died laughing
And the dead man said to the living woman

How happy we should be together
Over us the water will close again
But you weep and your hands tremble
None of us shall return

We landed again and started homeward
The lovers worshipped each other
And by couples all with lovely mouths
They walked at unequal distances
The dead men had chosen living women
And the living men
Dead women
An occasional juniper tree
Seemed like a ghost
The children rent the air
Blowing with hollow cheeks
Into their whistles of viburnum
Or elderberry
While the soldiers
Sang Tyrolean songs
Yodeling back and forth as people do
On the mountain

In the city
Our troupe dwindled little by little
We said
Au revoir
Till tomorrow
See you soon
Many entered beer parlors
Some left us

Devant une boucherie canine
Pour y acheter leur repas du soir

Bientôt je restai seul avec ces morts
Qui s'en allaient tout droit
Au cimitière
Où
Sous les Arcades
Je les reconnus
Couchés
Immobiles
Et bien vêtus
Attendant la sépulture derrière les vitrines

Ils ne se doutaient pas
De ce qui s'était passé
Mais les vivants en gardaient le souvenir
C'était un bonheur inespéré
Et si certain
Qu'ils ne craignaient point de le perdre

Ils vivaient si noblement
Que ceux qui la veille encore
Les regardaient comme leurs égaux
Ou même quelque chose de moins
Admiraient maintenant
Leur puissance leur richesse et leur génie
Car y a-t-il rien qui vous élève
Comme d'avoir aimé un mort ou une morte
On devient si pur qu'on en arrive
Dans les glaciers de la mémoire
A se confondre avec le souvenir
On est fortifié pour la vie
Et l'on n'a plus besoin de personne

At the dog butcher's
Where they were going to buy their evening meal

Soon I was left alone with the dead
They went straight
Toward the graveyard
There
Under the Arcades
I recognized them
Asleep
Unmoving
And beautifully dressed
Awaiting burial behind the panes of glass

They were unaware
Of what had happened
But the living remembered
It was an unexpected good fortune
And so certain
That they had no fear of losing it

They lived so nobly
That those who the evening before
Looked on them still as their equals
Or even as something less
Now admired
Their power their wealth and their genius
For is there anything so ennobling
As having loved a dead man or woman
You become so pure that you end up
In the glaciers of remembrance
Mingling with your memories
You are strengthened for life
And no longer do you need any one

Clotilde

L'anémone et l'ancolie
Ont poussé dans le jardin
Où dort la mélancolie
Entre l'amour et le dédain

Il y vient aussi nos ombres
Que la nuit dissipera
Le soleil qui les rend sombres
Avec elles disparaîtra

Les déités des eaux vives
Laissent couler leurs cheveux
Passe il faut que tu poursuives
Cette belle ombre que tu veux

Clotilde

Anemones and buttercups
Bloom in that garden
Where grief slumbers
Between love and disdain

Our shades too wander there
Until the night dispel them
And the sun vanish
That made them somber

Gods of spring water
Unbind their streaming hair
Pass for you must follow
That fair shadow you desire

Cortège

à M. Léon Bailby

Oiseau tranquille au vol inverse oiseau
Qui nidifie en l'air
A la limite où notre sol brille déjà
Baisse ta deuxième paupière la terre t'éblouit
Quand tu lèves la tête

Et moi aussi de près je suis sombre et terne
Une brume qui vient d'obscurcir les lanternes
Une main qui tout à coup se pose devant les yeux
Une voûte entre vous et toutes les lumières
Et je m'éloignerai m'illuminant au milieu d'ombres
Et d'alignements d'yeux des astres bien-aimés

Oiseau tranquille au vol inverse oiseau
Qui nidifie en l'air
A la limite où brille déjà ma mémoire
Baisse ta deuxième paupière
Ni à cause du soleil ni à cause de la terre
Mais pour ce feu oblong dont l'intensité ira s'augmentant
Au point qu'il deviendra un jour l'unique lumière

Un jour
Un jour je m'attendais moi-même
Je me disais Guillaume il est temps que tu viennes
Pour que je sache enfin celui-là que je suis
Moi qui connais les autres
Je les connais par les cinq sens et quelques autres

Procession

to M. Léon Bailby

Calm bird on inverted wing bird
Nesting in mid-air
At the limit where our soil still gleams
Lower your second eyelid earth dazzles you
When you lift your head

And I too close up I am sad and dull
A mist that has dimmed the lanterns
A hand suddenly placed before the eyes
An arch between you and all the lights
And I shall withdraw illuminating myself in the midst of
 shadows
And those ranks of eyes the beloved stars

Calm bird on inverted wing bird
Nesting in mid-air
At the limit where still my memory gleams
Lower your second eyelid
Neither for the sun or the earth
But for that oblong flame whose strength will increase
Until it becomes one day the unique light

One day
One day as I invited my soul
I said to myself William it's time to come
So I at last may find out who I am
I who know the others
I know them by five senses and by some others

Il me suffit de voir leurs pieds pour pouvoir refaire ces gens à
 milliers
De voir leurs pieds paniques un seul de leurs cheveux
Ou leur langue quand il me plaît de faire le médecin
Ou leurs enfants quand il me plaît de faire le prophète
Les vaisseaux des armateurs la plume de mes confrères
La monnaie des aveugles les mains des muets
Ou bien encore à cause du vocabulaire et non de l'écriture
Une lettre écrite par ceux qui ont plus de vingt ans
Il me suffit de sentir l'odeur de leurs églises
L'odeur des fleuves dans leurs villes
Le parfum des fleurs dans les jardins publics
O Corneille Agrippa l'odeur d'un petit chien m'eût suffi
Pour décrire exactement tes concitoyens de Cologne
Leurs rois-mages et la ribambelle ursuline
Qui t'inspirait l'erreur touchant toutes les femmes
Il me suffit de goûter la saveur du laurier qu'on cultive pour que
 j'aime ou que je bafoue
Et de toucher les vêtements
Pour ne pas douter si l'on est frileux ou non
O gens que je connais
Il me suffit d'entendre le bruit de leurs pas
Pour pouvoir indiquer à jamais la direction qu'ils ont prise
Il me suffit de tous ceux-là pour me croire le droit
De ressusciter les autres
Un jour je m'attendais moi-même
Je me disais Guillaume il est temps que tu viennes
Et d'un lyrique pas s'avançaient ceux que j'aime
Parmi lesquels je n'étais pas
Les géants couverts d'algues passaient dans leurs villes
Sous-marines où les tours seules étaient des îles
Et cette mer avec les clartés de ses profondeurs
Coulait sang de mes veines et fait battre mon cœur
Puis sur terre il venait mille peuplades blanches
Dont chaque homme tenait une rose à la main
Et le langage qu'ils inventaient en chemin

If I see their feet I can recreate those people by thousands
If I see their panicky feet a single hair of their head
Or their tongue when I feel like playing doctor
Or their children when I feel like playing prophet
The owners' ships the pens of my colleagues
The pennies of blind men the hands of the dumb
Or because of its words not the handwriting
A letter written by some one over twenty
It's enough that I smell the odor of their churches
The odor of the rivers in their cities
The fragrance of flowers in the city parks
O Cornelius Agrippa the scent of a little dog would have been
 enough for me
To describe precisely your fellow citizens of Cologne
Their wise kings and the long string of Ursulines
Who inspired in you the error concerning all women
It's enough that I sample their laurel for me to love or scoff
And from touching their clothes
I know beyond a doubt whether they're sensitive to drafts
O people familiar to me
If I hear the sound of their footsteps
I can forever point out what route they have taken
All these suffice for me to think I have the right
To restore to life the others
One day as I invited my soul
I said to myself William it's time to come
With lyric step those I loved drew near
And I was not among them
Giants draped with seaweed entered their cities
Underwater whose towers alone were islands
And that sea with the sparkle of its depths
Flowed as the blood in my veins and makes my heart beat
Then over the land came a thousand white tribes
Each man held a rose in his hand
And the language they invented on their journey

Je l'appris de leur bouche et je le parle encore
Le cortège passait et j'y cherchais mon corps
Tous ceux qui survenaient et n'étaient pas moi-même
Amenaient un à un les morceaux de moi-même
On me bâtit peu à peu comme on élève une tour
Les peuples s'entassaient et je parus moi-même
Qu'ont formé tous les corps et les choses humaines

Temps passés Trépassés Les dieux qui me formâtes
Je ne vis que passant ainsi que vous passâtes
Et détournant mes yeux de ce vide avenir
En moi-même je vois tout le passé grandir

Rien n'est mort que ce qui n'existe pas encore
Près du passé luisant demain est incolore
Il est informe aussi près de ce qui parfait
Présente tout ensemble et l'effort et l'effet

I learned from them and I still speak it
The procession marched by and I looked for my body there
All those who arrived and were not myself
Brought one by one the fragments of myself
They built me little by little as one raises a tower
The nations huddled together and I myself appeared
Formed by all bodies all human concerns

Time past time that has passed away You gods who
 shaped me
I live only passing by as you passed by
And turning my eyes from the empty future
In myself I see arising all the past

Nothing is dead but what has not yet existed
Tomorrow is dim beside the shining past
And formless beside an achieved perfection
That displays at once the effort and the effect

Marizibill

Dans la Haute-Rue à Cologne
Elle allait et venait le soir
Offerte à tous en tout mignonne
Puis buvait lasse des trottoirs
Très tard dans les brasseries borgnes

Elle se mettait sur la paille
Pour un maquereau roux et rose
C'était un juif il sentait l'ail
Et l'avait venant de Formose
Tirée d'un bordel de Changaï

Je connais gens de toutes sortes
Ils n'égalent pas leurs destins
Indécis comme feuilles mortes
Leurs yeux sont des feux mal éteints
Leurs cœurs bougent comme leurs portes

Marizibill

In the High Street at Cologne
She strolled up and down each twilight
Offering herself to everyone
A chick with style Then bored with sidewalks
Sat drinking late in one-eyed bars

She gave her all for a
Carroty fair-skinned pimp
A Jew who stank of garlic cloves
On his way home from Formosa
He'd lifted her from a Shanghai whorehouse

All kinds of people I've seen
That don't measure up to their destinies
Irresolute like dead leaves
Their eyes are flames almost gone out
Their hearts gape like their doorways

Le Voyageur

à Fernand Fleuret

Ouvrez-moi cette porte où je frappe en pleurant

La vie est variable aussi bien que l'Euripe

Tu regardais un banc de nuages descendre
Avec le paquebot orphelin vers les fièvres futures
Et de tous ces regrets de tous ces repentirs
 Te souviens-tu

Vagues poissons arqués fleurs surmarines
Une nuit c'était la mer
Et les fleuves s'y répandaient

Je m'en souviens je m'en souviens encore

Un soir je descendis dans une auberge triste
Auprès du Luxembourg
Dans le fond de la salle il s'envolait un Christ
Quelqu'un avait un furet
Un autre un hérisson
L'on jouait aux cartes
Et toi tu m'avais oublié

Te souviens-tu du long orphelinat des gares
Nous traversâmes des villes qui tout le jour tournaient
Et vomissaient la nuit le soleil des journées
O matelots ô femmes sombres et vous mes compagnons
 Souvenez-vous-en

The Traveler

to Fernand Fleuret

Open this door where I knock weeping

Life is uncertain like the sea around Euripos

You watched a bank of clouds descend
With the orphan steamer toward future fevers
And all those regrets all that repentance
 Do you remember

Waves arched fishes surmarine flowers
One night it was the sea
Where rivers widened

I remember I remember still

One evening I stopped at a dreary inn
Near the Luxembourg
In the depth of the room a Christ was soaring
Some one had a ferret
Another a hedgehog
We played cards
And you you had forgotten me

Do you remember the endless orphanage of railway stations
We crossed cities that all day revolved
And at night they vomited the sun
O sailors O dark women and you my companions
 Remember

Deux matelots qui ne s'étaient jamais quittés
Deux matelots qui ne s'étaient jamais parlé
Le plus jeune en mourant tomba sur le coté

O vous chers compagnons
Sonneries électriques des gares chant des moissonneuses
Traîneau d'un boucher régiment des rues sans nombre
Cavalerie des ponts nuits livides de l'alcool
Les villes que j'ai vues vivaient comme des folles

Te souviens-tu des banlieues et du troupeau plaintif des paysages

Les cyprès projetaient sous la lune leurs ombres
J'écoutais cette nuit au déclin de l'été
Un oiseau langoureux et toujours irrité
Et le bruit éternel d'un fleuve large et sombre

Mais tandis que mourants roulaient vers l'estuaire
Tous les regards tous les regards de tous les yeux
Les bords étaient déserts herbus silencieux
Et la montagne à l'autre rive était très claire

Alors sans bruit sans qu'on pût voir rien de vivant
Contre le mont passèrent des ombres vivaces
De profil ou soudain tournant leurs vagues faces
Et tenant l'ombre de leurs lances en avant

Les ombres contre le mont perpendiculaire
Grandissaient ou parfois s'abaissaient brusquement
Et ces ombres barbues pleuraient humainement
En glissant pas à pas sur la montagne claire

Qui donc reconnais-tu sur ces vieilles photographies
Te souviens-tu du jour où une abeille tomba dans le feu
C'était tu t'en souviens à la fin de l'été

Two sailors who had never parted
Two sailors who had never conversed
The youngest as he died sank tilting his scuppers

 O cherished companions
Electric bells of railway stations the song of reapers
Butcher's sled regiment of countless streets
Cavalry of bridges nights pale with alcohol
The cities I have glimpsed lived like madwomen

Do you remember the suburbs and the plaintive flock of
 landscapes

Cypresses flung their shadows beneath the moon
I listened to that night at summer's wane
A langorous fretful bird
And the eternal sound of a dark wide river

But dying and revolving toward the estuary
Were all the glances all the glances of all eyes
While the banks were deserted grassy silent
And the mountain on the other shore shone clear

Then silently and there was nothing alive to be seen
Against the mountain passed living shadows
In profile or suddenly turning vague faces
Thrusting the shadow of their lances forward

The shades against the perpendicular mountain
Grew or sometimes brusquely shrank
And those bearded shadows wept like men
Gliding step by step over the clear mountain

Who is it you recognize in those old photos
Remember the day a bee tumbled in the fire
It was you remember at summer's end

Deux matelots qui ne s'étaient jamais quittés
L'aîné portait au cou une chaîne de fer
Le plus jeune mettait ses cheveux blonds en tresse

Ouvrez-moi cette porte où je frappe en pleurant

La vie est variable aussi bien que l'Euripe

Two sailors who had never parted
The elder bore around his neck an iron chain
The younger wore his flaxen hair in a pigtail

Open this door where I knock weeping

Life is uncertain like the sea around Euripos

Marie

Vous y dansiez petite fille
Y danserez-vous mère-grand
C'est la maclotte qui sautille
Toutes les cloches sonneront
Quand donc reviendrez-vous Marie

Les masques sont silencieux
Et la musique est si lointaine
Qu'elle semble venir des cieux
Oui je veux vous aimer mais vous aimer à peine
Et mon mal est délicieux

Les brebis s'en vont dans la neige
Flocons de laine et ceux d'argent
Des soldats passent et que n'ai-je
Un cœur à moi ce cœur changeant
Changeant et puis encor que sais-je

Sais-je où s'en iront tes cheveux
Crépus comme mer qui moutonne
Sais-je ou s'en iront tes cheveux
Et tes mains feuilles de l'automne
Que jonchent aussi nos aveux

Je passais au bord de la Seine
Un livre ancien sous le bras
Le fleuve est pareil à ma peine
Il s'écoule et ne tarit pas
Quand donc finira la semaine

Marie

You danced there a little girl
Will you dance as grandmother
Hop and skip in the *maclotte*
All the bells will ring
But when will you return Marie

Masks become silent and
Music so far away
It is the sky singing
Let me love you and love you only a little
My unrest is delicious

Flocks wade the snow
Flakes of wool and of silver
Soldiers are marching and if I
Had a heart of my own O changing heart
Changing but what do I know

Do I know where your hair
Crinkling like a heavy sea
Do I know where your hair will vanish
Or your hands autumn leaves
That our vows too will scatter

I used to walk by the Seine
An old book under my arm
The river like my sorrow
Flows on without stopping
Will the week never draw to an end

La Blanche Neige

Les anges les anges dans le ciel
L'un est vêtu en officier
L'un est vêtu en cuisinier
Et les autres chantent

Bel officier couleur du ciel
Le doux printemps longtemps après Noël
Te médaillera d'un beau soleil
 D'un beau soleil

Le cuisinier plume les oies
 Ah! tombe neige
 Tombe et que n'ai-je
Ma bien-aimée entre mes bras

White Snow

Angels I see angels in heaven
One wears a uniform
One a chef's hat
Others are singing

Fair offieer color of sky
Long after Christmas spring
Will decorate you with a golden sun
 A golden sun

Cook plucks the geese
Scatter snow
Scatter ah my love if only
You were in my arms

Poème lu au mariage d'André Salmon

le 13 juillet 1909

En voyant des drapeaux ce matin je ne me suis pas dit
Voilà les riches vêtements des pauvres
Ni la pudeur démocratique veut me voiler sa douleur
Ni la liberté en honneur fait qu'on imite maintenant
Les feuilles ô liberté végétale ô seule liberté terrestre
Ni les maisons flambent parce qu'on partira pour ne plus revenir
Ni ces mains agitées travailleront demain pour nous tous
Ni même on a pendu ceux qui ne savaient pas profiter de la vie
Ni même on renouvelle le monde en reprenant la Bastille
Je sais que seuls le renouvellent ceux qui sont fondés en poésie
On a pavoisé Paris parce que mon ami André Salmon s'y marie

Nous nous sommes rencontrés dans un caveau maudit
Au temps de notre jeunesse
Fumant tous deux et mal vêtus attendant l'aube
Épris épris des mêmes paroles dont il faudra changer le sens
Trompés trompés pauvres petits et ne sachant pas encore rire
La table et les deux verres devinrent un mourant qui nous jeta le
 dernier regard d'Orphée
Les verres tombèrent se brisèrent
Et nous apprîmes à rire
Nous partîmes alors pèlerins de la perdition
A travers les rues à travers les contrées à travers la raison
Je le revis au bord du fleuve sur lequel flottait Orphélie

Poem Read at André Salmon's Wedding

July 13, 1909

When I saw the flags this morning I didn't say to myself
Behold the rich garments of the poor
Or democratic modesty desires to veil her sorrow from me
Or the liberty we honor is now causing people to imitate
The leaves O vegetable liberty the only earthly freedom
Or the houses flame because we are leaving and shall return no
 more
Or these waving hands will toil tomorrow for us all
Or even they've hanged those who didn't know how to profit
 from life
Or even they're renewing the world by taking the Bastille again
I know that the only people to renew the world are those
 grounded in poetry
They've adorned Paris with flags because my friend André
 Salmon is getting married there

We met first in an evil wine cellar
In the days of our youth
Both smoking both in terrible clothes and waiting for the dawn
In love in love with the same phrases whose meaning will have to
 be changed
Deceived deceived poor boys we didn't yet know how to laugh
The table and two glasses became a dying man who threw us the
 final glance of Orpheus
The glasses fell and shattered
And we learned how to laugh
We took our leave then pilgrims of perdition
Across streets across countries across reason
I saw him again by the river where Ophelia floated

Qui blanche flotte encore entre les nénuphars
Il s'en allait au milieu des Hamlets blafards
Sur la flûte jouant les airs de la folie
Je le revis près d'un moujik mourant compter les béatitudes
En admirant la neige semblable aux femmes nues
Je le revis faisant ceci ou cela en l'honneur des mêmes paroles
Qui changent la face des enfants et je dis toutes ces choses
Souvenir et Avenir parce que mon ami André Salmon se marie

Réjouissons-nous non pas parce que notre amitié a été le fleuve
 qui nous a fertilisés
Terrains riverains dont l'abondance est la nourriture que tous
 espèrent
Ni parce que nos verres nous jettent encore une fois le regard
 d'Orphée mourant
Ni parce que nous avons tant grandi que beaucoup pourraient
 confondre nos yeux et les étoiles
Ni parce que les drapeaux claquent aux fenêtres des citoyens qui
 sont contents depuis cent ans d'avoir la vie et de menues choses
 à défendre
Ni parce que fondés en poésie nous avons des droits sur les paroles
 qui forment et défont l'Univers
Ni parce que nous pouvons pleurer sans ridicule et que nous savons
 rire
Ni parce que nous fumons et buvons comme autrefois
Réjouissons-nous parce que directeur du feu et des poètes
L'amour qui emplit ainsi que la lumière
Tout le solide espace entre les étoiles et les planètes
L'amour veut qu'aujourd'hui mon ami André Salmon se marie

And still she floats pale among the water lilies
He went his way past wan Hamlets
Playing on a flute songs of madness
I saw him again beside a dying muzhik recite the beatitudes
Admiring snow like flesh of naked women
Again I saw him doing this or that in honor of those same phrases
That change the faces of children and I say all these things
Things past and things to come because my friend André Salmon
 is getting married

Let us rejoice not because our friendship was the river that
 enriched us
River lands whose abundance is the nourishment all hope for
Or because our glasses throw us once again the gaze of dying
 Orpheus
Or because we have grown so tall that many might confuse our
 eyes with the stars
Or because flags flap at the windows of citizens content for a
 century to have their lives and small things to defend
Or because grounded in poetry we have rights over those phrases
 that shape and destroy the Universe
Or because we can weep without absurdity and know how to
 laugh
Or because we smoke and drink as long ago
Let us rejoice because the director of fire and of poets
Love who fills as light does
All solid space between the stars and planets
Love determines that today my friend André Salmon gets
 married

L' *Adieu*

J'ai cueilli ce brin de bruyère
L'automne est morte souviens-t'en
Nous ne nous verrons plus sur terre
Odeur du temps brin de bruyère
Et souviens-toi que je t'attends

The Farewell

I picked this spray of heather
Autumn is dead remember
Never more on earth we two together
Breath of time spray of heather
Remember I wait for you

Salomé

Pour que sourie encore une fois Jean-Baptiste
Sire je danserais mieux que les séraphins
Ma mère dites-moi pourquoi vous êtes triste
En robe de comtesse à coté du Dauphin

Mon cœur battait battait très fort à sa parole
Quand je dansais dans le fenouil en écoutant
Et je brodais des lys sur une banderole
Destinée à flotter au bout de son bâton

Et pour qui voulez-vous qu'à présent je la brode
Son bâton refleurit sur les bords du Jourdain
Et tous les lys quand vos soldats ô roi Hérode
L'emmenèrent se sont flétris dans mon jardin

Venez tous avec moi là-bas sous les quinconces
 Ne pleure pas ô joli fou du roi
Prends cette tête au lieu de ta marotte et danse
N'y touchez pas son front ma mére est déjà froid

Sire marchez devant trabants marchez derrière
Nous creuserons un trou et l'y enterrerons
Nous planterons des fleurs et danserons en rond
Jusqu'à l'heure ou j'aurai perdu ma jarretière
 Le roi sa tabatière
 L'infante son rosaire
 Le curé son bréviaire

Salomé

To see John the Baptist smile once more
Sire I would outdance the seraphim
Tell me mother why you are grieving
Though dressed like a countess at the Dauphin's side

When he spoke my heart beat how it beat
I listened as I danced over the fennel
I embroidered lilies upon a banner
To float from the tip of his staff

For whom shall I embroider them now
His staff blooms again on Jordan's banks
When your soldiers led him away King Herod
The lilies in my garden withered

Under the quincunx everyone come with me
 Weep not charming jester
Take this head in your hands for a bauble and dance
Touch it not mother the brow is cold

Sire march first and halberdiers follow
We shall dig a hole and bury it
We shall plant flowers and dance in a ring
Till the hour when I lose my garter
 The king his snuffbox
 Infanta her rosary
 Priest his breviary

La Porte

La porte de l'hôtel sourit terriblement
Qu'est-ce que cela peut me faire ô ma maman
D'être cet employé pour qui seul rien n'existe
Pi-mus couples allant dans la profonde eau triste
Anges frais débarqués à Marseille hier matin
J'entends mourir et remourir un chant lointain
Humble comme je suis qui ne suis rien qui vaille

Enfant je t'ai donné ce que j'avais travaille

The Door

The hotel door smiles its terrible smile
What can it mean to me my mother
To be that clerk for whom alone nothing exists
Pi-mus fish coupled in the deep sad water
Fresh angels disembarked at Marseilles yesterday morning
I hear a distant song that dies over and over
Humble as I am who am nothing worthwhile

Child I gave you what I had now labor

Merlin et la vieille Femme

Le soleil ce jour-là s'étalait comme un ventre
Maternel qui saignait lentement sur le ciel
La lumière est ma mère ô lumière sanglante
Les nuages coulaient comme un flux menstruel

Au carrefour où nulle fleur sinon la rose
Des vents mais sans épine n'a fleuri l'hiver
Merlin guettait la vie et l'éternelle cause
Qui fait mourir et puis renaître l'univers

Une vieille sur une mule à chape verte
S'en vint suivant la berge du fleuve en aval
Et l'antique Merlin dans la plaine déserte
Se frappait la poitrine en s'écriant Rival

O mon être glacé dont le destin m'accable
Dont ce soleil de chair grelotte veux-tu voir
Ma Mémoire venir et m'aimer ma semblable
Et quel fils malheureux et beau je veux avoir

Son geste fit crouler l'orgueil des cataclysmes
Le soleil en dansant remuait son nombril
Et soudain le printemps d'amour et d'héroïsme
Amena par la main un jeune jour d'avril

Les voies qui viennent de l'ouest étaient couvertes
D'ossements d'herbes drues de destins et de fleurs
Des monuments tremblants près des charognes vertes
Quand les vents apportaient des poils et des malheurs

Merlin and the Old Woman

That day the sun sprawled like a maternal
Belly bleeding slowly across the sky
The light is my mother O bloodstained light
The clouds flowed like a menstrual flux

At the crossroads where no flower but a thornless
Compass rose of the winds adorned winter with flowers
Merlin watched for life and the cause eternal
Of the death and renewal of the universe

An old woman on a mule that bore a green cope
Came following downstream the river's course
And ancient Merlin in the deserted plain
Beat on his breast and shrieked out Rival

O my frozen self whose fate subdues me
And whose sun of flesh shivers do you gladly see
My Memory my peer ride toward me with love
And what child sad and winsome I long to have

His gesture crumbled the pride of upheavals
The dancing sun shimmied its navel
And suddenly love's heroic springtime
Came leading by the hand a young April day

The roads from the west were dotted with bones
With plants sprouting fates and flowers
With monuments trembling beside green carrion
When the winds were blowing fluff and sorrows

Laissant sa mule à petits pas s'en vint l'amante
A petits coups le vent défripait ses atours
Puis les pâles amants joignant leurs mains démentes
L'entrelacs de leurs doigts fut leur seul laps d'amour

Elle balla mimant un rythme d'existence
Criant Depuis cent ans j'espérais ton appel
Les astres de ta vie influaient sur ma danse
Morgane regardait du haut du mont Gibel

Ah! qu'il fait doux danser quand pour vous se déclare
Un mirage où tout chante et que les vents d'horreur
Feignent d'être le rire de la lune hilare
Et d'effrayer les fantômes avant-coureurs

J'ai fait des gestes blancs parmi les solitudes
Des lémures couraient peupler les cauchemars
Mes tournoiements exprimaient les béatitudes
Qui toutes ne sont rien qu'un pur effet de l'Art

Je n'ai jamais cueilli que la fleur d'aubépine
Aux printemps finissants qui voulaient défleurir
Quand les oiseaux de proie proclamaient leurs rapines
D'agneaux mort-nés et d'enfants-dieux qui vont mourir

Et j'ai vieilli vois-tu pendant ta vie je danse
Mais j'eusse été tôt lasse et l'aubépine en fleurs
Cet avril aurait eu la pauvre confidence
D'un corps de vieille morte en mimant la douleur

Et leurs mains s'élevaient comme un vol de colombes
Clarté sur qui la nuit fondit comme un vautour
Puis Merlin s'en alla vers l'est disant Qu'il monte
Le fils de la Mémoire égale de l'Amour

MERLIN AND THE OLD WOMAN

Dismounting his love skipped daintily forward
Daintily did the wind smooth her attire
The pale lovers joined their maddened hands
In a gesture that was their sole gest of love

As she danced she aped a rhythm of existence
She cried For a century I waited your call
The stars of your life poured light on my dance
Morgana watched from the top of Mount Gibel

Ah! how sweet to dance when for you there unfolds
A mirage filled with singing and when winds of horror
Enact the laugh of the mirthful moon
And would frighten away all ghostly heralds

I made white gestures in the wilderness
Lemurs ran swarming through my nightmares
My leaps and twirls expressed that bliss
Which is an effect of art and nothing more

I never plucked any but hawthorn petals
Toward the end of springtimes shedding their blossoms
When birds of prey proclaimed their pillage
Of doomed infant gods and stillborn lambs

You see me grown old while you live I dance
But I would have soon wearied and the hawthorn flowers
This April would have had a meager trust
The corpse of an old woman who died aping sorrow

And their hands hovered like a flight of doves
Whose brightness night pounced upon like a vulture
Then Merlin turned eastward saying May he ascend
The son of Memory that is Love's peer

Qu'il monte de la fange ou soit une ombre d'homme
Il sera bien mon fils mon ouvrage immortel
Le front nimbé de feu sur le chemin de Rome
Il marchera tout seul en regardant le ciel

La dame qui m'attend se nomme Viviane
Et vienne le printemps des nouvelles douleurs
Couché parmi la marjolaine et les pas-d'âne
Je m'éterniserai sous l'aubépine en fleurs

Whether he rise from the clay or be man's shadow
He is surely my son my immortal work
His brow clouded with fire alone he will walk
The road to Rome with his face toward heaven

The lady awaiting me is called Vivian
And when comes a springtime of new sorrow
Couched among coltsfoot and sweet marjoram
For ever I live on beneath the hawthorn flowers

Saltimbanques

à Louis Dumur

Dans la plaine les baladins
S'éloignent au long des jardins
Devant l'huis des auberges grises
Par les villages sans églises

Et les enfants s'en vont devant
Les autres suivent en rêvant
Chaque arbre fruitier se résigne
Quand de très loin ils lui font signe

Ils ont des poids ronds ou carrés
Des tambours des cerceaux dorés
L'ours et le singe animaux sages
Quêtent des sous sur leur passage

Mountebanks

to Louis Dumur

Across the plain mountebanks
Withdraw past garden walls
By doors of gray inns
Through villages without steeples

The children lead the way and
The others follow in a dream
Each fruit tree resigns itself
When they hail it from afar

Weights they carry round or square
Drums and gold hoops
Those wise beasts the bear and monkey
Beg pennies along the road

Le Larron

Maraudeur étranger malheureux malhabile
Voleur voleur que ne demandais-tu ces fruits
Mais puisque tu as faim que tu es en exil
Il pleure il est barbare et bon pardonnez-lui

LARRON

Je confesse le vol des fruits doux des fruits mûrs
Mais ce n'est pas l'exil que je viens simuler
Et sachez que j'attends de moyennes tortures
Injustes si je rends tout ce que j'ai volé

VIEILLARD

Issu de l'écume des mers comme Aphrodite
Sois docile puisque tu es beau Naufragé
Vois les sages te font des gestes socratiques
Vous parlerez d'amour quand il aura mangé

CHŒUR

Maraudeur étranger malhabile et malade
Ton père fut un sphinx et ta mère une nuit
Qui charma de lueurs Zacinthe et les Cyclades
As-tu feint d'avoir faim quand tu volas les fruits

LARRON

Possesseurs de fruits mûrs que dirai-je aux insultes
Ouïr ta voix ligure en nénie ô maman
Puisqu'ils n'eurent enfin la pubère et l'adulte
De prétexte sinon de s'aimer nuitamment

The Thief

Freebooter foreigner awkward and ill-starred
Thief why would you not ask us for our fruit
But seeing you are hungry and are in exile
He weeps he is a barbarian and a good man forgive him

THIEF

I confess to the theft of tender ripe fruit
But it is no exile's role I imitate
Know that I expect only middling tortures
Unjust if I return all I have stolen

OLD MAN

Born of the sea foam like Aphrodite
Be gentle as you are handsome Castaway
The elders implore you with Socratic gestures
Speak of love to him after he has eaten

CHOROS

Freebooter foreigner awkward and sickly
A sphinx was your father and your mother a night
Who charmed with her glimmers Zante and the Cyclades
Did you feign hunger when you ravished our fruit

THIEF

Owners of ripe fruit how reply to these jeers
I hear your Ligurian voice O my mother lamenting
For they had no occasion the maid and the grown man
To seek each other's love if not by night

LE LARRON

Il y avait des fruits tout ronds comme des âmes
Et des amandes de pomme de pin jonchaient
Votre jardin marin où j'ai laissé mes rames
Et mon couteau punique au pied de ce pêcher

Les citrons couleur d'huile et à saveur d'eau froide
Pendaient parmi les fleurs des citronniers tordus
Les oiseaux de leur bec ont blessé vos grenades
Et presque toutes les figues étaient fendues

L'ACTEUR

Il entra dans la salle aux fresques qui figurent
L'inceste solaire et nocturne dans les nues
Assieds-toi là pour mieux ouïr les voix ligures
Au son des cinyres des Lydiennes nues

Or les hommes ayant des masques de théâtre
Et les femmes ayant des colliers où pendait
La pierre prise au foie d'un vieux coq de Tanagre
Parlaient entre eux le langage de la Chaldée

Les autans langoureux dehors feignaient l'automne
Les convives c'étaient tant de couples d'amants
Qui dirent tour à tour Voleur je te pardonne
Reçois d'abord le sel puis le pain de froment

Le brouet qui froidit sera fade à tes lèvres
Mais l'outre en peau de bouc maintient frais le vin blanc
Par ironie veux-tu qu'on serve un plat de fèves
Ou des beignets de fleurs trempés dans du miel blond

Une femme lui dit Tu n'invoques personne
Crois-tu donc au hasard qui coule au sablier
Voleur connais-tu mieux les lois malgré les hommes
Veux-tu le talisman heureux de mon collier

THE THIEF

Fruit rounded like souls lay scattered
And pinecone almonds littered
Your sea garden where I posed my oars
And left my Punic knife beneath the peach tree

Oil-tinted lemons tasting of cool water
Swayed among the blossoms of the twisted grove
The birds have pecked your pomegranates
And nearly all the figs were split

ACTOR

He entered the frescoed hall that pictures
The solar nocturnal incest wrapped in clouds
Be seated listen to Ligurian voices
And to zithers plucked by nude Lydian women

Now the men who had donned their theater masks
And the women wearing necklaces where hung
The stone from an old fighting cock of Tanagra
Addressed each other in the Chaldean tongue

A languid south wind feigned autumn out of doors
The banquet guests were so many amorous pairs
Who said one by one Thief you are forgiven
Here is the salt and here the wheaten bread

Broth growing cold will seem dull to your lips
But a goatskin bottle keeps the white wine chill
Do you wish them ironically to serve a dish of beans
Or fritters of flowers dipped in blond honey

A woman spoke to him You invoke no one
Do you believe in chance that flows through the hourglass
Are you versed in the laws in spite of men
Thief do you want the amulet from my necklace

Larron des fruits tourne vers moi tes yeux lyriques
Emplissez de noix la besace du héros
Il est plus noble que le paon pythagorique
Le dauphin la vipère mâle ou le taureau

Qui donc es-tu toi qui nous vins grâce au vent scythe
Il en est tant venu par la route ou la mer
Conquérants égarés qui s'éloignaient trop vite
Colonnes de clins d'yeux qui fuyaient aux éclairs

CHŒUR

Un homme bègue ayant au front deux jets de flammes
Passa menant un peuple infime pour l'orgueil
De manger chaque jour les cailles et la manne
Et d'avoir vu la mer ouverte comme un œil

Les puiseurs d'eau barbus coiffés de bandelettes
Noires et blanches contre les maux et les sorts
Revenaient de l'Euphrate et les yeux des chouettes
Attiraient quelquefois les chercheurs de trésors

Cet insecte jaseur ô poète barbare
Regagnait chastement à l'heure d'y mourir
La forêt précieuse aux oiseaux gemmipares
Aux crapauds que l'azur et les sources mûrirent

Un triomphe passait gémir sous l'arc-en-ciel
Avec de blêmes laurés debout dans les chars
Les statues suant les scurriles les agnelles
Et l'angoisse rauque des paonnes et des jars

Les veuves précédaient en égrenant des grappes
Les évêques noirs révérant sans le savoir
Au triangle isocèle ouvert au mors des chapes
Pallas et chantaient l'hymne à la belle mais noire

THE THIEF

Filcher of fruit gaze at me with lyric eyes
Heap with walnuts the hero's begging sack
He is nobler than Pythagorean peacock
Than the dolphin the male viper or the bull

Who are you blown hither by Scythian winds
So many have wandered this way by sea or land
Conquerors men who were lost or too swiftly withdrew
Columns of glances flew past on the lightning

CHOROS

A stammering man whose forehead bore twin flames
Passed leading a mean crowd their pride
Was to feed each day on quail and manna
And to have glimpsed the sea naked as an eye

Bearded men drawers of water who wear black-and-white
Head bands against mischief or spells
Returned from the Euphrates and the eyes of owls
Lured an occasional treasure-seeker

Chatter of insects O barbarian poet
Swelled chastely at the dying hour
In the precious woods where birds lay jewel-buds
And azure and pools bring toads to ripeness

A triumph passed groaning beneath the rainbow
Pale charioteers stood wreathed with laurel
There were sweating statues buffoons ewe-lambs
And the discordant anguish of peacocks and ganders

Widows nibbling bunches of grapes walked before
Black bishops who worshipped unknowingly
Pallas of the isosceles triangle and blazoned cope
And those widows hymned the black but comely

LE LARRON

Les chevaucheurs nous jetèrent dans l'avenir
Les alcancies pleines de cendre ou bien de fleurs
Nous aurons des baisers florentins sans le dire
Mais au jardin ce soir tu vins sage et voleur

Ceux de ta secte adorent-ils un signe obscène
Belphégor le soleil le silence ou le chien
Cette furtive ardeur des serpents qui s'entr'aiment

L'ACTEUR

Et le larron des fruits cria Je suis chrétien

CHŒUR

Ah! Ah! les colliers tinteront cherront les masques
Va-t'en va-t'en contre le feu l'ombre prévaut
Ah! Ah! le larron de gauche dans la bourrasque
Rira de toi comme hennissent les chevaux

FEMME

Larron des fruits tourne vers moi tes yeux lyriques
Emplissez de noix la besace du héros
Il est plus noble que le paon pythagorique
Le dauphin la vipère mâle ou le taureau

CHŒUR

Ah! Ah! nous secouerons toute la nuit les sistres
La voix ligure était-ce donc un talisman
Et si tu n'es pas de droite tu es sinistre
Comme une tache grise ou le pressentiment

Puisque l'absolu choit la chute est une preuve
Qui double devient triple avant d'avoir été
Nous avouons que les grossesses nous émeuvent
Les ventres pourront seuls nier l'aséité

THE THIEF

Riders flung to us in a future time
Clay spheres stuffed with ashes or with flowers
In silence we shall have Florentine kisses
But to the garden this evening you came a thief and wise

Do those of your sect adore an obscene sign
Belphegor the sun or silence or the dog
The stealthy desire of serpents intertwined

ACTOR

And the filcher of fruit cried out I am Christian

CHOROS

Ah! the necklaces will tinkle the masks will fall
Go against the fire a shadow prevails
Ah! the thief on the left in the gust of wind
Will laugh at you like a horse that whinnies

WOMAN

Filcher of fruit gaze at me with lyric eyes
Heap with walnuts the hero's begging sack
He is nobler than Pythagorean peacock
Than the dolphin the male viper or the bull

CHOROS

Ah! all night we shall rattle the sistra
Did you think the Ligurian voice a talisman
And if you are not to the right you are sinister
Like a foreboding or a gray stain

Since the absolute falls the fall is a proof
What doubles is triple before having been
We avow that pregnancies move us
Bellies alone will refute aseity

Vois les vases sont pleins d'humides fleurs morales
Va-t'en mais dénudé puisque tout est à nous
Ouïs du chœur des vents les cadences plagales
Et prends l'arc pour tuer l'unicorne ou le gnou

L'ombre équivoque et tendre est le deuil de ta chair
Et sombre elle est humaine et puis la nôtre aussi
Va-t'en le crépuscule a des lueurs légères
Et puis aucun de nous ne croirait tes récits

Il brillait et attirait comme la pantaure
Que n'avait-il la voix et jupes d'Orphée
Et les femmes la nuit feignant d'être des taures
L'eussent aimé comme on l'aima puisqu'en effet

Il était pâle il était beau comme un roi ladre
Que n'avait-il la voix et les jupes d'Orphée
La pierre prise au foie d'un vieux coq de Tanagre
Au lieu du roseau triste et du funèbre faix

Que n'alla-t-il vivre à la cour du roi d'Édesse
Maigre et magique il eût scruté le firmament
Pâle et magique il eût aimé des poétesses
Juste et magique il eut épargné les démons

Va-t'en errer crédule et roux avec ton ombre
Soit! la triade est mâle et tu es vierge et froid
Le tact est relatif mais la vue est oblongue
Tu n'as de signe que le signe de la croix

See the vases are 'filled with moist flower emblems
Go but denuded since everything is ours
Hear plagal cadences upon the gale
And take the bow to kill the unicorn or gnu

The equivocal soft shadow is your flesh that grieves
And is somber it is human as ours is too
Go for twilight reveals gentle glimmers
Indeed none of us would believe your tales

He gleamed and enticed like a magic stone
If only he had Orpheus' voice and robe
The women at night pretending to be heifers
Would have loved him as they loved him for indeed

He was pale he was handsome like a leprous king
If only he had Orpheus' voice and robe
The gallstone of an old Tanagrine rooster
Not the sad reed and funereal load

If only he had gone to the king of Edessa's court
Thin and magical he'd have perused the heavens
Pale and magical have loved poetesses
Just and magical have spared demons

Go wander naïve and red-haired with your shadow
So be it! the triad is male and you are virginal and cold
Touch is relative but sight is oblong
You have no sign but the sign of the cross

Le Vent nocturne

Oh! les cimes des pins grincent en se heurtant
Et l'on entend aussi se lamenter l'autan
Et du fleuve prochain à grand'voix triomphales
Les elfes rire au vent ou corner aux rafales
Attys Attys Attys charmant et débraillé
C'est ton nom qu'en la nuit les elfes ont raillé
Parce qu'un de tes pins s'abat au vent gothique
La forêt fuit au loin comme une armée antique
Dont les lances ô pins s'agitent au tournant
Les villages éteints méditent maintenant
Comme les vierges les vieillards et les poètes
Et ne s'éveilleront au pas de nul venant
Ni quand sur leurs pigeons fondront les gypaètes

Night Wind

Oh! the pine tops creak as they scrape their boughs together
I hear too the south wind lamenting
And from the river triumphal voices
Of elves who laugh at the wind or shout with each gust
Attis Attis Attis charming untidy
It is your name they have mocked in the night
Because one of your pines falls in the gothic wind
The forest withdraws in flight like an ancient army
Whose lances O pines wave as they turn
Villages are extinguished and now they meditate
Like virgins old men or poets
They will not wake for anyone who comes
But slumber though vultures swoop on their pigeons

Lul de Faltenin

à Louis de Gonzague Frick

Sirènes j'ai rampé vers vos
Grottes tiriez aux mers la langue
En dansant devant leurs chevaux
Puis battiez de vos ailes d'anges
Et j'écoutais ces chœurs rivaux

Une arme ô ma tête inquiète
J'agite un feuillard défleuri
Pour écarter l'haleine tiède
Qu'exhalent contre mes grands cris
Vos terribles bouches muettes

Il y a là-bas la merveille
Au prix d'elle que valez-vous
Le sang jaillit de mes otelles
A mon aspect et je l'avoue
Le meurtre de mon double orgueil

Si les bateliers ont ramé
Loin des lèvres à fleur de l'onde
Mille et mille animaux charmés
Flairent la route à la rencontre
De mes blessures bien-aimées

Leurs yeux étoiles bestiales
Éclairent ma compassion
Qu'importe ma sagesse égale
Celle des constellations
Car c'est moi seul nuit qui t'étoile

Lul of Faltenin

to *Louis de Gonzague Frick*

Sirens I clambered toward your caves
You thrust your tongues out at the waves
And danced before their horses
Then clapped your angel wings while I
Listened to those rival choirs

A weapon O my restless brow
I agitate a withered bough
And fan the tepid breath
Exhaled against my shrill cries
By your fearful quiet mouths

There waits down yonder a wonder
What are you compared to it
Blood leaps from my heraldic wounds
At my approach and I confess
The slaying of my double pride

If the boatmen rowed away
From lips that stir the water
More than a thousand charmed beasts
Scent the trail when they encounter
My cherished wounds

Their eyes starlike bestial
Illumine my compassion
But no matter my wisdom
Equals that of stars
Night I am the one who constellates you

Sirènes enfin je descends
Dans une grotte avide J'aime
Vos yeux Les degrés sont glissants
Au loin que vous devenez naines
N'attirez plus aucun passant

Dans l'attentive et bien-apprise
J'ai vu feuilloler nos forêts
Mer le soleil se gargarise
Où les matelots désiraient
Que vergues et mâts reverdissent

Je descends et le firmament
S'est changé très vite en méduse
Puisque je flambe atrocement
Que mes bras seuls sont les excuses
Et les torches de mon tourment

Oiseaux tiriez aux mers la langue
Le soleil d'hier m'a rejoint
Les otelles nous ensanglantent
Dans le nid des Sirènes loin
Du troupeau d'étoiles oblongues

Sirens at last I clamber down
Into a gaping cave I love
Your eyes The stairs are slippery
From afar turned into dwarves
You no longer lure the passerby

In the watchful well-learned
Sea gargles the sun
I have seen our forests slowly leaf
Where sailors once yearned
That yard and mast grow green again

I descend and the firmament
Has swiftly changed to a sea medusa
Because I flame atrociously
And my arms are the sole excuse
And torches of my torment

Birds thrusting your tongues out at the sea
Yesterday's sun caught up with me
We are stained with heraldic blood
In the sirens' nest far far
From all flocks of oblong stars

La Tzigane

La tzigane savait d'avance
Nos deux vies barrées par les nuits
Nous lui dîmes adieu et puis
De ce puits sortit l'Espérance

L'amour lourd comme un ours privé
Dansa debout quand nous voulûmes
Et l'oiseau bleu perdit ses plumes
Et les mendiants leurs *Ave*

On sait très bien que l'on se damne
Mais l'espoir d'aimer en chemin
Nous fait penser main dans la main
A ce qu'a prédit la tzigane

The Gypsy

The gypsy knew ahead of time
Night's shadow on our lives
We bade her farewell and
Then hope welled from hiding

Heavy as a tame bear
Love danced at our command
The bluebird shed its plumes
And the beggars their *Aves*

One knows when one is damned
Still the hope of love along the way
Makes us ponder hand in hand
What the gypsy foretold

L'Ermite

à Félix Fénéon

Un ermite déchaux près d'un crâne blanchi
Cria Je vous maudis martyres et détresses
Trop de tentations malgré moi me caressent
Tentations de lune et de logomachies

Trop d'étoiles s'enfuient quand je dis mes prières
O chef de morte O vieil ivoire Orbites Trous
Des narines rongées J'ai faim Mes cris s'enrouent
Voici donc pour mon jeûne un morceau de gruyère

O Seigneur flagellez les nuées du coucher
Qui vous tendent au ciel de si jolis culs roses
Et c'est le soir les fleurs de jour déjà se closent
Et les souris dans l'ombre incantent le plancher

Les humains savent tant de jeux l'amour la mourre
L'amour jeu des nombrils ou jeu de la grande oie
La mourre jeu du nombre illusoire des doigts
Seigneur faites Seigneur qu'un jour je m'énamoure

J'attends celle qui me tendra ses doigts menus
Combien de signes blancs aux ongles les paresses
Les mensonges pourtant j'attends qu'elle les dresse
Ses mains énamourées devant moi l'Inconnue

Seigneur que t'ai-je fait Vois Je suis unicorne
Pourtant malgré son bel effroi concupiscent
Comme un poupon chéri mon sexe est innocent
D'être anxieux seul et debout comme une borne

The Hermit

to Félix Fénéon

A barefoot hermit beside a whitened skull
Cried out I curse you martyrs and agonies
Too many temptations lure me against my will
Temptations of the moon and logomachies

Too many stars run off when I recite my prayers
O woman's head Old ivory O sockets Caves
Of fretted nostrils My voice grows harsh I starve
Then here for my fasting is a crumb of gruyère

O Lord flog the sunset clouds
Flaunting for you sweet rosy bottoms
Twilight falls already day's blossoms close
And shadowy mice bewitch the floor

Men know so many games mora amor
Amor game of navels or game of mother goose
Mora game of a knavish sum of fingers
Lord let me Lord one day fall in love

I wait for a woman who will offer me slender fingers
So many signals with white nails indolence
And lies yet I wait till she raise
Enamored hands before me she who is Unknown

Lord how did I offend you See I am unicorn
Yet in spite of its lovely lusting fright
Like a cherished baby my sex is innocent
Anxious alone and upright like a milestone

L'ERMITE

Seigneur le Christ est nu jetez sur lui
La robe sans couture éteignez les ardeurs
Au puits vont se noyer tant de tintements d'heures
Quand isochrones choient des gouttes d'eau de pluie

J'ai veillé trente nuits sous les lauriers-roses
As-tu sué du sang Christ dans Gethsémani
Crucifié réponds Dis non Moi je le nie
Car j'ai trop espéré en vain l'hématidrose

J'écoutais à genoux toquer les battements
Du cœur le sang roulait toujours en ses artères
Qui sont de vieux coraux ou qui sont des clavaires
Et mon aorte était avare éperdument

Une goutte tomba Sueur Et sa couleur
Lueur Le sang si rouge et j'ai ri des damnés
Puis enfin j'ai compris que je saignais du nez
A cause des parfums violents de mes fleurs

Et j'ai ri du vieil ange qui n'est point venu
De vol très indolent me tendre un beau calice
J'ai ri de l'aile grise et j'ôte mon cilice
Tissé de crins soyeux par de cruels canuts

Vertuchou Riotant des vulves des papesses
De saintes sans tétons j'irai vers les cités
Et peut-être y mourir pour ma virginité
Parmi les mains les peaux les mots et les promesses

Malgré les autans bleus je me dresse divin
Comme un rayon de lune adoré par la mer
En vain j'ai supplié tous les saints aémères
Aucun n'a consacré mes doux pains sans levain

Et je marche Je fuis ô nuit Lilith ulule

THE HERMIT

Lord Christ is naked throw down upon him
The seamless robe quench every ardor
In the well are drowned so many tolling hours
When isochronal raindrops fall

I kept watch thirty nights beneath the oleanders
Christ did you sweat blood at Gethsemane
You who were crucified Say no You deny it
I hoped too much and vainly the hemathidrosis

I knelt and listened to my pulsing heart
Knock loudly through my arteries the blood still beat
Through those ancient corals those clavaria
And my aorta was a distracted miser

A drop fell Sweat And its color
A glimmer The blood so red that I chuckled at the damned
Then saw it was my nose that bled
From the violent perfume of my flowers

And I mocked the old angel who never once leaned
From his lazy flight to hand me a fair chalice
I mocked the gray wing and then shed the hairshirt
Woven of shiny horsehair by cruel silk weavers

By thunder Smirking at the sex of popesses
And titless lady saints I am off to the city
Perhaps to die there for my virginity
Among hands and hides words and promises

In spite of blue south winds I arise divine
Like a moonbeam cherished by the waves
I implored all saints lacking feast days but in vain
None would bless my sweet unleavened loaves

And I wander I flee O night for Lilith howls

Et clame vainement et je vois de grands yeux
S'ouvrir tragiquement O nuit je vois tes cieux
S'étoiler calmement de splendides pilules

Un squelette de reine innocente est pendu
A un long fil d'étoile en désespoir sévère
La nuit les bois sont noirs et se meurt l'espoir vert
Quand meurt le jour avec un râle inattendu

Et je marche je fuis ô jour l'émoi de l'aube
Ferma le regard fixe et doux de vieux rubis
Des hiboux et voici le regard des brebis
Et des truies aux tétins roses comme des lobes

Des corbeaux éployés comme des tildes font
Une ombre vaine aux pauvres champs de seigle mûr
Non loin des bourgs où des chaumières sont impures
D'avoir des hiboux morts cloués à leur plafond

Mes kilomètres longs Mes tristesses plénières
Les squelettes de doigts terminant les sapins
Ont égaré ma route et mes rêves poupins
Souvent et j'ai dormi au sol des sapinières

Enfin O soir pâmé Au bout de mes chemins
La ville m'apparut très grave au son des cloches
Et ma luxure meurt à présent que j'approche
En entrant j'ai béni les foules des deux mains

Cité j'ai ri de tes palais tels que des truffes
Blanches au sol fouillé de clairières bleues
Or mes désirs s'en vont tous à la queue leu leu
Ma migraine pieuse a coiffé sa cucuphe

Car toutes sont venues m'avouer leurs péchés
Et Seigneur je suis saint par le vœu des amantes

THE HERMIT

Vainly she calls and I see huge eyes
Widen sadly O night I see your skies
Tranquilly starred with resplendent pills

The skeleton of an innocent queen sways
From a long stellar wire in somber despair
Night and the woods are black green hope dies
When dies the day with an unexpected rattle

And I wander I flee O day for dawn's unease
Has shut the ruby eyes of owls
Staring and gentle now the sheep and the sows
With rosy teats like ear lobes turn to gaze

Crows deployed in tittle cast vain
Shadows on humble fields of rye
Not far from country towns where shanties are stained
With dead owls nailed to their ceilings

My long kilometers My absolute grief
Skeleton fingers at the pine bough's tip
Have confused my path and my naïve dreams
Often and stretched on the ground I dreamed of fir groves

At last O swooning twilight At the end of my road
Gravely to a sound of bells the city appeared
And now my lewdness dies as I draw near
I entered and with lifted hands blessed the crowds

City I mocked each palace that gleams
Like truffles on soil funneled by blue glades
Now my desires helter-skelter all run away
My pious migraine has donned its tea leaves

For all the women came to tell me their sins
And Lord by the vows of lovers I am saint

Zélotide et Lorie Louise et Diamante
Ont dit Tu peux savoir ô toi l'effarouché

Ermite absous nos fautes jamais vénielles
O toi le pur et le contrit que nous aimons
Sache nos cœurs sache les jeux que nous aimons
Et nos baisers quintessenciés comme du miel

Et j'absous les aveux pourpres comme leur sang
Des poétesses nues des fées des fornarines
Aucun pauvre désir ne gonfle ma poitrine
Lorsque je vois le soir les couples s'enlaçant

Car je ne veux plus rien sinon laisser se clore
Mes yeux couple lassé au verger pantelant
Plein du râle pompeux des groseilliers sanglants
Et de la sainte cruauté des passiflores

Zélotide and Lorie Louise and Diamante
Said You understand O you the startled one

Hermit absolve our faults which are always mortal
O you the pure the contrite whom we adore
Look into our hearts and know the games we love
And our kisses quintessential like honey

And I absolve avowals scarlet as the blood of these
Naked poetesses fornarinas and fairies
My breast swells with no shabby desire
When I see the couples embracing at twilight

For I no longer want anything but to close
My eyes weary couple panting in the grove
Full of the pompous rattle of blood-stained currant boughs
And the saintly cruelty of passionflowers

Automne

Dans le brouillard s'en vont un paysan cagneux
Et son bœuf lentement dans le brouillard d'automne
Qui cache les hameaux pauvres et vergogneux

Et s'en allant là-bas le paysan chantonne
Une chanson d'amour et d'infidélité
Qui parle d'une bague et d'un cœur que l'on brise

Oh! l'automne l'automne a fait mourir l'été
Dans le brouillard s'en vont deux silhouettes grises

Autumn

Through mist a knock-kneed peasant and his
Bullock slowly pass through mist of autumn
That veils shabby villages

And as he goes his way the peasant hums
A song of love and faithlessness
That tells of a ring and a breaking heart

Autumn autumn has brought on summer's death
Through mist pass two gray silhouettes

L'Émigrant de Landor Road

à André Billy

Le chapeau à la main il entra du pied droit
Chez un tailleur très chic et fournisseur du roi
Ce commerçant venait de couper quelques têtes
De mannequins vêtus comme il faut qu'on se vête

La foule en tous les sens remuait en mêlant
Des ombres sans amour qui se traînaient par terre
Et des mains vers le ciel plein de lacs de lumière
S'envolaient quelquefois comme des oiseaux blancs

Mon bateau partira demain pour l'Amérique
Et je ne reviendrai jamais
Avec l'argent gagné dans les prairies lyriques
Guider mon ombre aveugle en ces rues que j'aimais

Car revenir c'est bon pour un soldat des Indes
Les boursiers ont vendu tous mes crachats d'or fin
Mais habillé de neuf je veux dormir enfin
Sous des arbres pleins d'oiseaux muets et de singes

Les mannequins pour lui s'étant déshabillés
Battirent leurs habits puis les lui essayèrent
Le vêtement d'un lord mort sans avoir payé
Au rabais l'habilla comme un millionnaire

Au-dehors les années
Regardaient la vitrine
Les mannequins victimes
Et passaient enchaînées

The Emigrant from Landor Road

to André Billy

His hat in his hand and right foot first he strode
Into the stylish store of a royal haberdasher
That merchant had just severed several heads
Of dummies dressed in the latest manner

The crowd swayed in all directions mingling
Loveless shadows that dragged over the earth
And toward a sky full of lakes of light
Occasionally hands took flight like white birds

My boat leaves for America tomorrow
 And never shall I return
With money earned on the lyric prairies
To guide a blind shadow through streets I once loved

Homecoming is fine for the soldier from India
Gamblers have sold all my rare gold hardware
But clad in new clothes I want at last to slumber
Beneath trees full of monkeys and songless birds

For his sake the dummies disrobed
Shook out their raiment and arrayed him
The marked-down suit of a lord deceased without paying
Suited him like a millionaire

 Outside the years
 Peered through the pane
 At the victim dummies
 And passed on in chains

Intercalées dans l'an c'étaient les journées veuves
Les vendredis sanglants et lents d'enterrements
De blancs et de tout noirs vaincus des cieux qui pleuvent
Quand la femme du diable a battu son amant

Puis dans un port d'automne aux feuilles indécises
Quand les mains de la foule y feuillolaient aussi
Sur le pont du vaisseau il posa sa valise
 Et s'assit

Les vents de l'Océan en soufflant leurs menaces
Laissaient dans ses cheveux de longs baisers mouillés
Des émigrants tendaient vers le port leurs mains lasses
Et d'autres en pleurant s'étaient agenouillés

Il regarda longtemps les rives qui moururent
Seuls des bateaux d'enfant tremblaient à l'horizon
Un tout petit bouquet flottant à l'aventure
Couvrit l'Océan d'une immense floraison

Il aurait voulu ce bouquet comme la gloire
Jouer dans d'autres mers parmi tous les dauphins
 Et l'on tissait dans sa mémoire
 Une tapisserie sans fin
 Qui figurait son histoire

 Mais pour noyer changées en poux
Ces tisseuses têtues qui sans cesse interrogent
 Il se maria comme un doge
Aux cris d'une sirène moderne sans époux

Gonfle-toi vers la nuit O Mer Les yeux des squales
Jusqu'à l'aube ont guetté de loin avidement
Des cadavres de jours rongés par les étoiles
Parmi le bruit des flots et les derniers serments

In the year's procession were widowed days
Funereal Fridays bloody and slow
White ones and others all black vanquished by rainy skies
When the devil's wife has been beating her lover

In an autumnal port with its hesitant foliage
When the hands of the crowd were also like leaves
He placed his suitcase on the ship's deck
 And sat himself down

The winds of Ocean breathed their threats
And left in his hair long damp kisses
Emigrants stretched weary hands toward the harbor
Or wept and knelt down

Long he looked at the shores that died
Only toy boats trembled on the horizon
He would have wanted that bouquet like glory
And to frolic in other seas among all the dolphin

He could have wished that bouquet to frolic
Like glory in other seas among all the dolphin
 And there wove in his memory
 A tapestry endless
 That pictured his story

 But to change into lice and to drown
Those persistent weavers who ask without ceasing
 Like a doge he wedded
To the shrieks of a modern spinster siren

Swell O Sea toward nightfall The eyes of sharks
Till dawn have watched hungrily from afar
While the stars nibble dead days
Among the noise of waves and last promises

Rosemonde

à André Derain

Longtemps au pied du perron de
La maison où entra la dame
Que j'avais suivie pendant deux
Bonnes heures à Amsterdam
Mes doigts jetèrent des baisers

Mais le canal était désert
Le quai aussi et nul ne vit
Comment mes baisers retrouvèrent
Celle à qui j'ai donné ma vie
Un jour pendant plus de deux heures

Je la surnommai Rosemonde
Voulant pouvoir me rappeler
Sa bouche fleurie en Hollande
Puis lentement je m'en allai
Pour quêter la Rose du Monde

Rosemonde

to André Derain

Long at the foot of those stairs
Where I lost
Her whom I spent two
Hours pursuing in Amsterdam
My fingers blew kisses

Canal was forsaken
Embankment too no one saw
If my kisses had found
One who took from my life
More than two hours

I named her Rosemonde
Lest I forget
Mouth flowered in Holland
Then slowly I took my way
Seeking the rose of the world
La rose du monde

Le Brasier

à Paul-Napoléon Roinard

J'ai jeté dans le noble feu
Que je transporte et que j'adore
De vives mains et même feu
Ce Passé ces têtes de morts
Flamme je fais ce que tu veux

Le galop soudain des étoiles
N'étant que ce qui deviendra
Se mêle au hennissement mâle
Des centaures dans leurs haras
Et des grand'plaintes végétales

Où sont ces têtes que j'avais
Où est le Dieu de ma jeunesse
L'amour est devenu mauvais
Qu'au brasier les flammes renaissent
Mon âme au soleil se dévêt

Dans la plaine ont poussé des flammes
Nos cœurs pendent aux citronniers
Les têtes coupées qui m'acclament
Et les astres qui ont saigné
Ne sont que des têtes de femmes

Le fleuve épinglé sur la ville
T'y fixe comme un vêtement
Partant à l'amphion docile
Tu subis tous les tons charmants
Qui rendent les pierres agiles

The Brazier

to Paul-Napoléon Roinard

I have flung to the noble fire
Which I transport and I adore
Living hands and even that
Late Past those heads of the dead
Flame I do what you desire

The sudden gallop of the stars
What will be and nothing more
Mingles with the male cry
Of centaurs on their ranches
And huge vegetable laments

Where are the heads I had
Where is the god of my youth
Love has turned to wickedness
Let flames glow on the brazier
My soul strips naked in the sun

Over the plain flames sprang up
Our hearts sway from the lemon trees
The severed heads acclaiming me
The stars that bled
Are only women's heads

The river stapled to the town
Holds you imprisoned like a gown
Thus obeying Amphion
You suffer the charming tones
That quicken stones

*

Je flambe dans le brasier à l'ardeur adorable
Et les mains des croyants m'y rejettent multiple innombrablement
Les membres des intercis flambent auprès de moi
Éloignez du brasier les ossements
Je suffis pour l'éternité à entretenir le feu de mes délices
Et des oiseaux protègent de leurs ailes ma face et le soleil

O Mémoire Combien de races qui forlignent
Des Tyndarides aux vipères ardentes de mon bonheur
Et les serpents ne sont-ils que les cous des cygnes
Qui étaient immortels et n'étaient pas chanteurs
Voici ma vie renouvelée
De grands vaisseaux passent et repassent
Je trempe une fois encore mes mains dans l'Océan

Voici le paquebot et ma vie renouvelée
Ses flammes sont immenses
Il n'y a plus rien de commun entre moi
Et ceux qui craignent les brûlures

*

Descendant des hauteurs où pense la lumière
Jardins rouant plus haut que tous les ciels mobiles
L'avenir masqué flambe en traversant les cieux

Nous attendons ton bon plaisir ô mon amie

J'ose à peine regarder la divine mascarade

Quand bleuira sur l'horizon la Désirade

Au-delà de notre atmosphère s'élève un théâtre
Que construisit le ver Zamir sans instrument
Puis le soleil revint ensoleiller les places

*

I flame in the adorable heat of the brazier
Hands of believers thrust me down manifold countlessly
Limbs of torn martyrs burn near me
Banish from the brazier those bones of the dead
I shall forever suffice to stoke the fires of my delight
Birds with their wings shelter my face and the sun

O Memory How many strains decline
From the Tyndarides to the ardent vipers of my good luck
But are the serpents only necks of those swans
Who were immortal and not singers
Here is my renewed life
Great ships pass and pass again
I dip my hands once again in the Ocean

Here is the steamer and here my renewed life
Its flames are immense
I no longer have anything in common
With those who dread burns

*

Descending from heights where meditates the light
Gardens wheeling higher than all the unstable skies
The masked future aflame crosses the sky

We await your good pleasure my love

I scarcely dare gaze at the divine masquerade

When on the horizon will the island Désirade turn blue

Beyond our atmosphere rises a theater
Erected without tools by the worm Shamir
Then the sun returned to brighten the squares

D'une ville marine apparue contremont
Sur les toits se reposaient les colombes lasses

Et le troupeau de sphinx regagne la sphingerie
A petits pas Il orra le chant du pâtre toute la vie
Là-haut le théâtre est bâti avec le feu solide
Comme les astres dont se nourrit le vide

 Et voici le spectacle
Et pour toujours je suis assis dans un fauteuil
Ma tête mes genoux mes coudes vain pentacle
Les flammes ont poussé sur moi comme des feuilles

Des acteurs inhumains claires bêtes nouvelles
Donnent des ordres aux hommes apprivoisés
 Terre
O Déchirée que les fleuves ont reprisée

J'aimerais mieux nuit et jour dans les sphingeries
Vouloir savoir pour qu'enfin on m'y dévorât

Of a seaside city looming against the mountain
On the rooftops weary doves reposed

And the flock of sphinxes regains the sphinxery
Slowly They will hear all their lives the shepherd's song
Up there the theater is built of dense fire
Like stars that nourish empty space

 And here is the show
And for ever I am seated in the theater stall
My head knees and elbows vain five-pointed star
Flames shoot from me like leaves

Inhuman actors bright new beasts
Are giving orders to tamed men
 Earth
O rent earth the rivers have mended you

I would rather night and day in the sphinxeries
Desire to know and at last be devoured there

Rhénanes

Mon verre est plein d'un vin trembleur comme une flamme
Écoutez la chanson lente d'un batelier
Qui raconte avoir vu sous la lune sept femmes
Tordre leurs cheveux verts et longs jusqu'à leurs pieds

Debout chantez plus haut en dansant une ronde
Que je n'entende plus le chant du batelier
Et mettez près de moi toutes les filles blondes
Au regard immobile aux nattes repliées

Le Rhin le Rhin est ivre où les vignes se mirent
Tout l'or des nuits tombe en tremblant s'y refléter
La voix chante toujours à en râle-mourir
Ces fées aux cheveux verts qui incantent l'été

Mon verre s'est brisé comme un éclat de rire

MAI

Le mai le joli mai en barque sur le Rhin
Des dames regardaient du haut de la montagne
Vous êtes si jolies mais la barque s'éloigne
Qui donc a fait pleurer les saules riverains

Or des vergers fleuris se figeaient en arrière
Les pétales tombés des cerisiers de mai

Rhénanes

RHENISH NIGHT

My glass glows with a wine that flickers like flame
Listen to the boatman's slow song
He has seen seven maids in the moonlight
Twisting their long green hair

Up dancers form a ring sing louder
Drown out the boatman's song
And bring me all the blonde young girls
With their cool glance and braided hair

The Rhine the drunken Rhine mirrors vineyards
Night's gold trembles in his stream
Still I hear that death-rattle song
Of green-haired witches casting spells on summer

My glass has shattered like a burst of laughter

MAY

May fair May sailing the Rhine
Ladies kept watch from the high mountains
How handsome you are but the ship sails on
Who made the river willows weep

Flowering orchards congealed in our wake
Petals shed by cherry boughs

Sont les ongles de celle que j'ai tant aimée
Les pétales flétris sont comme ses paupières

Sur le chemin du bord du fleuve lentement
Un ours un singe un chien menés par des tziganes
Suivaient une roulotte trainée par un âne
Tandis que s'éloignait dans les vignes rhénanes
Sur un fifre lointain un air de régiment

Le mai le joli mai a paré les ruines
De lierre de vigne vierge et de rosiers
Le vent du Rhin secoue sur le bord les osiers
Et les roseaux jaseurs et les fleurs nues des vignes

LA SYNAGOGUE

Ottomar Scholem et Abraham Lœweren
Coiffés de feutres verts le matin du sabbat
Vont à la synagogue en longeant le Rhin
Et les coteaux où les vignes rougissent là-bas

Ils se disputent et crient des choses qu'on ose à peine traduire
Bâtard conçu pendant les règles ou Que le diable entre dans ton
 père
Le vieux Rhin soulève sa face ruisselante et se détourne pour
 sourire
Ottomar Scholem et Abraham Lœweren sont en colère

Parce que pendant le sabbat on ne doit pas fumer
Tandis que les chrétiens passent avec des cigares allumés
Et parce qu'Ottomar et Abraham aiment tous deux
Lia aux yeux de brebis et dont le ventre avance un peu

Pourtant tout à l'heure dans la synagogue l'un après l'autre

Are the fingernails of one I loved
Wilted petals are like her eyelids

Along the stream's edge slowly along the trail
Came a bear a monkey a dog at the heel
Of gypsies and a cart a donkey drew
While fading through the Rhenish vineyards
A far fife played a regimental air

May fair May has adorned the ruins
With ivy with creeper and with roses
A Rhine wind ruffles the river osiers
The gossipy reeds and the vines' bare flowers

THE SYNAGOGUE

Ottomar Scholem and Abraham Loeweren
In green felt hats of a sabbath morning
On their way to the synagogue stroll along the Rhine
Beneath hills where the vines are reddening

Their shouts are scarcely translatable
Bastard conceived at the wrong time of month or May the devil
 possess your father
The old Rhine lifts wet face and hides a smile
When they grow angry

Because they may not smoke on the sabbath
And Christians are passing with lit cigars
Because Ottomar and Abraham both adore
Lia of the sheep's eyes and protruding belly

Yet at the synagogue they will kiss the Torah

Ils baiseront la thora en soulevant leur beau chapeau
Parmi les feuillards de la fête des cabanes
Ottomar en chantant sourira à Abraham

Ils déchanteront sans mesure et les voix graves des hommes
Feront gémir un Léviathan au fond du Rhin comme une voix
 d'automne
Et dans la synagogue pleine de chapeaux on agitera les loulabim
Hanoten ne Kamoth bagoim tholahoth baleoumim

LES CLOCHES

Mon beau tzigane mon amant
Écoute les cloches qui sonnent
Nous nous aimions éperdument
Croyant n'être vus de personne

Mais nous étions bien mal cachés
Toutes les cloches à la ronde
Nous ont vus du haut des clochers
Et le disent à tout le monde

Demain Cyprien et Henri
Marie Ursule et Catherine
La boulangère et son mari
Et puis Gertrude ma cousine

Souriront quand je passerai
Je ne saurai plus où me mettre
Tu seras loin Je pleurerai
 J'en mourrai peut-être

In turn and lift lovely hats
Among boughs hung for the Feast of the Tabernacle
Ottomar as he sings will smile at Abraham

Flat unrhythmic their deep tones
Make a Leviathan groan from the depths of the Rhine like
 voice of autumn
While beyond the hats someone waves loulabim
Hanoten ne Kamoth bagoim tholahoth baleoumim

BELLS

My fair gypsy my love
Listen to the bells
We loved madly
Thinking no one knew

But we hid ourselves poorly
All the bells around
Saw from their steeples
And are telling the world

Tomorrow Cyprian Henry
Mary Ursula Catherine
The bakeress her husband
And cousin Gertrude

Will smile as I pass by
I won't know what to do
With you far away I shall cry
 And maybe even die

LA LORELEY

à Jean Sève

A Bacharach il y avait une sorcière blonde
Qui laissait mourir d'amour tous les hommes à la ronde

Devant son tribunal l'évêque la fit citer
D'avance il l'absolvit à cause de sa beauté

O belle Loreley aux yeux pleins de pierreries
De quel magicien tiens-tu ta sorcellerie

Je suis lasse de vivre et mes yeux sont maudits
Ceux qui m'ont regardée évêque en ont péri

Mes yeux ce sont des flammes et non des pierreries
Jetez jetez aux flammes cette sorcellerie

Je flambe dans ces flammes ô belle Loreley
Qu'un autre te condamne tu m'as ensorcelé

Évêque vous riez Priez plutot pour moi la Vierge
Faites-moi donc mourir et que Dieu vous protège

Mon amant est parti pour un pays lointain
Faites-moi donc mourir puisque je n'aime rien

Mon cœur me fait si mal il faut bien que je meure
Si je me regardais il faudrait que j'en meure

Mon cœur me fait si mal depuis qu'il n'est plus là
Mon cœur me fit si mal du jour où il s'en alla

L'évêque fit venir trois chevaliers avec leurs lances
Menez jusqu'au couvent cette femme en démence

THE LORELEI

to Jean Sève

In Bacharach there lived a witchlike blonde
Who let languish from love all the men around

Before his tribunal the bishop bade her appear
Already he absolved a lady so fair

Fair Lorelei your eyes are costly gems
Say from what source your sorcery comes

I weary of life accursed are my eyes
All perish bishop who encounter my gaze

My eyes are filled with flames not costly gems
Fling fling their magic spell into the flames

I burn in those flames fair Lorelei
I am bewitched another must preside

Bishop you grow merry Pray to Mary instead
God will reward you if you grant me death

To a far country my love has gone
Condemn me to die for I love no one

My heart grieves me so that I must die
Should I glimpse my own face I must die

My heart grieves me so now he is not here
My heart grieved me so the day he took leave

The bishop has summoned three knights with their weapons
Lead to the convent this demented woman

Va-t'en Lore en folie va Lore aux yeux tremblants
Tu seras une nonne vêtue de noir et blanc

Puis ils s'en allèrent sur la route tous les quatre
La Loreley les implorait et ses yeux brillaient comme des astres

Chevaliers laissez-moi monter sur ce rocher si haut
Pour voir une fois encore mon beau château

Pour me mirer une fois encore dans le fleuve
Puis j'irai au couvent des vierges et des veuves

Là-haut le vent tordait ses cheveux déroulés
Les chevaliers criaient Loreley Loreley

Tout là-bas sur le Rhin s'en vient une nacelle
Et mon amant s'y tient il m'a vue il m'appelle

Mon cœur devient si doux c'est mon amant qui vient
Elle se penche alors et tombe dans le Rhin

Pour avoir vu dans l'eau la belle Loreley
Ses yeux couleur du Rhin ses cheveux de soleil

SCHINDERHANNES

à Marius-Ary Leblond

Dans la forêt avec sa bande
Schinderhannes s'est désarmé
Le brigand près de sa brigande
Hennit d'amour au joli mai

Benzel accroupi lit la Bible
Sans voir que son chapeau pointu

Go mad Lore go Lore with trembling gaze
You shall be a nun in black and white guise

Then they went down the high road all the four
The Lorelei whose face gleamed like a star

Cried Lords let me climb this lofty stone
So I may see my fine castle again

So I may see myself once more in the waves
Before I join a convent of maids and old wives

On high the wind twisted her unbound hair
Lorelei Lorelei The knights shouted to her

Below on the Rhine a ship comes sailing
My love is upon it he sees me he is calling

My heart softens so now that he arrives
She faltered then and plummeted into the waves

For she had glimpsed in the water the fair Lorelei
Eyes color of the Rhine hair like sunlight

SCHINDERHANNES

to Marius-Ary Leblond

Deep in the forest with his gang
Schinderhannes stows his arms away
The highwayman near his highway spouse
Neighs lustily the month is May

Benzel squats and reads the Bible
Unaware that his pointed hat

A plume d'aigle sert de cible
A Jacob Born le mal foutu

Juliette Blaesius qui rote
Fait semblant d'avoir le hoquet
Hannes pousse une fausse note
Quand Schulz vient portant un baquet

Et s'écrie en versant des larmes
Baquet plein de vin parfumé
Viennent aujourd'hui les gendarmes
Nous aurons bu le vin de mai

Allons Julia la mam'zelle
Bois avec nous ce clair bouillon
D'herbes et de vin de Moselle
Prosit Bandit en cotillon

Cette brigande est bientôt soûle
Et veut Hannes qui n'en veut pas
Pas d'amour maintenant ma poule
Sers-nous un bon petit repas

Il faut ce soir que j'assassine
Ce riche juif au bord du Rhin
Au clair des torches de résine
La fleur de mai c'est le florin

On mange alors toute la bande
Pète et rit pendant le dîner
Puis s'attendrit à l'allemande
Avant d'aller assassiner

With its eagle feather is a target
For Jacob Born to sling things at

Juliette Blaesius burps pretends
It was a hiccup she let out
Hannes utters a discordant shout
When Schulz comes bringing in a bucket

And then he hollers shedding tears
O bucket full of perfumed wine
If the police should come today
We'll have downed the wine of May

Come on Julia my mamzelle
Drink with us this decanted mess
Of herbs and Moselle wine Prosit
My bandit in a lady's dress

That highway floozy is soon drunk
And turns to Hannes who turns his back
Let's have no petting now my chick
Fix us a tasty little snack

Tonight I must go forth and slay
That wealthy Jew beside the Rhine
And all by the light of resin torches
The florin is the flower of May

And so they pitch in the whole gang
Farts and guffaws throughout the meal
Then they turn tender German fashion
Before sallying forth to slay and steal

RHÉNANE D'AUTOMNE

à Toussaint-Luca

Les enfants des morts vont jouer
Dans le cimetière
Martin Gertrude Hans et Henri
Nul coq n'a chanté aujourd'hui
Kikiriki

Les vieilles femmes
Tout en pleurant cheminent
Et les bons ânes
Braillent hi han et se mettent à brouter les fleurs
Des couronnes mortuaires

C'est le jour des morts et de toutes leurs âmes
Les enfants et les vieilles femmes
Allument des bougies et des cierges
Sur chaque tombe catholique
Les voiles des vieilles
Les nuages du ciel
Sont comme des barbes de biques

L'air tremble de flammes et de prières

Le cimetière est un beau jardin
Plein de saules gris et de romarins
Il vous vient souvent des amis qu'on enterre
Ah! que vous êtes bien dans le beau cimetière
Vous mendiants morts saouls de bière
Vous les aveugles comme le destin
Et vous petits enfants morts en prière

Ah! que vous êtes bien dans le beau cimetière

AUTUMN RHÉNANE

to Toussaint-Luca

Dead men's children play
In the cemetery
Martin Gertrude Hans and Henry
No cock has crowed today
Kikiriki

The old women
Weep as they walk
The meek donkeys
Bray hee haw and nip the flowers
That wreathe the tombstones

On this the feast of all souls
Children and wives
Light tapers
By each Catholic grave
The women's veils
The clouds above them
Wave like a goat's beard

Flame and prayer shake the air

The cemetery is a fair garden
Of gray willow and rosemary
Those we have buried come to mind
How softly you sleep in your garden graves
Beggars who died drinking beer
You who were blind as fate
And little children dead in prayer

How softly you sleep in the fair cemetery

Vous bourgmestres vous bateliers
Et vous conseillers de régence
Vous aussi tziganes sans papiers
La vie vous pourrit dans la panse
La croix vous pousse entre les pieds

Le vent du Rhin ulule avec tous les hiboux
Il éteint les cierges que toujours les enfants rallument
Et les feuilles mortes
Viennent couvrir les morts

Des enfants morts parlent parfois avec leur mère
Et des mortes parfois voudraient bien revenir

Oh! je ne veux pas que tu sortes
L'automne est plein de mains coupées
Non non ce sont des feuilles mortes
Ce sont les mains des chères mortes
Ce sont tes mains coupées

Nous avons tant pleuré aujourd'hui
Avec ces morts leurs enfants et les vieilles femmes
Sous le ciel sans soleil
Au cimetière plein de flammes

Puis dans le vent nous nous en retournâmes

A nos pieds roulaient des châtaignes
Dont les bogues étaient
Comme le cœur blessé de la madone
Dont on doute si elle eut la peau
Couleur des châtaignes d'automne

Mayors and boatmen
Privy councillors
And all you gypsies without passports
Life seethes in your guts
The cross shoots up at our feet

A Rhine wind hoots with the owls
Puffs out the candles the young relight them
And now dead leaves
Blanket the graves

Ghost children cry to their mothers
Ghost women yearn to walk

But I shall not let you return
Autumn is full of severed hands
No no they are leaves
They are ghost hands once cherished
Your severed hands

We have mourned so today
With the dead with their children and wives
Under a sunless sky
In a graveyard dotted with flame

Then struggled homeward through the gale

Chestnuts lay scattered along our way
Burred like the
Virgin's wounded heart
But it is doubtful whether her skin
Was color of autumn chestnuts

LES SAPINS

Les sapins en bonnets pointus
De longues robes revêtus
 Comme des astrologues
Saluent leurs frères abattus
Les bateaux qui sur le Rhin voguent

Dans les sept arts endoctrinés
Par les vieux sapins leurs aînés
 Qui sont de grands poètes
Ils se savent prédestinés
A briller plus que des planètes

A briller doucement changés
En étoiles et enneigés
 Aux Noëls bienheureuses
Fêtes des sapins ensongés
Aux longues branches langoureuses

Les sapins beaux musiciens
Chantent des noëls anciens
 Au vent des soirs d'automne
Ou bien graves magiciens
Incantent le ciel quand il tonne

Des rangées de blancs chérubins
Remplacent l'hiver les sapins
 Et balancent leurs ailes
L'été ce sont de grands rabbins
Ou bien de vieilles demoiselles

Sapins médecins divagants
Ils vont offrant leurs bons onguents
 Quand la montagne accouche

FIR TREES

Fir trees in the peaked bonnets
And trailing robes
 Of astrologers
Hail their felled brothers
The boats sailing the Rhine

Raised in the seven arts
By the old firs their elders
 Who are great poets
They know themselves fated
To outshine the planets

To gleam subtly changed
Into stars all snowy
 On Christmas eves
To dream
Along langorous boughs

Fir trees fair musicians
Sing ancient carols
 In wind of autumn evenings
Or as grave magicians
Hurl spells on the thunder

Winter transforms them
To rows of white cherubim
 Rocking their wings
Summer to tall rabbis
Or aged spinsters

The pungent salves
Of these traveling doctors
 Heal the mountain in labor

De temps en temps sous l'ouragan
Un vieux sapin geint et se couche

LES FEMMES

Dans la maison du vigneron les femmes cousent
Lenchen remplis le poêle et mets l'eau du café
Dessus — Le chat s'étire après s'être chauffé
— Gertrude et son voisin Martin enfin s'épousent

Le rossignol aveugle essaya de chanter
Mais l'effraie ululant il trembla dans sa cage
Ce cyprès là-bas a l'air du pape en voyage
Sous la neige — Le facteur vient de s'arrêter

Pour causer avec le nouveau maître d'école
— Cet hiver est très froid le vin sera très bon
— Le sacristain sourd et boiteux est moribond
— La fille du vieux bourgmestre brode une étole

Pour la fête du curé La forêt là-bas
Grâce au vent chantait à voix grave de grand orgue
Le songe Herr Traum survint avec sa sœur Frau Sorge
Kaethi tu n'as pas bien raccommodé ces bas

— Apporte le café le beurre et les tartines
La marmelade le saindoux un pot de lait
— Encore un peu de café Lenchen s'il te plaît
— On dirait que le vent dit des phrases latines

— Encore un peu de café Lenchen s'il te plaît
— Lotte es-tu triste O petit cœur — Je crois qu'elle aime
— Dieu garde — Pour ma part je n'aime que moi-même
— Chut A présent grand-mère dit son chapelet

At times in a storm
An old fir creaks and sinks down to slumber

THE WOMEN

At the vine-grower's house the women sew
Lenchen fill the stove we shall want
Coffee—Cat stretches on the hearth
—So Gertrude and Martin at last will marry

From his cage the blind nightingale tried to sing
But an owl hooted and he trembled
Your cypress has a papal air
In the snow—Look the mailman's stopped he's

Chatting with the new schoolmaster
—This bitter weather means good wine
—Poor lame deaf sexton on his deathbed
—You know the mayor's daughter is embroidering a stole

For Father's birthday Outside the forest
Played low organ music in the wind
As Herr Dream arrived with his sister Frau Sorrow
Kaethi what a way to darn stockings

—You may serve the coffee now some bread and butter
Marmalade lard a pitcher of milk
—More coffee please Lenchen
—You'd think that the wind was speaking in Latin

—More coffee please Lenchen
—Lotte little heart why so sad?—Is it love?
—God forbid—I for one love only myself
—Hush grandmother is telling her beads

— *Il me faut du sucre candi Leni je tousse*
— *Pierre mène son furet chasser les lapins*
Le vent faisait danser en rond tous les sapins
Lotte l'amour rend triste — Ilse la vie est douce

La nuit tombait Les vignobles aux ceps tordus
Devenaient dans l'obscurité des ossuaires
En neige et repliés gisaient là des suaires
Et des chiens aboyaient aux passants morfondus

Il est mort écoutez La cloche de l'église
Sonnait tout doucement la mort du sacristain
Lise il faut attiser le poêle qui s'éteint
Les femmes se signaient dans la nuit indécise

Septembre 1901-mai 1902

—Have you a sugar lump Leni for my cough?
—Pierre's gone hunting with his ferret
Now wind danced the fir trees in a ring outside
Lotte love saddens—O Ilsa life is sweet

As night descended vineyards with contorted vines
In the darkness became charnel-houses
Where shrouds lay folded and snowy
The dogs bayed at each frozen passerby

Listen he is dead Softly the church bell
Tolled for the sexton
Lisa poke the stove or it will go out
And they crossed themselves in the enigmatic night

September 1901–May 1902

Signe

Je suis soumis au Chef du Signe de l'Automne
Partant j'aime les fruits je déteste les fleurs
Je regrette chacun des baisers que je donne
Tel un noyer gaulé dit au vent ses douleurs

Mon Automne éternelle ô ma saison mentale
Les mains des amantes d'antan jonchent ton sol
Une épouse me suit c'est mon ombre fatale
Les colombes ce soir prennent leur dernier vol

Sign

I serve the Lord of Autumn's Sign
And therefore love fruits loathe flowers
I regret each kiss given
Like the shaken nut tree that tells the wind its sorrows

My eternal Autumn O my soul's season
The hands of last year's lovers strew your soil
A woman pursues me she is my fated shadow
Doves tonight take their last flight

Un Soir

Un aigle descendit de ce ciel blanc d'archanges
 Et vous soutenez-moi
Laisserez-vous trembler longtemps toutes ces lampes
 Priez priez pour moi

La ville est métallique et c'est la seule étoile
 Noyée dans tes yeux bleus
Quand les tramways roulaient jaillissaient des feux pâles
 Sur des oiseaux galeux

Et tout ce qui tremblait dans tes yeux de mes songes
 Qu'un seul homme buvait
Sous les feux de gaz roux comme la fausse oronge
 O vêtue ton bras se lovait

Vois l'histrion tire la langue aux attentives
 Un fantôme s'est suicidé
L'apôtre au figuier pend et lentement salive
 Jouons donc cet amour aux dés

Des cloches aux sons clairs annonçaient ta naissance
 Vois
Les chemins sont fleuris et les palmes s'avancent
 Vers toi

One Evening

An eagle descended from skies white with archangels
 Uphold me
Will you let all those lamps flicker for long
 Pray pray for me

The city is metallic and it's the only star
 Drowned in your blue eyes
When trolley cars rumbled pale sparks flew upward
 Over mangy birds

And everything flickering in your eyes of my dreams
 Drained by one man only
Under gas lamps ruddy as mock orange agaric
 You all arrayed your arm curved toward me

See the actor stick out his tongue at the women staring
 A ghost has killed himself
The apostle hangs from the fig tree his saliva spills slowly
 Then why not hazard our love on a dice throw

Bells with shrill music announced your birth
 See
The paths are all flowered and palms are advancing
 Toward you

La Dame

Toc toc Il a fermé sa porte
Les lys du jardin sont flétris
Quel est donc ce mort qu'on emporte

Tu viens de toquer à sa porte
 Et trotte trotte
 Trotte la petite souris

The Lady

Knock knock He has shut his door
The garden lilies are faded
Who is that corpse they're carrying off

You were just knocking at his door
 And trot trot
 Trot little mouse

Les Fiançailles

à Picasso

Le printemps laisse errer les fiancés parjures
Et laisse feuilloler longtemps les plumes bleues
Que secoue le cyprès où niche l'oiseau bleu

Une Madone à l'aube a pris les églantines
Elle viendra demain cueillir les giroflées
Pour mettre aux nids des colombes qu'elle destine
Au pigeon qui ce soir semblait le Paraclet

Au petit bois de citronniers s'énamourèrent
D'amour que nous aimons les dernières venues
Les villages lointains sont comme leurs paupières
Et parmi les citrons leurs cœurs sont suspendus

*

Mes amis m'ont enfin avoué leur mépris
Je buvais à pleins verres les étoiles
Un ange a exterminé pendant que je dormais
Les agneaux les pasteurs des tristes bergeries
De faux centurions emportaient le vinaigre
Et les gueux mal blessés par l'épurge dansaient
Étoiles de l'éveil je n'en connais aucune
Les becs de gaz pissaient leur flamme au clair de lune
Des croque-morts avec des bocks tintaient des glas
A la clarté des bougies tombaient vaille que vaille
Des faux cols sur des flots de jupes mal brossées
Des accouchées masquées fêtaient leurs relevailles

The Betrothal

to Picasso

Spring lets foresworn lovers wander
And blue feathers leaf slowly down
Shaken from the cypress where the bluebird nests

Madonna plucked the eglantines at dawn
Tomorrow she will come and gather gillyflowers
And place them on the nests of those doves she destines
For the pigeon who this evening seemed the Holy Ghost

In the little lemon grove there fell in love
With love that we love the latest dove comers
Like their eyelids are towns in the distance
And among the lemons their hearts are swaying

 *

My friends have at last avowed to me their scorn
I drained tall tumblers full of stars
While I was sleeping an angel did away
With the lambs the shepherds of dreary sheepfolds
False centurions carried off the vinegar
And beggars sorely stung by spurge were dancing
Of stars that give warning I know not one
Gas lamps pissed their flame by moonlight
Undertakers clinked a knell on their beer mugs
By candlelight fell for better or worse
False collars upon streams of poorly brushed skirts
Masked women fêted their giving birth

La ville cette nuit semblait un archipel
Des femmes demandaient l'amour et la dulie
Et sombre sombre fleuve je me rappelle
Les ombres qui passaient n'étaient jamais jolies

*

Je n'ai plus même pitié de moi
Et ne puis exprimer mon tourment de silence
Tous les mots que j'avais à dire se sont changés en étoiles
Un Icare tente de s'élever jusqu'à chacun de mes yeux
Et porteur de soleils je brûle au centre de deux nébuleuses
Qu'ai-je fait aux bêtes théologales de l'intelligence
Jadis les morts sont revenus pour m'adorer
Et j'espérais la fin du monde
Mais la mienne arrive en sifflant comme un ouragan

*

J'ai eu le courage de regarder en arrière
Les cadavres de mes jours
Marquent ma route et je les pleure
Les uns pourrissent dans les églises italiennes
Ou bien dans de petits bois de citronniers
Qui fleurissent et fructifient
En même temps et en toute saison
D'autres jours ont pleuré avant de mourir dans des tavernes
Où d'ardents bouquets rouaient
Aux yeux d'une mulâtresse qui inventait la poésie
Et les roses de l'électricité s'ouvrent encore
Dans le jardin de ma mémoire

*

The city seemed an archipelago that night
Women asked for love and for fealty
And dark dark river I remember
The shadows passing by were never pretty

*

I no longer even pity myself
Am unable to express my silent anguish
All the words I wanted to say have changed to stars
An Icarus would fly into each of my eyes
And wafter of suns I burn in the midst of two nebulae
What have I done to the theological beasts of the mind
Once the dead returned to adore me
I awaited the end of the world
But mine arrives whistling like a hurricane

*

I have been brave enough to look back
The corpses of my days
Dot my journey and I mourn them
Some rot in Italian churches
Or in little lemon groves
That flower and bear fruit
All at once and in every season
Others wept before dying in taverns
Where blazing bouquets crumbled
Before the eyes of a mulatto girl who invented poetry
And the roses of electricity still unfold
In the garden of my memory

*

Pardonnez-moi mon ignorance
Pardonnez-moi de ne plus connaître l'ancien jeu des vers
Je ne sais plus rien et j'aime uniquement
Les fleurs à mes yeux redeviennent des flammes
Je médite divinement
Et je souris des êtres que je n'ai pas créés
Mais si le temps venait où l'ombre enfin solide
Se multipliait en réalisant la diversité formelle de mon amour
J'admirerais mon ouvrage

*

J'observe le repos du dimanche
Et je loue la paresse
Comment comment réduire
L'infiniment petite science
Que m'imposent mes sens
L'un est pareil aux montagnes au ciel
Aux villes à mon amour
Il ressemble aux saisons
Il vit décapité sa tête est le soleil
Et la lune son cou tranché
Je voudrais éprouver une ardeur infinie
Monstre de mon ouïe tu rugis et tu pleures
Le tonnerre te sert de chevelure
Et tes griffes répètent le chant des oiseaux
Le toucher monstrueux m'a pénétré m'empoisonne
Mes yeux nagent loin de moi
Et les astres intacts sont mes maîtres sans épreuve
La bête des fumées a la tête fleurie
Et le monstre le plus beau
Ayant la saveur du laurier se désole

*

Forgive my ignorance
Forgive me for having forgotten the old game of verses
I no longer know anything and can only love
Flowers before my eyes become flames once more
Divinely I meditate
And smile at beings I never created
But if the time came when the shadow tangible at last
Multiplied and achieved my love's diverse forms
Then I would admire my labors

*

I observe the Sunday calm
And praise indolence
How how to reduce
The infinitely little knowledge
That my senses impose upon me
One of them is like mountains or the sky
Like cities or like my love
He resembles the seasons
And lives beheaded his head is the sun
And the moon his slit throat
I long to compass an infinite ardor
Monster of my hearing you weep and roar
Your hair is thunder
And your claws echo bird song
Monstrous touch has pierced and poisons me
My eyes swim far away
And the inviolate stars are my unproven masters
The beast of vapors has a flowery head
And the most beautiful monster
The one who tastes of laurel is disconsolate

*

A la fin les mensonges ne me font plus peur
C'est la lune qui cuit comme un œuf sur le plat
Ce collier de gouttes d'eau va parer la noyée
Voici mon bouquet de fleurs de la Passion
Qui offrent tendrement deux couronnes d'épines
Les rues sont mouillées de la pluie de naguère
Des anges diligents travaillent pour moi à la maison
La lune et la tristesse disparaîtront pendant
Toute la sainte journée
Toute la sainte journée j'ai marché en chantant
Une dame penchée à sa fenêtre m'a regardé longtemps
M'éloigner en chantant

*

Au tournant d'une rue je vis des matelots
Qui dansaient le cou nu au son d'un accordéon
J'ai tout donné au soleil
Tout sauf mon ombre

Les dragues les ballots les sirènes mi-mortes
A l'horizon brumeux s'enfonçaient les trois-mâts
Les vents ont expiré couronnés d'anémones
O Vierge signe pur du troisième mois

*

Templiers flamboyants je brûle parmi vous
Prophétisons ensemble ô grand maître je suis
Le désirable feu qui pour vous se dévoue
Et la girande tourne ô belle ô belle nuit

Liens déliés par une libre flamme Ardeur
Que mon souffle éteindra O Morts à quarantaine

Lies at the last frighten me no longer
There's the moon that sizzles like an egg in the pan
That necklace of water will adorn the drowned girl
And here is my bouquet of passionflowers
Tenderly offering two crowns of thorns
The streets are awash with fresh rain
Busy angels labor for me at home
The moon and grief will vanish during
All the blessèd day
All the blessèd day I have walked singing
A lady leaned from her window and watched for a long while
As I withdrew into the distance singing

*

At a turn in the road I saw sailors
Dancing bare-necked to the sound of an accordion
All to the sun I have given
All but my shadow

Dragnets cotton bales half-dead sirens
At the misty horizon vanished a three-masted schooner
The winds have died down wreathed with anemones
O Virgin immaculate sign of the third month

*

Flamboyant knights templars I burn among you
Together great master let's prophesy I am
The desirable fire that consigns itself to you
And the girandole turns O lovely lovely night

Fetters loosened by a free flame Ardor
That my breath will snuff out O those dead at forty

Je mire de ma mort la gloire et le malheur
Comme si je visais l'oiseau de la quintaine

Incertitude oiseau feint peint quand vous tombiez
Le soleil et l'amour dansaient dans le village
Et tes enfants galants bien ou mal habillés
Ont bâti ce bûcher le nid de mon courage

I take aim with my death at suffering and renown
As if I had in view the bird of the quintain

Uncertainty faked painted bird when you tottered
Love and the sun danced in the village
And your gallant children in fine or wretched clothing
Built this funeral pyre the nest of my courage

Clair de Lune

Lune mellifluente aux lèvres des déments
Les vergers et les bourgs cette nuit sont gourmands
Les astres assez bien figurent les abeilles
De ce miel lumineux qui dégoutte des treilles
Car voici que tout doux et leur tombant du ciel
Chaque rayon de lune est un rayon de miel
Or caché je conçois la très douce aventure
J'ai peur du dard de feu de cette abeille Arcture
Qui posa dans mes mains des rayons décevants
Et prit son miel lunaire à la rose des vents

Clair de Lune

Moon dribbling honey upon lips of lunatics
Orchards and country towns tonight grow greedy
Stars resemble bees
Of a luminous liquid that drips from trellises
Each honey beam oozes from heaven
Taking its own sweet time
Hidden I glimpse the sweet adventure
But I fear the fiery sting of that bee Arcturus
He has flung me deceiving beams
And culled his moon honey from the compass rose of the winds

1909

La dame avait une robe
En ottoman violine
Et sa tunique brodée d'or
Était composée de deux panneaux
S'attachant sur l'épaule

Les yeux dansants comme des anges
Elle riait elle riait
Elle avait un visage aux couleurs de France
Les yeux bleus les dents blanches et les lèvres très rouges
Elle avait un visage aux couleurs de France

Elle était décolletée en rond
Et coiffée à la Récamier
Avec de beaux bras nus

N'entendra-t-on jamais sonner minuit

La dame en robe d'ottoman violine
Et en tunique brodée d'or
Décolletée en rond
Promenait ses boucles
Son bandeau l'or
Et traînait ses petits souliers à boucles

Elle était si belle
Que tu n'aurais pas osé l'aimer

1909

The lady's dress was
Of purple corded silk
And her gold-broidered tunic
Was formed of two panels
Fitted at the shoulder

Her eyes danced like angels
She laughed she laughed
Her face showed France's colors
Blue eyes white teeth and lips of scarlet
Her face showed France's colors

Her dress was scooped low front and back
Her hair was waved *à la Récamier*
And O the fair bare arms she had

Will midnight never toll the hour

The lady clad in the purple corded silk
And the gold-broidered tunic
Scooped low front and back
Tossed her curls
Her gold bandeau
And trailed wee buckled shoes

She was so beautiful
You wouldn't have dared love her

J'aimais les femmes atroces dans les quartiers énormes
Ou naissaient chaque jour quelques êtres nouveaux
Le fer était leur sang la flamme leur cerveau
J'aimais j'aimais le peuple habile des machines
Le luxe et la beauté ne sont que son écume
Cette femme était si belle
Qu'elle me faisait peur

I used to love dreadful women in crowded slums
Where each day a few new creatures were born
Iron was their blood and flame their brain
I loved I loved the clever tribe of machines
Luxury and beauty are only their spume
That woman was so beautiful
She frightened me

A la Santé

I

Avant d'entrer dans ma cellule
Il a fallu me mettre nu
Et quelle voix sinistre ulule
Guillaume qu'es-tu devenu

Le Lazare entrant dans la tombe
Au lieu d'en sortir comme il fit
Adieu adieu chantante ronde
O mes années ô jeunes filles

II

Non je ne me sens plus là
 Moi-même
Je suis le quinze de la
 Onzième

Le soleil filtre à travers
 Les vitres
Ses rayons font sur mes vers
 Les pitres

Et dansent sur le papier
 J'écoute
Quelqu'un qui frappe du pied
 La voûte

At the Santé

I

Before entering my prison cell
I had to undress
What sinister voice howled
Guillaume you have fallen

Lazarus descends into the tomb
Instead of leaving it
Farewell songs and dances
My youth O my loves

II

No I am no longer
 Myself
Only the fifteenth of the
 Eleventh

Sun filters through
 Windows
His light on my verses plays
 Like a clown

And dances over the paper
 Hush
Some one raps with his foot on
 The ceiling

III

Dans une fosse comme un ours
Chaque matin je me promène
Tournons tournons tournons toujours
Le ciel est bleu comme une chaîne
Dans une fosse comme un ours
Chaque matin je me promène

Dans la cellule d'à côté
On y fait couler la fontaine
Avec les clefs qu'il fait tinter
Que le geôlier aille et revienne
Dans la cellule d'à côté
On y fait couler la fontaine

IV

Que je m'ennuie entre ces murs tout nus
Et peints de couleurs pâles
Une mouche sur le papier à pas menus
Parcourt mes lignes inégales

Que deviendrai-je ô Dieu qui connais ma douleur
Toi qui me l'as donnée
Prends en pitié mes yeux sans larmes ma pâleur
Le bruit de ma chaise enchaînée

Et tous ces pauvres cœurs battant dans la prison
L'Amour qui m'accompagne
Prends en pitié surtout ma débile raison
Et ce désespoir qui la gagne

III

Every morning I pace
My pit like a bear
Turn turn again turn
Sky glitters like a chain
Every morning I pace
My pit like a bear

In the cell next to mine
Water is running
The jailer clinks his keys
As he comes and goes
In the cell next to mine
Water is running

IV

How weary I am surrounded by bare walls
 That are washed in pale colors
A fly on the paper minces
 Between my uneven verses

What will become of me God who knows my anguish
 You who gave it to me
Pity these tearless eyes my pallor
 The chair rattling its chains

And all poor hearts throbbing in prison
 May Love that never abandons me
Pity above all my faint reason
 And the grief that subdues it

V

Que lentement passent les heures
Comme passe un enterrement

Tu pleureras l'heure où tu pleures
Qui passera trop vitement
Comme passent toutes les heures

VI

J'écoute les bruits de la ville
Et prisonnier sans horizon
Je ne vois rien qu'un ciel hostile
Et les murs nus de ma prison

Le jour s'en va voici que brûle
Une lampe dans la prison
Nous sommes seuls dans ma cellule
Belle clarté Chère raison

Septembre 1911

V

How slowly time passes
As a funeral passes

You will regret this hour of tears
It will leave only too soon
Like all other hours

VI

I hear city noises
Prisoner with no horizon
I see only a hostile sky
And the bare walls of my prison

Day ends now a lamp
Burns in the prison
We alone share my cell
Lovely light Precious reason

September 1911

Automne malade

Automne malade et adoré
Tu mourras quand l'ouragan soufflera dans les roseraies
Quand il aura neigé
Dans les vergers

Pauvre automne
Meurs en blancheur et en richesse
De neige et de fruits mûrs
Au fond du ciel
Des éperviers planent
Sur les nixes nicettes aux cheveux verts et naines
Qui n'ont jamais aimé

Aux lisières lointaines
Les cerfs ont bramé

Et que j'aime ô saison que j'aime tes rumeurs
Les fruits tombant sans qu'on les cueille
Le vent et la forêt qui pleurent
Toutes leurs larmes en automne feuille à feuille
 Les feuilles
 Qu'on foule
 Un train
 Qui roule
 La vie
 S'écoule

Sickly Autumn

Autumn sickly and adored
You will die when tempests shake the rose garden
After it has snowed
In orchards

Poor autumn
Expire in whiteness and in wealth
Of snow and ripe fruit
In the depth of the sky
Hawks float
Above nixies with green hair dwarves
Who have never loved

By distant forests
Stags have belled

How I love O season how I love your distant murmurs
Fruit dropping ungathered
Wind and wood weeping
All their tears in autumn leaf by leaf
 Leaves
 Trodden down
 A train
 That passes
 Life
 Speeds on

Hôtels

La chambre est veuve
Chacun pour soi
Présence neuve
On paye au mois

Le patron doute
Payera-t-on
Je tourne en route
Comme un toton

Le bruit des fiacres
Mon voisin laid
Qui fume un âcre
Tabac anglais

O La Vallière
Qui boite et rit
De mes prières
Table de nuit

Et tous ensemble
Dans cet hôtel
Savons la langue
Comme à Babel

Fermons nos portes
A double tour
Chacun apporte
Son seul amour

Hotels

In this widowed room
You're on your own
A new arrival
Paying nothing down

The landlord suspects
We'll never pay
Like a spinning top
I turn round and round

Clamor of cabs
My ugly neighbor
Who puffs a sour
English pipe

O La Vallière
Who limps and sneers
At my prayers
O bedside table

And altogether
In this hotel
We know the language
They spoke at Babel

Close your doors
With a double lock
Each man harbors
His only love

Cors de Chasse

Notre histoire est noble et tragique
Comme le masque d'un tyran
Nul drame hasardeux ou magique
Aucun détail indifférent
Ne rend notre amour pathétique

Et Thomas de Quincey buvant
L'opium poison doux et chaste
A sa pauvre Anne allait rêvant
Passons passons puisque tout passe
Je me retournerai souvent

Les souvenirs sont cors de chasse
Dont meurt le bruit parmi le vent

Hunting Horns

Our history is noble and tragic
Like the mask of a tyrant
No hazardous or magic drama
No trifling detail
Can make our love pathetic

And Thomas de Quincey sipping
Sweet opium chaste and poisonous
Brooded on his unhappy Anne
Let us pass since everything passes
But I shall often turn again

Memories are hunting-horns
Whose notes die on the wind

Vendémiaire

Hommes de l'avenir souvenez-vous de moi
Je vivais à l'époque où finissaient les rois
Tour à tour ils mouraient silencieux et tristes
Et trois fois courageux devenaient trismégistes

Que Paris était beau à la fin de septembre
Chaque nuit devenait une vigne où les pampres
Répandaient leur clarté sur la ville et là-haut
Astres mûrs becquetés par les ivres oiseaux
De ma gloire attendaient la vendange de l'aube

Un soir passant le long des quais déserts et sombres
En rentrant à Auteuil j'entendis une voix
Qui chantait gravement se taisant quelquefois
Pour que parvînt aussi sur les bords de la Seine
La plainte d'autres voix limpides et lointaines

Et j'écoutai longtemps tous ces chants et ces cris
Qu'éveillait dans la nuit la chanson de Paris

J'ai soif villes de France et d'Europe et du monde
Venez toutes couler dans ma gorge profonde

Je vis alors que déjà ivre dans la vigne Paris
Vendangeait le raisin le plus doux de la terre
Ces grains miraculeux qui aux treilles chantèrent

Et Rennes répondit avec Quimper et Vannes
Nous voici ô Paris Nos maisons nos habitants

Vendémiaire

You who are not yet born remember me
I lived when kings died out
One by one they departed silent mournful
And thrice courageous became trismegist

How gorgeous was Paris toward the end of September
Each night became a vine whose leaves
Spread brightness over the city above
Ripe stars nibbled by the drunken birds
Of my fame awaited dawn's harvest

One evening past quais lonely and dark
Going home to Auteuil I heard a voice
Sing gravely when it paused
Other voices clear yet distant
Answered along the Seine

Long I listened to their plaints and cries
Waked on the night by the song of Paris

I am thirsty come to me cities of France Europe and the world
Flow down my deep throat

I saw then Paris already drunken in the vineyard
Harvest earth's sweetest fruit
Those marvelous grapes singing from the arbor

Rennes answered with Quimper and Vannes
We are here Paris Our houses our people

Ces grappes de nos sens qu'enfanta le soleil
Se sacrifient pour te désaltérer trop avide merveille
Nous t'apportons tous les cerveaux les cimetières les murailles
Ces berceaux pleins de cris que tu n'entendras pas
Et d'amont en aval nos pensées ô rivières
Les oreilles des écoles et nos mains rapprochées
Aux doigts allongés nos mains les clochers
Et nous t'apportons aussi cette souple raison
Que le mystère clôt comme une porte la maison
Ce mystère courtois de la galanterie
Ce mystère fatal fatal d'une autre vie
Double raison qui est au-delà de la beauté
Et que la Grèce n'a pas connue ni l'Orient
Double raison de la Bretagne où lame à lame
L'océan châtre peu à peu l'ancien continent

Et les villes du Nord répondirent gaiement

O Paris nous voici boissons vivantes
Les viriles cités où dégoisent et chantent
Les métalliques saints de nos saintes usines
Nos cheminées à ciel ouvert engrossent les nuées
Comme fit autrefois l'Ixion mécanique
Et nos mains innombrables
Usines manufactures fabriques mains
Où les ouvriers nus semblables à nos doigts
Fabriquent du réel à tant par heure
Nous te donnons tout cela

Et Lyon répondit tandis que les anges de Fourvières
Tissaient un ciel nouveau avec la soie des prières

Désaltère-toi Paris avec les divines paroles
Que mes lèvres le Rhône et la Saône murmurent
Toujours le même culte de sa mort renaissant
Divise ici les saints et fait pleuvoir le sang

Our clustered senses ripened in the sun
Will quench your thirst greedy wonder
We bring you all the brains graveyards and high walls
Cradles full of wails you will never hear
From upstream our thoughts O rivers
Ears of schools hands folded together
With tapered fingers our hands the steeples
And the subtle reasoning
That mystery shuts upon like the door to a house
Courtly mystery of love
Fatal fatal mystery of another life
Reason twice over and beyond beauty
Unknown to Greece or the Orient
Known only to Brittany where wave upon wave
Ocean castrates the ancient continent

The cities of the North replied gaily

We are here Paris living draughts
Manly cities where rattle and sing
Metallic saints in our sainted factories
Chimneys in the open air impregnate the clouds
As did long ago Ixion the mechanical
And our hands innumerable
Mills works factories hands
Where workers naked like our fingers
Manufacture reality at so much an hour
All this we give you

Lyons spoke while the angels of Fourvières
Wove a new sky with the silk of prayers

Slake your thirst Paris upon sacred words
Murmured by my lips the Rhone and the Saône
Here always the same rites of his death renascent
Divide the saints and shower blood

Heureuse pluie ô gouttes tièdes ô douleur
Un enfant regarde les fenêtres s'ouvrir
Et des grappes de têtes à d'ivres oiseaux s'offrir

Les villes du Midi répondirent alors

Noble Paris seule raison qui vis encore
Qui fixes notre humeur selon ta destinée
Et toi qui te retires Méditerranée
Partagez-vous nos corps comme on rompt des hosties
Ces très hautes amours et leur danse orpheline
Deviendront ô Paris le vin pur que tu aimes

Et un râle infini qui venait de Sicile
Signifiait en battement d'ailes ces paroles

Les raisins de nos vignes on les a vendangés
Et ces grappes de morts dont les grains allongés
Ont la saveur du sang de la terre et du sel
Les voici pour ta soif ô Paris sous le ciel
Obscurci de nuées faméliques
Que caresse Ixion le créateur oblique
Et où naissent sur la mer tous les corbeaux d'Afrique
O raisins Et ces yeux ternes et en famille
L'avenir et la vie dans ces treilles s'ennuyent

Mais où est le regard lumineux des sirènes
Il trompa les marins qu'aimaient ces oiseaux-là
Il ne tournera plus sur l'écueil de Scylla
Où chantaient les trois voix suaves et sereines

Le détroit tout à coup avait changé de face
Visages de la chair de l'onde de tout
Ce que l'on peut imaginer
Vous n'êtes que des masques sur des faces masquées

Blessing of rain warm drops O sorrow
A child watches windows opening
And clustered heads appear to drunken birds

The cities of the South then answered

Noble Paris the one philosophy still surviving
That tempers our mood to your destiny
And you ebbing Mediterranean
Partake of our broken bodies as of the Host
These high passions and their orphan dance
Will become O Paris the pure wine you crave

From Sicily arose an endless rattle
With beating of wings

Our vines are harvested
These clusters of dead whose oval grapes
Have the savor of blood of earth or of salt
Await you Paris beneath a sky
Shadowed with starveling clouds
That Ixion crooked creator caresses
Where Africa's crows fly forth on the sea
O harvest and dull clannish eyes
Life and the future grow weary in these arbors

But where are the shining glances of sirens
Harpies who gulled the sailors they desired
No more upon Scylla's reef
Where sang the three voices suave and tranquil

The straits were suddenly transformed
Faces of flesh of water of all
That one can imagine
You are only masks upon masked faces

Il souriait jeune nageur entre les rives
Et les noyés flottant sur son onde nouvelle
Fuyaient en le suivant les chanteuses plaintives
Elles dirent adieu au gouffre et à l'écueil
A leurs pâles époux couchés sur les terrasses
Puis ayant pris leur vol vers le brûlant soleil
Les suivirent dans l'onde où s'enfoncent les astres

Lorsque la nuit revint couverte d'yeux ouverts
Errer au site où l'hydre a sifflé cet hiver
Et j'entendis soudain ta voix impérieuse
O Rome
Maudire d'un seul coup mes anciennes pensées
Et le ciel où l'amour guide les destinées

Les feuillards repoussés sur l'arbre de la croix
Et même la fleur de lys qui meurt au Vatican
Macèrent dans le vin que je t'offre et qui a
La saveur du sang pur de celui qui connaît
Une autre liberté végétale dont tu
Ne sais pas que c'est elle la suprême vertu

Une couronne du trirègne est tombée sur les dalles
Les hiérarques la foulent sous leurs sandales
O splendeur démocratique qui pâlit
Vienne la nuit royale où l'on tuera les bêtes
La louve avec l'agneau l'aigle avec la colombe
Une foule de rois ennemis et cruels
Ayant soif comme toi dans la vigne éternelle
Sortiront de la terre et viendront dans les airs
Pour boire de mon vin par deux fois millénaire

La Moselle et le Rhin se joignent en silence
C'est l'Europe qui prie nuit et jour à Coblence
Et moi qui m'attardais sur le quai à Auteuil
Quand les heures tombaient parfois comme les feuilles

He smiled the young swimmer between the straits
And the drowned followed in his wake
Fleeing those plaintive singers
Who said farewell to whirlpool and reef
To their pale lovers couched on terraces
Took flight toward the burning sun
And followed the dead where stars plunge into the wave

When night returning with a thousand eyes
Wandered to the site where the hydra hissed this winter
And suddenly I heard your imperious voice
O Rome
Curse my former thoughts
And heaven where love guides the fates

Withes sprung from the tree of the cross
Even fleur-de-lis withering in the Vatican
Have steeped in the wine I offer you
It tastes of His blood he who recognized
As supreme virtue a natural
Liberty you have never known

A tiara has fallen to the flagstones
The hierarchs spurn it with their sandals
O democratic splendor fading
When royal night comes and we slay the beasts
Wolf with lamb eagle with dove
A horde of kings fierce enemies
Thirsting like you in the eternal vine
Will quit their tombs for the air
To drink my two-thousand-year-old wine

Moselle and Rhine meet in silence
It is Europe praying day and night at Coblenz
And I who tarried on the quai at Auteuil
While the hours fell like leaves

Du cep lorsqu'il est temps j'entendis la prière
Qui joignait la limpidité de ces rivières

O Paris le vin de ton pays est meilleur que celui
Qui pousse sur nos bords mais aux pampres du nord
Tous les grains ont mûri pour cette soif terrible
Mes grappes d'hommes forts saignent dans le pressoir
Tu boiras à longs traits tout le sang de l'Europe
Parce que tu es beau et que seul tu es noble
Parce que c'est dans toi que Dieu peut devenir
Et tous mes vignerons dans ces belles maisons
Qui reflètent le soir leurs feux dans nos deux eaux
Dans ces belles maisons nettement blanches et noires
Sans savoir que tu es la réalité chantent ta gloire
Mais nous liquides mains jointes pour la prière
Nous menons vers le sel les eaux aventurières
Et la ville entre nous comme entre des ciseaux
Ne reflète en dormant nul feu dans ses deux eaux
Dont quelque sifflement lointain parfois s'élance
Troublant dans leur sommeil les filles de Coblence

Les villes répondaient maintenant par centaines
Je ne distinguais plus leurs paroles lointaines
Et Trèves la ville ancienne
A leur voix mêlait la sienne
L'univers tout entier concentré dans ce vin
Qui contenait les mers les animaux les plantes
Les cités les destins et les astres qui chantent
Les hommes à genoux sur la rive du ciel
Et le docile fer notre bon compagnon
Le feu qu'il faut aimer comme on s'aime soi-même
Tous les fiers trépassés qui sont un sous mon front
L'éclair qui luit ainsi qu'une pensée naissante
Tous les noms six par six les nombres un à un
Des kilos de papier tordus comme des flammes
Et ceux-là qui sauront blanchir nos ossements

From autumn vines I heard the prayer
Where their limpid waters meet

O Paris the wine of your country is better than
What grows on our banks yet on northern shores
My grapes await your terrible thirst
My clusters of strong men drip in the winepress
You will drain with deep draughts all Europe's blood
Because you are beautiful and you alone noble
Because in you God can be manifest
And in their fine houses
Whose lights twinkle at dusk upon our two streams
In their checkered houses
My vine-growers ignorant that you are reality praise you
Now our liquid-hands joined in prayer
Lead erring waters toward the sea
The city between us as between scissors
Casts in its sleep no light upon the two rivers
Whose distant murmurs occasionally
Trouble in dream the maids of Coblenz

The cities answered now by hundreds
I no longer made out their distant words
Ancient Trèves
Mingled her voice with theirs
Essence of universe flavors my wine
Seas animals and plants
Cities fates singing stars
Men kneeling on the shore of heaven
And docile iron a trusty friend
Fire one should cherish like a brother
All proud dead who are one under my brow
Lightning that glitters like a newborn thought
All names six by six all numbers one by one
Kilos of paper twisted like flames
And those that will whiten our bones

Les bons vers immortels qui s'ennuient patiemment
Des armées rangées en bataille
Des forêts de crucifix et mes demeures lacustres
Au bord des yeux de celle que j'aime tant
Les fleurs qui s'écrient hors de bouches
Et tout ce que je ne sais pas dire
Tout ce que je ne connaîtrai jamais
Tout cela tout cela changé en ce vin pur
Dont Paris avait soif
Me fut alors présenté

Actions belles journées sommeils terribles
Végétation Accouplements musiques éternelles
Mouvements Adorations douleur divine
Mondes qui vous ressemblez et qui nous ressemblez
Je vous ai bus et ne fus pas désaltéré

Mais je connus dès lors quelle saveur a l'univers

Je suis ivre d'avoir bu tout l'univers
Sur le quai d'où je voyais l'onde couler et dormir les bélandres

Écoutez-moi je suis le gosier de Paris
Et je boirai encore s'il me plaît l'univers

Écoutez mes chants d'universelle ivrognerie

Et la nuit de septembre s'achevait lentement
Les feux rouges des ponts s'éteignaient dans la Seine
Les étoiles mouraient le jour naissait à peine

The pleasing lines of immortal verse patiently growing weary
Armies ranked for battle
Forests of crosses and my lake dwellings
On the shore of eyes of her I love
Flowers crying from mouths
And all I cannot say
All I shall never know
All all metamorphosed into that pure wine
To appease thirsty Paris
Was offered to me then

Deeds fine days uneasy sleep
Vegetation Couplings eternal music
Motion Worship divine sorrow
Worlds that resemble us and yourselves
Though I have drained you I am thirsty still

But I know the savor of the universe

I reel on universe
Along the quai where I saw waves flow and barges rock

Hear me I am the gullet of Paris
I shall drain you again if I wish

Hear my songs of universal drunkenness

The September night slowly ended
Red lights on bridges were quenched in the Seine
Stars died day began slowly

Notes

[Bracketed numbers refer to entries in the bibliography.]

ZONE, page 2

First published in *Les Soirées de Paris*, no. 11 (December, 1912).

Lines 1-24. Apollinaire in his thirty-third year, like Dylan Thomas, Villon, Dante, and others at about the same age, sums up his life, as he strolls through twentieth-century Paris. The rhythm of the free-verse lines suggests the pace of a man walking. Various references to the external world situate the poem in place and time. In line 2, I have not kept the literal meaning of *ce matin*, "this morning." The city landscape that changes as the poet walks through it corresponds to different stages in his life. At first he is enclosed in the present moment, surrounded by monuments to modernity, many of which are personified.

Lines 25-41. The young street (l. 25) is his point of departure into an evocation of his youth. Apollinaire associates Catholic images with his childhood. The blue and white in which his mother dressed her son are Mary's colors (l. 26). The same memory, and in almost the same words, launches "Prière," published posthumously in *Œuvres poétiques* ([1], p. 576). Memories of youth and youthful devotion become an invocation of Christ which suggests the litany, or the poems of Péguy. (For a discussion of resemblances between "Zone" and Cendrars' "Pâques à New-York," see Madame Durry [18], p. 234 ff.) The invocation dissolves into a fantasy that is underlined by plays on words. In the phrase *la double potence* (l. 37), *potence* is *double* not only because both honor and eternity are exhibited there, but because *potence* has at least two meanings, "gallows" and "bracket"; other meanings are suggested by the word's Latin origin, *potentia*, "power" and "prop," or "stay." The description of Christ "qui monte au ciel" (l. 40) suggests at once an apotheosis and a flying machine: the verb *monter* means any kind of ascension, whether spiritual or physical, natural or supernatural.

Lines 42-70. In their statement "s'il sait voler qu'on l'appelle voleur" (l. 47), the devils make a pun on *voler* "to fly" and *voler* "to steal." Their sneering wit adds both a light touch and a Dantean dimension. Many images and names—Simon Magus and the other famous flyers (ll. 46 and 49), the clock whose hands run backward, Hradchen, the Jewish neighborhoods, the mosaic portrait of the poet, the amusing adjectival forms of place-names—have already occurred in Apollinaire's own stories in prose, in *L'Hérésiarque et Cie* [2]. The gathering of the birds includes several legendary winged creatures that represent man's past moments of imagination and vision. *Les périlleux détroits* abandoned by the sirens are literally "the perilous straits" (l. 67). The Christ who is an airplane represents, in contrast to sirens, roc, and phoenix, a modern variety of exaltation. At the same time, the Futuristic fusion of man and plane is superimposed upon an outgrowth of all the past, and most probably, as Michel Décaudin observes, upon a Christian image: Apollinaire may have seen, in the museum at Cologne, two medieval paintings that show Christ flying through the sky upon a winged cross, surrounded by fluttering angels (Michel Décaudin [14], p. 87).

Lines 71-120. Abruptly the poet returns to the present. Crowds, busses, accentuate his solitude. He is ashamed of his own desires, tormented by a need for both spiritual and human love, assailed by scenes from his past which comment on his present unrest. Some of his memories are moments of revelation, some are remembered seemingly for no reason, some are treated with reverence, some with buffoonery. I did not attempt to carry over into English the amusing forms in the line "L'un est Nissard il y a un Mentonasque et deux Turbiasques" (l. 92). The last scene from his past, briefly mentioned (ll. 113 and 114), is an event that affected Apollinaire deeply. He was accused of stealing works of art from the Louvre and had to spend several days in prison before being cleared of the charge, an ordeal he has described in a group of lyrics placed near the end of *Alcools* and ambiguously entitled "A la Santé." I translated as "judge" the *juge d'instruction*— "the examining magistrate" who interrogates the accused to determine whether there should be a trial (l. 113). A passage follows that comments on the array of memories and sums up the poet's life, in a fashion comparable to the self-examination of "A la Santé" and also to such nostalgic evocations as "Le Voyageur" and "Le Pont Mirabeau."

Lines 121-134. Once more the poet returns to the present. He walks through a Jewish part of town and thinks about the fate of refugees in Paris, a favorite theme, for he too is a foreigner, had trouble finding jobs, and was unable to become a French citizen, though he had no trouble joining the army. The *édredon rouge* (l. 127), writes Madame Durry [18], pp. 79-80), refers to a red quilt presented to Apollinaire by his mother. As in some other moments of seriousness, Apollinaire lightens his description of exiles (a theme he shares with Baudelaire) by a verbal joke. The line "Ils espèrent gagner de l'argent dans l'Argentine" (l. 125) contains a pun on *argent*, "money" or "silver," and *Argentine* "Argentina." The refugees are mainly Jewish. One of the unproved tales about Apollinaire is that he was partly Jewish. A more likely explanation of his interest in Jewish lore and in the Wandering Jew, is that, as a foreigner and of illegitimate birth, he felt spiritually akin to an outcast people who managed to preserve their identity.

Lines 135-153. Dusk comes, and nightfall. Fragments of the present pierce the poet's reverie—a bar, a restaurant, the streetwalkers who do not make him feel less lonely. In early dawn he makes his way homeward, when milkmen are clinking their *bidons*, "cans" containing about five liters (l. 145). The fading night is like a Romantic courtesan such as those Baudelaire wrote of in his early poems. The names Métive, Ferdine, Lea contrast ironically with the pitiful ugliness of the real women observed by the poet. He likens his life to an *eau-de-vie* (l. 149), an image that, like Balzac's *Peau de Chagrin*, suggests a quantity that is limited and continually dwindling. *Eau de vie* was the tentative title of this collection of verse before Apollinaire finally settled on the subtler *Alcools*. The pun on "brandy" and "water of life" is not translatable. At the end of the poem the poet's charity extends, not only to all the other exiles besides himself assembled in the Paris of 1912, refugees, Jews, streetwalkers, and the Christ one abandons along with one's childhood, but to the far-away savages in whose primitive carvings the poet sees himself and the modern world reflected.

Lines 154-55. The last brief lines suggest withdrawal into sleep or death. As the poet exits, the sun rises. A play on sounds exists in the original—*cou coupé* which gives a sense of inevitability to the image, lost in the translation. A similar image occurs in the sixth poem of "Les Fiançailles" but with, I think, a different meaning. In

"Zone," the sun's slit throat is comparable to those nineteenth-century images of a sick or dying sun, contained in poems of Baudelaire, Rimbaud, Laforgue, which imply a mystical correspondence between onlooker and landscape. The twentieth-century poet seems more ebullient, more reconciled to the terms of his existence than did his predecessors. In his poem the image of the sun (for an expanded version, see "Les Doukhobors" ([1], p. 715) affirms the violence of life and its continual renewal.

LE PONT MIRABEAU, page 14

First published in *Les Soirées de Paris*, no. 1 (February, 1912).

Mario Roques has pointed out the technical resemblance between this poem and a thirteenth-century *chanson de toile*, "Gaieté et Oriour," which Apollinaire could have read in Gaston Paris' *Chrestomathie du Moyen Age*. However, as Michel Décaudin observes, the most striking resemblance is to stanza xxiii of Villon's *Grand Testament*, which contains the line "Allé s'en est, et je demeure."

The poet laments musically, in a set form, the passing of time and of love. Throughout the poem, syntax and sound couple the images of bridge and poet, and of river and emotion. By a reluctant act of memory the poet recalls past passion, reluctant because he would rather give himself entirely to the present, although he remains aware that the present also will one day become the past, that time and being are in conflict. As the images change and develop, so, after each stanza, the refrain has a different meaning. The succession of sorrow, joy, indifference suggests the very act of love, as do the images of bridge and river. Apollinaire's lack of confidence in love's endurance and in human stability, his blurring of those perspectives that various points in time make available to us, recall another lesser lyric from *Alcools*, "La Tzigane." I am also reminded of Aragon's "Il n'y a pas d'amour heureux."

LA CHANSON DU MAL-AIMÉ, page 16

First published in *Mercure de France*, no. 285 (May 1, 1909), without dedication, and followed by the date 1903.

As the introductory stanza indicates, a first version took shape in 1903. Internal evidence suggests that the poem in its entirety may

have been written in 1904. Michel Décaudin finds in the poem a mixture of moods—Apollinaire's fury after his first trip to London to see Annie and his sadness after his second trip, when she had decided to leave for America. He and Adéma observe that the beginning of the poem may describe London in November, the month of Apollinaire's first trip, and that the last part certainly describes Paris in June, the month of Apollinaire's return to France after his second trip to London in May. A study of the poem's structure has been made by Professor Breunig ("Le Roman du Mal-Aimé" [8]). When the poem was included in *Alcools*, it was dedicated to Paul Léautaud. According to the latter, when Apollinaire mentioned to him that he had sent a poem to the *Mercure de France*, but that it had been ignored by the editors, Léautaud looked it up and had it published ("La Chanson du Mal-Aimé" [24]).

Best known of Apollinaire's poems, and perhaps best loved, this long lament for Annie Playden, the English girl who would not have him, is composed entirely of octosyllabic quintains, with a uniform pattern of end rhymes. The sole technical variant the poet allows himself is the occasional substitution of assonance for rhyme. The poem avoids monotony or sentimentality by its consciousness of the poet's role, the quality of its imagery and the general tone—ambiguous, grotesque, musical, at times nostalgic, at times grotesquely humorous. Six years later, looking back on his unhappiness over Annie, Apollinaire evokes a young man who wanted both fame and love, "poète inconnu au milieu d'autres poètes inconnus, elle loin et ne pouvant venir à Paris," a young man who was to achieve the one far more easily than the other: "J'en souffris beaucoup, témoin ce poème ou je me croyais mal aimé tandis que c'était moi qui aimais mal" (*Tendre comme le souvenir* [3], p. 70).

Epigraph. Although a more precise translation of *le* in line 5 is "it" rather than "him," the poet's love is not only a passion but a god (see stanza 18) who dies and is renewed like the phoenix. In this poem, states of mind are repeatedly externalized and exorcised through personification.

Stanzas 1-8. The poet defines, in a series of contrasting images, what it is to be *mal-aimé*, "poorly loved." He first recalls two encounters in London, one with a young gangster, the other, with a drunken woman who resembled his love—shameless, elusive, inhuman —and then recalls two examples taken from antiquity of heroes who

were, unlike himself, well loved.

Stanza 2. The biblical image comments ironically on the pursuer as well as on the pursued.

Stanza 5. *Inhumaine* is a euphuistic term, a traditional epithet of the cruel beloved. Here it is used on two levels: Annie is at once cruel and literally inhuman.

Stanza 7. The Hindu origins of Sacontale and her royal spouse Doushmanta have been identified by Jeanine Moulin [28].

Stanza 8. *Ombres* "shadows" is a recurring image throughout the poem. Here it suggests several themes—memory, resemblance, and the illusions caused by love. The shadows are faithless because they are not what they appear to be.

Stanzas 9-12. A passage follows in which the poet attempts vainly to reject the past. Lethe is opposed to Helen and the coldness of the rejected heart to the warmth of the Saviour. Memory merges with the woman remembered and she with those illusions that resemble her.

Stanza 9. A prey to anger and regret, the poet shifts his attitude within one stanza. The renowned poor are the great men who have died: all that remains to them are the shadows, or shades, they have become. One thinks of Helen and of the renown that lives after death.

Stanza 10. "The forty of Sebaste" were forty Christian soldiers garrisoned at Sebaste in Armenia. They were martyred in 320 by being exposed naked on a frozen lake. The poet's heart has undergone a similar martyrdom, exposure to cruel memories. His sufferings are worse than those of the martyrs because the god of love has proved deceitful. Thus he turns momentarily to thoughts of the Easter sun, the symbol of Christ.

Stanza 11. *Mon beau navire* may describe not only the poet's faculty of memory, which is the muse that inspires his poems, but perhaps also the object remembered, namely, Annie, who is one aspect of the muse. Baudelaire describes a woman as a "beau navire." As in Rimbaud's "Bateau Ivre," a journey that began auspiciously has ended badly.

Stanza 12. "Avec la femme qui s'éloigne" could refer not only to Annie, but also to the woman who staggered from the tavern. A fusion of identities and of points in time characterizes the entire poem.

Stanza 13. This recurrent stanza provides transitions between vari-

ous parts of the poem and gives to contrasting sections a sense of continuity. The Milky Way, described in terms of terrestial waters that flow with milk and honey, and the drowned bodies which are still moved by love, recall a stanza from "Le Bateau Ivre":

> Et dès lors, je me suis baigné dans le Poème
> De la Mer, infusé d'astres et lactescent,
> Devorant les azurs verts; où, flottaison blême
> Et ravie, un noyé pensif parfois descend.

The image of other women looming on the poet's horizon like nebulae suggests the theme of love's renewal, announced by the phoenix. Religion and love are linked to astronomy: as medieval pilgrims followed "le chemin de St. Jacques" west to Galicia, so the poet follows the Milky Way toward some outer-space sanctuary of love.

Stanzas 14-18. The Aubade, a rural invitation to love adorned with classical allusions and recalling past happiness, is the first of three titled insertions. Although each of the three is provided with at least one introductory stanza, only the Aubade is followed by a stanza of commentary.

Stanza 15. *Pâquette* is short for *pâquerette*, "Easter daisy," and harks back to the invocation of the Easter sun.

Stanza 16. Contains two mild plays on words: *Vénus* and *revenus*, the noun *rose* and the adjective *rose*. Apollinaire himself probably coined the verb *feuilloler*, which occurs again in both "L'Émigrant de Landor Road" and "Les Fiançailles."

Stanza 18. Pan, love, and Christ are presented in close juxtaposition and in a logical progression. By relating earthly to heavenly love, Apollinaire ennobles his subject matter. The manner is modern; the concept, traditional. The stanza situates us, for the first time, in Paris, which is the poem's present.

Stanza 19. Prelude to a passage of transition, this stanza recurs once more at the end of the poem, and provides the poem's title. *Mal-aimé*, "ill-loved," I have translated here as "unhappy lover" and, in its second and final occurrence, as "poorly loved." "Les hymnes d'esclave aux murènes" is a mysterious line, difficult to translate. Moray eels are voracious, savage, brightly colored; the Mediterranean variety has been considered a *pièce de résistance* from Roman times.

Do the fisher slaves sing alluring hymns to their prey, or are they themselves the destined victims? In support of the second interpretation, Maurice Piron recalls the Roman anecdote about Vedius Pollion who punished his servants by throwing them to the eels in his fish tanks. Piron recalls, too, a stanza from Victor Hugo's "L'Homme heureux" (*Odes et Ballades*, IV, 8), which Apollinaire may have echoed:

> Je m'ennuie au forum, je m'ennuie aux arènes;
> Je demande à tous: Que fait-on?
> Je fais jeter par jour un esclave aux murènes,
> Et je m'amuse à peine à ce jeu de Caton.

What makes the line memorable in its mystery is the typically Apollinairean confusion between hunter and hunted. The ambiguity of the French is hard, if not impossible, to preserve in English. The eels are subtly compared to the queens, the years, the sirens, and the state of mind of the poorly loved. The stanza as a whole describes the dangerous vocation of the poet. The source of his inspiration is a destructive force which, in the long run, will turn against him. Or perhaps the *mal-aimé* has simply chosen the wrong songs (those of love) to sing. In either case he is a new Orpheus. Elsewhere, Apollinaire warns the poet:

> La femelle de l'alcyon,
> L'Amour, les volantes Sirènes,
> Savent de mortelles chansons
> Dangereuses et inhumaines.
> N'oyez pas ces oiseaux maudits,
> Mais les Anges du paradis.

> ("Orphée," *Le Bestiaire*,
> *Œuvres*, 26)

Stanza 20. These lines renew the commentary on the Aubade and link it to the theme of faithfulness which will furnish the excuse for the song of the Zaporogian Cossacks. The fair images, the memories that resemble her (or him) can be taken as ironical references to the beginning of the poem, to the hoodlum and to the drunken woman

who resemble the poet's love. Ironical also, to some degree, is the mention of the faithful wife. The story of the widow who builds for her dead husband a grandiose tomb or who weeps daily by his grave, has been made fun of by La Fontaine and Voltaire, among others. Apollinaire's comparison of his role to that of the widow, like his vision of Annie as a boy, contributes to the portrayal of love as a baffling emotion. The confusion between the sexes and the description of things by their opposites occur throughout the poem.

Stanzas 21-26. Three stanzas introduce the Cossacks' song. Michel Décaudin suggests Apollinaire may have known one of the Russian painter Repin's pictures of the Cossacks writing to the Sultan by candlelight, may have come across some French translation, now lost, of the letter attributed to them. A number of such letters exist. All are Polish forgeries. The last two stanzas of their letter were not in the first version of the Chanson, but were added to the proofs of *Alcools*. The description of the Sultan's birth is reminiscent of the birth of Gargantua.

According to Georges Schmits [36], the Cossacks are models of fidelity, like Penelope, Sacontale, the wife of Mausoleus, the bulldog, and the ivy. Originally a warrior tribe that peopled the Ukraine and the banks of the Don, they were used in the fifteenth century by Muscovite princes to colonize the steppes and to oppose the Turkish and Tartar invasions. They refused all compromise with the invaders, including the Sultan of Constantinople. Schmits notes also that Barabbas, who was condemned for murder and sedition, became a slang term for "villain," that the devil always presides at the witches' sabbath (which I have translated as "revels"), that the rotten fish of Salonike may describe the corruption of the Balkan town, that the Sultan's birth suggests that of Croniamantal in *Le Poète assassiné*, that Podolia is a region in Poland which the Sultan obtained in 1672 (and therefore "butcher of Podolia" means, not "one from" but "one who ruined" Podolia), that *amant*, "lover," contains a play on *amant des plaies* "one who lives with, that is, one who is covered with wounds and perhaps loves them" and *aman*, an ablution used by the Turks.

Stanza 27. The abrupt reappearance of the recurrent stanza provides a bitterly humorous transition between the insulting Cossack song and the subsequent passage on lovesickness which lies at the heart of the poem.

Stanzas 28-41. In five stanzas at the center of the Chanson, Apol-
linaire describes, more directly than elsewhere, his desire for a rec-
onciliation with Annie, his awareness that all is over, his feelings of
revulsion and attraction. Two stanzas denouncing his love and two
lamenting his own unhappiness precede and follow a stanza implor-
ing her return.

Stanza 28. *Vos baisers florentins* contains a double meaning: the
Florentines were reputed moneylenders and traitors.

Stanza 29. This stanza is no more complimentary than the one pre-
ceding it. Stars and sirens are ambiguous images in Apollinaire's poetry,
and the gifts of fairy godmothers are of dubious value.

Stanza 30. The bridge is the poet's gesture or his words asking
her to return—a bridge across time, distance, and lack of understand-
ing. *Le Pont Mirabeau*, which was written later, fuses the images of
bridge and poet in a comparable manner.

Stanza 31. His heart and head are casks of the Danaïdes because he
fills them over and over with love. His emotions are futilely expended
on Annie.

Stanza 32. *Ma blanche rade*, literally "my white roadstead." *La Dési-
rade* is an island in the Antilles whose name encloses the word "desire."

A curious sequence follows. The images of grief (stanzas 33-35),
of the poet's shadow (stanzas 36 and 37), and of springtime (stanzas
38 and 39) undergo a kind of deification, and in the obscure language
of prophecy, foretell his eventual healing.

Stanza 33. The Pyraustas is a fabulous insect, supposed to live in fire.
Pyr is repeated as *feux* in the next line. "Aegipans" is an epithet of
both pans and satyrs; the whole line does little more than repeat the
preceding line as a joke. "Et les destins damnés ou faustes"—*fauste*,
coined by Apollinaire, suggests either the Latin *faustus*, "auspicious" or
"Faustian." In favor of the second interpretation are the pattern of
repetition already set up in the two preceding lines and the association
of ideas: the will-o'-the-wisp led Faust to Walpurgis Night in Goethe's
poem. Apollinaire may well have had in mind both "auspicious" and
"damned" (or even "barely saved"). Compare his use of *sainte* in "Les
Fiançailles" (p. 170, and note, p. 266).

Stanza 35. *Malheur*, which has been translated as "unhappiness,"
means "bad luck" or "misfortune."

Stanzas 36-37. The shadow, the snake, and the shadowy wife recall,
not only the myth of the poet Orpheus, but also passages in Valéry's

La Jeune Parque, published eight years after the Chanson.

Stanza 38. Bees and fire are associated also in "Le Voyageur." There the image suggests sadness, the destruction of what is bright and good and sweet, and is explicitly linked with autumn. A bee falls into the fire as "brightness falls from the air," or as Baudelaire plunges "dans les froides ténèbres." Here, to the contrary, the burning of the tomb-like beehives announces the return of springtime.

Stanza 39. The *Argyraspids*, literally "with silver shields," were Alexander the Great's bodyguard. The repetition of the epithet in the next line is another learned joke, like that contained in stanza 33. "Dendrophori" is the name of certain gods (like Sylvanus), the name of people who carry sacred trees in processions and of members of certain guilds (such as the carpenters') during the Roman empire. Here, perhaps, because pale and mysterious, dendrophori may refer to rural gods who hibernate in winter and whose most faithful worshippers are the poor.

Stanzas 40-48. In a restatement of his unhappiness (stanzas 40 and 41) Apollinaire links a vulgar and a religious image. These give added dimension to his portrayal of love and furnish an introduction to the song of "The Seven Swords" (stanzas 42-48).

Stanza 40. "Et moi j'ai le cœur aussi gros" contains a play on words: *avoir le cœur gros*, "to have a heavy heart," is used by Apollinaire first in the figurative sense of "sad" and then literally as "big." The image of the heart pierced by seven swords, as Michael Décaudin notes, is not new. In "Rhénane d'automne" which appeared the same year 1909, the Madonna's heart is likened to a chestnut in its spiky shell. And other poets, notably Baudelaire, Leconte de Lisle, Laforgue, had used the image.

Stanza 41. The swords *sans morfil*, "without a wire-edge," suggest not only a phallic symbol but an emotion that bludgeons and tears rather than pierces (cf. instructions to soldiers not to sharpen their bayonets because blunted they will do more damage).

Stanza 42. The names of the seven swords have been modified in an attempt to make the same sorts of half-poetic, half-obscene, plays on words in English. "Pâline," the name of the first sword in the original, is probably an anagram or a portmanteau word. *Ghibelline*, with its bloody connotations, is an appropriate epithet for a "bloody destiny." Maurice Piron has observed that *Ghibelline* may be a verbal play formed on *Gibel*, an alternate name for Etna where Vulcan had his

forges, and that Apollinaire had already shown his acquaintance with this place-name in "Merlin et la vieille Femme." For a useful synthesis of the scholarly work done on "Les Sept Épées," see T. E. Marshall, "Composition and Structure of Guillaume Apollinaire's Alcools" [27].

Stanza 43. "Noubosse," the name of the second sword, suggests *faire la nouba* and *se donner une bosse*, both of which mean "to go on a spree." It suggests also the image of a hump or swelling. "Carabosse," another play on *bosse*, is the name of the evil fairy who gives unfortunate presents to the hero.

Stanza 44. One interpretation of the mysterious *chibriape* is that it may be a deformation of "Cypriot," containing also the word *priape*, "Priapus." Hermes, instead of being *trismégiste*, "three times great," his usual epithet (and one exploited in "Crépuscule" and "Vendémiaire"), becomes a dwarf.

Stanza 45. The fourth sword "Malourène" can be read also as *Ma Lou reine*, "my queen Lou." The appearance of Lou, one of Apollinaire's later loves, in a poem celebrating his unhappy passion for Annie Playden, is prophetic indeed, since he had not yet met her when he published the Chanson. However, it carries out a theme announced in the introductory stanza: the poet's love is renascent, like the phoenix.

Stanza 47. "La sixième métal de gloire," "the sixth metal of glory," can also read as "la sixième m'étale de gloire," "the sixth covers me with glory."

Stanzas 49-59. Following the final appearance of the recurrent stanza (49) is a passage that puts the poet's unhappiness in a larger frame of reference—that of human destiny in general (stanzas 50 and 51), the story of Luitpold (stanzas 52-54), the frequently quoted evocation of modern Paris (stanzas 55-58), the second recurring stanza (59).

Stanza 50. "To lost music" can qualify either the preceding or following phrase. In the punctuated first version, it qualifies the preceding one.

Stanza 51. Note the parallel between the shivering stars and the glowworms that waver. These images of trembling light, ominous heralds of the future, underline the uncertainty in human lives.

Stanza 53. In the original: "Près d'un château sans châtelaine," a relationship is set up between *château* and *châtelaine* similar to the one immediately following, between *barque* and *barcaroles*.

Stanzas 55-58. The oft-quoted final stanzas describe the poet turn-

ing from his memories to the city around him. The mood contrasts with
the recollection of London that opens the poem, but the same tech-
nique of an animate, sympathizing landscape is used.

LES COLCHIQUES, page 38

First published in *La Phalange*, no. 17 (November 15, 1907), with
"La Tzigane" and "Lul de Faltenin."

These approximate alexandrines with their sonorous rhymes were
probably composed during Apollinaire's stay in Germany in the fall of
1901 or in 1902. As crocuses poison the cows, so his sweetheart's eyes
poison the poet. Countless are the flowers, and countless her glances.
The image of the lady's eyes that can wound or poison the worshipper
dates at least from troubador poetry. The related image of the circle,
announced by the word *cerne*, "eye-ring," is suggested also by the
mothers who are daughters of their daughters. Time is circular. The
generations repeat. Even love repeats. The final comment about the
cows that leave the meadows forever is ambiguous: perhaps they leave
because they have been poisoned and will die, thus breaking the circle.
Otherwise, being cows, they will assuredly return.

PALAIS, page 40

First published in *Revue littéraire de Paris et de Champagne*, no. 32
(November, 1905), with the title "Dans le Palais de Rosemonde."
Although the dedication to Max Jacob appears only in *Alcools*, it may
indicate the source of the poem's inspiration.

Apollinaire attempts to comment on the poetic process by means of
fantasy, but achieves merely a series of progressively morbid images,
except for the last stanza. The quatrains, composed of rhyming alex-
andrines, are typical of his early verse.

Stanza 1. The palace, which Henry II of England built for his
mistress Rosemonde, as Michel Décaudin points out, is evoked by the
poet in several other poems.

Stanza 3. The agapes or love-feasts (with their Greek menu of lamb
and rezina) are contrasted, in the final stanza, with the Pentecosts.
Love as inspiration is contrasted with the Holy Spirit, and the poet as
lover with the poet as apostle. In "Rosemonde," the girl's name sug-
gests a comparable contrast between terrestrial loves and the Rose of
Heaven.

CHANTRE, page 44

This single line was added on the proofs of *Alcools*.

The title *Chantre* means "singer" (especially in the sense of "poet") or "cantor."

"Et l'unique cordeau des trompettes marines" is an alexandrine containing two puns: *cordeau*, "cord," is also *cor d'eau*, "horn of water" (and possibly *corps d'eau*, "body of water"); *trompette marine* is a "trumpet marine" (i.e., a medieval musical instrument with a single string) or, literally, a "marine trumpet."

The poem has been praised, especially by André Rouveyre, in *Amour et Poésie d'Apollinaire*, for its lyric qualities, for the likeness between the shape of the trumpet marine and that of the cord, between the sound of the trumpet marine and the cantor's voice.

Besides the surprise effect caused by the *jeux d'analogies*, there is that caused by the trumpet marine itself which has an awkward shape and a glum note. In *Le Bourgeois Gentilhomme*, M. Jourdain's liking for the trumpet marine is a source of comedy (II, i). It is the contrast between the trumpet marine's comic connotations and the evocative title and lyric alexandrine derived from it that inspire Michel Décaudin's shrewd comment on Apollinaire's poetics: "Son principal ressort est pour lui la surprise, c'est-à-dire non seulement l'émerveillement, mais aussi le rire, l'étonnement devant l'insolite. Ce qu'on a souvent pris pour un penchant à la mystification n'est que l'expression de cette vertu poétique de la surprise" ([14], p. 113).

CRÉPUSCULE, page 46

First published in *Les Argonautes*, no. 9 (February, 1909), with "Saltimbanques," and without dedication.

The poem may have been written before Apollinaire and Marie Laurencin met in 1908. The images suggest not only her paintings but those of Picasso. As Michel Décaudin observes, the fairy-tale atmosphere suggests Germany and also the poetry of Max Jacob.

These octosyllabic quatrains, which are embellished with varying rhyme schemes (ABBA, CCDD, EFEF), inner rhyme ("Et dans l'étang"), assonance, and alliteration, describe musically the making of a poem. The scenes with Columbine and Harlequin evoke twilight and characterize the poet. When day dies and the shadows of the dead

draw near, Columbine admires her own naked beauty (or its reflection). Her counterpart, Harlequin, takes advantage of the fading light to play his magic tricks. The assembly of sorcerers, magicians, and fairies are his peers who will admire or criticize his performance. The rest of the cast have other reactions to him. The hanged man abets him. The blind man (or woman) who rocks a fair infant cannot see the baby, much less the performance. The doe passes by, wondering, but indifferent to all but her fawns. The dwarf is envious as Harlequin seems to swell.

The poem's appeal is primarily visual until the final word of the final stanza, when the poet takes leave of his fantasy, and of us, with a pun. *Trismégiste*, "three times great," is an epithet of Hermes Trismegistus, supposed author of the Hermetic books which concern cabalistic ideas as well as magic, astrology, and alchemy, and so has come to signify, in Apollinaire's often esoteric vocabulary, "a learned magician." The epithet literally describes Harlequin's stature as three times his ordinary size. On another level, it refers to those powers of magic or of mirrors that allow him to grow. The ambiguities contained in *trismégiste* are an ironic contrast to the word with which it rhymes, *triste*, "sad." Harlequin grows literally before the onlookers' eyes and takes on stature as well in their imagination. He speaks a secret language, invokes the supernatural, prophesies, turns common objects to gold, or like the poet, gives the illusion of doing these things.

ANNIE, page 48

First published in *Les Soirées de Paris*, no. 8 (September, 1912), with "Le Voyageur" and "Cors de Chasse," and entitled "Fanny."

The free-verse form, with its lines of varying lengths and its unexpected rhymes, adds to the humor. The poet imagines himself meeting Annie in a new guise, in an East Texas landscape that bears a striking resemblance to France. His geography, as Michel Décaudin notes, is a little vague. Either he has misplaced Mobile, or he imagines Texas to be even bigger than it is. His portrayal of Annie as a Mennonite is a mild kidding of her strict Anglican background, and his comment that "La dame et moi suivons presque le même rite," may be a way of saying the opposite.

LA MAISON DES MORTS, page 50

First published as a story in prose, with the title "L'Obituaire," and without dedication, in *Le Soleil*, (August 31, 1907).

The poet, like Vergil in Dante's poem, intermediates between the dead and the living, but unlike the Augustan poet, Apollinaire is alive, and the story takes place in this world. Accordingly, the dead are not unhappy exiles, or pilgrims, or blessed spirits; they are courteous visitors, indistinguishable from the living. The image of the dummies that describes them before they wake anticipates the victim dummies of "L'Émigrant de Landor Road" and, as in the latter poem, introduces a note of fantasy.

The language is playful and exploits various techniques: the naïve misstatement "Et la terre plate à l'infini / Comme avant Galilée" (stanza 3, ll. 7 and 8); the too-appropriate detail, "Un ange en diamant brisa toutes les vitrines" (stanza 3, l. 10); the redundant expression. The resemblance between the living and the dead gives rise to ironic language and to some ironic situations .The *chevau-légers*, "light horsemen," no longer part of the French army after 1815, are anachronistic and ghostly (stanza 9, l. 3). The dead wrangle "avec autant de vigueur que les vivants" (stanza 20, l. 6). Descriptive of both living and dead is the phrase "C'était à mourir de rire" (stanza 24, l. 7), a joke Apollinaire had already used in his story, "La Serviette des Poètes," where he describes a tubercular poet coughing his heart out "avec des mines à mourir de rire" [2] (p. 201). A living woman tells him that he comes too late—because she is married, not because her suitor is dead. She declares, "Je pleure et je voudrais mourir" (stanza 23, last line), wanting to escape, not to the dead man, but from the living husband. Conversations present ironic contrasts on the subject of time: "Je vous attendrai / Dix ans vingt ans s'il le faut," says the student (stanza 13, ll. 1 and 2). "Je vous attendrai / Toute votre vie," replies the dead woman (stanza 14, ll. 1 and 2). In the same spirit are the goodbyes: "Au revoir / A demain / A bientôt" (stanza 27, ll. 4-6). The confusion between living and dead creates a peculiar atmosphere; in comparison with their vividness, reality fades: "Un genévrier parfois / Faisait l'effet d'un fantôme" (stanza 26, ll. 8 and 9). This same atmosphere prevails when the living, fortified by the memory of a dead love, return to the ordinary world of beer parlors and dog butchers.

The poet's concern with memory is first indicated at the beginning of the third stanza: when the eyes of the dead light up, "Rapide comme ma mémoire" (stanza 3, l. 2). Memory and consciousness itself are almost identified. Later the student says to his dead love, "Ni le temps ni l'absence / Ne nous feront oublier nos promesses" (stanza 16, ll. 5 and 6) and names the two greatest enemies of memory. Near the end of the poem, the remembering of those who are no longer subject to change preserves them, as a glacier would, undecayed; it preserves also the ones who remember.

CLOTILDE, page 64

First published in *Les Soirées de Paris*, no. 6 (July, 1912), with "Marie-Sybille" (later, "Marizibill") and "Rosemonde."

In these highly literary quatrains composed of seven- and eight-syllable lines and *rimes croisées*, an allegorical garden of love, where grow "l'anémone et l'ancolie," is evoked musically and untranslatably. *Ombre*, as in "La Chanson du Mal-Aimé," suggests at once "ghost" and "shadow"; when it refers to the poet's own shadow, it partakes mysteriously of his identity. It is a seeming paradox that night should dispel the shadows and the sun make them dark. "Les déités des eaux vives," as Professor Breunig points out, occurs also in the story *Que-vlove? Déités*, "mythological deities," is a poetic word, not uncommon in *fin de siècle* verse.

CORTÈGE, page 66

First published in *Poème et Drame*, Vol. I (November, 1912), without dedication.

The title refers to the central passage of the poem, where Apollinaire describes himself as composed of all humanity, past and present. The theme suggests unanimism, a poetic movement begun around 1908 by Jules Romains and others, which relates the individual personality to the collective soul. Apollinaire's humorous yet earnest, deliberate yet informal free verse comes closer than the Abbaye poets (in my opinion) to catching the tone of voice of the original unanimist, Walt Whitman:

> I find I incorporate gneiss, coal, long-threaded moss,
> fruits, grains, esculent roots,

And am stucco'd with quadrupeds and birds all over,
And have distanced what is behind me for good reasons,
But call any thing back again when I desire it.

("Song of Myself," part 31)

Lines 1 and 2. The bird image in the first stanza suggests an airplane or one of the birds in "Zone." It may have been suggested to Apollinaire, as Michel Décaudin points out, by *Le Monde Enchanté*, a travel book containing medieval and renaissance accounts of journeys to foreign lands. One passage describes a little seabird that lays its eggs high in the air; another, the medieval belief that the bird of paradise lived eternally in the air. Birds dwell in the same rarefied atmosphere in "Le Brasier." And, in "L'Émigrant de Landor Road," the stars themselves are given birdlike (or perhaps fishlike) habits, when they nibble the corpses in the sea.

Lines 3-5. "Notre sol" contains a double meaning: *sol*, "earth," and *sol* (Latin), "sun." Michel Décaudin quotes from *L'Enchanteur Pourrissant* a passage that shows the growth not only of an image but of a verbal play:

Les aigles . . .
. . .
Croyant voir, sur le sol, un soleil écrasé,
Éblouis, ont baissés leur seconde paupière.

If the bird in "Cortège" is an eagle, he may be kin to the eagle pouncing from the horizon in "Zone" and to the eagle descending from a snowy sky in "Un Soir."

Lines 6-11. "Et moi aussi de près . . ." I too, says the poet elliptically, I am at once darkness and light, like the earth, like the bird. At a distance I dazzle, but close up I am sad and dull. This second stanza, with its image of the soul in darkness surrounded by the watching stars, suggests work of a younger poet, Pierre Reverdy, who admired Apollinaire:

Ils sont encore tous là derrière
Les regards étoilés
Tous les noms confondus
Les rires étouffés

228

Les numéros perdus
Enfin le vent brutal les a tous dispersés
Et seul il s'en allait dans l'ombre sans écho

(from "Comme on Change," *Sources du
Vent*, 1929)

The country Apollinaire explored occasionally, Reverdy dwelt in always.

Lines 17-18. The oblong flame that appears in the third stanza is a saviour—Christ, perhaps man, or even a new creation or a final destruction. Michel Décaudin observes that in "Lul de Faltenin" the stars are *oblongues* and that in a poem from *Il y a*, Icarus is a *dieu oblong*; thus, the adjective describes a trail of light left by an astral body. It suggests also the flying saints of old paintings and the paths traced on a film which has been exposed for an hour or two under a starry sky. "Oblong" is used to describe motion and perhaps also the growth in intensity of the fire which will eventually swallow all other fires.

Line 19 *et seq*. Abruptly Apollinaire switches gears and uses language reminiscent of Whitman. Also like Whitman's are the curious mixture of curiosity and compassion, and the sense of humor. The error concerning all women, which was inspired in Cornelius Agrippa by the long line of Ursulines (i.e., St. Ursula and all her ladies, who were slain by the Huns), is the point of view he expressed in a youthful eulogy of women, *De Nobilitate et Praecellentia femini Sexus*, an attitude not shared, observes Décaudin, by the author of "La Chanson du Mal-Aimé."

MARIZIBILL, page 72

First published in *Les Soirées de Paris*, no. 6 (July, 1912), with "Clotilde" and "Rosemonde" under the title "Marie-Sybille."

The form, octosyllabic quintains, is similar to that of "La Chanson du Mal-Aimé" and "Marie." "Marizibill" appears in other works of Apollinaire, notably in a story from *L'Hérésiarque et Cie*, where the alternate spelling is explained as the pronunciation of Marie-Sybille in Cologne ("Amphion Faux-Messie" [2], p. 233).

Stanza 5. The "brasseries borgnes" recall the London and Paris of "La Chanson du Mal-Aimé." However, the personification of a man-

made landscape, which appears occasionally in *Alcools*, is hardly a trademark of Apollinaire. Léon-Paul Fargue, a slightly older contemporary, exploited the same kind of imagery to a much greater degree during these same years. In *Tancrède* (1911), he describes

> Le petit restaurant malingre
> Tiède comme un
> Baiser malsain
>
> ("Divers Objets")

But it is in *Poèmes* (1912) that Fargue's imaginative use of personification emerges as a source of fantasy in such phrases as "Le phare qui tourne à pleins poings son verre de sang dans les étoiles . . ." ("Le rampe s'allume").

Line 6. *Se mettre sur la paille*, "to go broke," is used also in the literal sense, "to lie down in the straw."

Lines 11-15. The last stanza is another way of expressing that compassion for humanity which one finds in the central portion of "Cortège." The imagery echoes that of other poems: dead leaves suggest partings in "Rhénane d'automne" and in "L'Émigrant de Landor Road"; eyes and fire, the resurrection in "La Maison des Morts"; hearts and doors, loneliness, in "Hôtels"; in several of the Rhineland poems, the wind is loud with voices. Here, the dead leaves, the eyes like glowing coals, the hearts and doorways suggest that people like Marizibill are already dead and in Limbo or the second circle of Hell, driven vainly on by winds of desire.

LE VOYAGEUR, page 74

First published in *Les Soirées de Paris*, no. 8 (September, 1912), with "Fanny" (later, "Annie") and "Cors de Chasse," and without dedication. Fernand Fleuret, to whom "Le Voyageur" is dedicated in *Alcools*, describes the poem as one of the duets he and Apollinaire used to improvise while walking about the streets of Paris. But his story may be an exaggeration.

Line 1. "Ouvrez-moi cette porte"—In "La Porte," "la porte de l'hôtel sourit terriblement"; in "Hôtels," each man lives behind shut doors. One finds also, in Pierre Reverdy's poetry, doors that open (or close) upon life.

Line 2. "La vie est variable aussi bien que l'Euripe"—literally, "life is uncertain, as well as Euripos." Euripos is a strait between Boeotia and the isle of Euboea where Aristotle supposedly drowned. Here it suggests death. Once more Apollinaire treats an ancient metaphor in a modern manner, this time, the voyage of life, which is the controlling image of the poem. One finds the same metaphor in Reverdy's "D'Un autre Ciel" (*La Lucarne Oval*, 1916), treated in much the same manner.

Line 4. "Le paquebot orphelin" may be, like "le bateau ivre," the poet's image of himself. The "fièvres futurs," like shores passing by, instantly become *regrets* and *repentirs*. Time is likened to the passing shore also in "Mai."

Line 7. "Surmarine" is a coined word, an example of a coinage that is musical and pleasingly evocative, not discordant.

Lines 11-31. The seemingly haphazard collection of memories builds to a cumulative effect and announces the structure Apollinaire will use in "Zone." Again, some of the images are like those in "Zone": the soaring Christ, the flock of landscapes, troupes of streets and bridges, nights pale with *alcool*. One is also reminded of "Vendémiaire" as of the flaming cities. "Le long orphelinat des gares," harking back to the orphan steamer, once more brings in the linked themes of loneliness and travel.

Lines 32-47. Toward the end of this free-verse poem is a series of four quatrains of alexandrines, rhyming ABBA, which may belong to an earlier period. The eyes are the ripples in the river. I translated "Des ombres vivaces" as "living shadows"; "lively shades" might bring out more strongly the paradox contained in this phrase. The ghostly army suggests one of Ossian's. Michel Décaudin, however, finds the image related to ghosts in the Rhineland poems.

Lines 51-53. About the two sailors, Décaudin makes one of his luminous remarks: they remind him of an old photo of Apollinaire and his brother as children, dressed in sailor's costume (reproduced in Pascal Pia's *Apollinaire par lui-même* [30], p. 24).

Lines 49 and 50. The two most beautiful lines in this poem, which is less ambitious than "Zone" or "Vendémiaire" and more beautiful, in my opinion, than either, are those about the bee that falls into the fire when the year is dwindling and rushing into winter. Was the fire lit in a room—or was it a bonfire built in the garden to destroy summer's residue? The glitter and hum of the bee link it to the image of fire. At

the same time, sweetness, harvest, virtue, life itself are consumed in the bee's death. Apollinaire, at thirty-two, is aware of mortality.

MARIE, page 80

First published in *Les Soirées de Paris*, no. 9 (October, 1912).

"Marie," like "Le Pont Mirabeau," celebrates the uncertainty of love, which is at the mercy of time and of the changing heart. See especially the closing lines, where the Seine and the poet's sorrow are compared, and time seems to stand still.

Lines 1-5. The *maclotte* is a Walloon dance, danced in the region of Stavelot where Apollinaire spent the summer of his nineteenth year. The first lines evoke a Maria whom he met at Stavelot, but already at the end of the first stanza the poet is thinking of Marie Laurencin and of their quarrels.

Line 6. In the second stanza, an alexandrine, inserted among the octosyllabic quintains, gives onomatopoeic stress to the poet's love (as he would like it to be), prolonging it till it fades away like music.

LA BLANCHE NEIGE, page 82

First published in *Alcools*.

The irregular lines, occasional rhyme, and the fairy-tale imagery (which evokes for Professor Breunig a Rhineland scene) contribute to make the first part of "La Blanche Neige" a nursery song. If the Christmas goose and domestic angels evoke German (or Danish) fairy tales, the sun's medal seems to be Apollinaire's embellishment. The ending, which may allude to Annie, has always reminded me, because of the concisely stated correspondence between weather (or invoked weather) and the lover's desire, of a sixteenth-century English lyric:

> O Western wind, when wilt thou blow
>> That the small rain down can rain?
> Christ, that my love were in my arms,
>> And I in my bed again!

and of Housman's embroidery upon the same theme:

> The weeping Pleiades wester,
> And I lie down alone.

POÈME LU AU MARIAGE D'ANDRÉ SALMON, page 84

First published in *Vers et Prose*, XXVII (October-December, 1911).

Apollinaire's own story about the composition of this free-verse poem that reminds one of Whitman is that he wrote it upstairs in a double-decker bus on his way to the Salmons' wedding, while his friend René Dalize talked to him continually (Philippe Soupault [38]). The story is perhaps more significant of Apollinaire's attitude toward himself and of his delight in exaggeration than of his actual methods of composition. Although he seems to have written entire passages of poetry at first jet, he also rewrote considerably (Moulin [28]; Décaudin [14]; corrected copy of *Alcools*, Tzara collection). A manuscript version of "Poème lu au mariage d'André Salmon" indicates the poem underwent many changes [15]).

Line 12. Michel Décaudin finds the phrase "caveau maudit," "cursed wine cellar," unsuitable for the Café du Départ where the gay and hospitable *Soirées de la Plume* were held, and he conjectures that the adjective *maudit* refers to the poverty of the two young writers. Madame Durry relates ([18], p. 18) that André Salmon told her "caveau maudit" meant at the time a meeting place for poets, because involvement in poetry was "un engagement sérieux." Probably, too, the phrase owes something to Verlaine, who had been a devotee of the Café du Départ a generation earlier, and to his title for the poets he loved (including himself), "les poètes maudits."

L'ADIEU, page 88

First published in *Le Festin d'Ésope*, no. 2 (December, 1903).

For variants of "Adieu," see notes to the Pléiade edition of the *Œuvres Poétiques* and especially Décaudin, *Le Dossier d'Alcools*. In earlier versions, as quotation marks and spacing indicate, lines 1-3 are spoken by one person (living?), lines 4 and 5 by another (dead?). The final version, although it was first published with a space after line 3, suggests equally well that lines 1, 3, and 4 are spoken by the living person, lines 2 and 5 by the dead one. Or perhaps there is no longer a dialogue taking place.

"Adieu" bears a faint resemblance to Hugo's poem for his dead daughter, "Demain, dès l'aube . . ." but Apollinaire's farewell to the dead, or perhaps to a lost love (probably Marie Dubois of Stavelot), contains more mystery than does Hugo's, partly because the modern poet's

octosyllables are more concise and elliptic than the Romantic poet's alexandrines. As in other poems of Apollinaire, the barrier between the living and the dead has been let down. The poem may be a sentimental dialogue, but the distinction between the sexes has been lost. All minor details of context are blurred. What remains is the gesture of farewell, as poignant as that on a Roman stele, framed by the autumnal season and the sad wild landscape one associates with heather.

SALOMÉ, page 90

First published in *Vers et Prose*, IV (December, 1905, January-February, 1906), with "L'Émigrant de Landor Road," "Les Cloches," and "Mai."

Apollinaire had already written a story about the death of Salomé, and he may have read Laforgue's story about her in the *Moralités Légendaires*, which was republished in 1903. Salomé was a popular heroine-villain in Symbolist literature. The story, as Apollinaire presents it here, is ambiguous. Is Salomé simply daft? Do her words conceal a (sadistic) passion for the Evangelist? Does she rejoice or does she despair? Is the poet perhaps really concerned not with Salomé at all but with John the Baptist, like himself a victim of women? The loosely rhyming quatrains, composed of alexandrines and a lone decasyllable, are followed by three remarkable half lines. These prolong the final rhyme, speed up the rhythm and the flow of images, and underline the increasing disorder that marks the poem's ending.

LA PORTE, page 92

First published in *Vers et Prose*, XXXI (October-December, 1912), with "Le Larron," "Dans le Palais de Rosemonde" (later, "Palais"), "Marie," "L'Adieu," and "La Dame."

These rhyming alexandrines concern Apollinaire's youth in Paris when he was first trying to make his way.

Line 4. Pi-mus fish, having only one eye apiece, swim in couples. Similarly, with pihi birds, who have only one wing (see "Zone"). Apollinaire picked up these details in a translation from the Chinese which he read in the *Journal asiatique* (January-February, 1896).

Line 5. The pun on "angels" and "angelfish" may be more obvious in English than in French.

MERLIN ET LA VIEILLE FEMME, page 94

First published in *Les Rubriques nouvelles*, no. 6 (June, 1912).

"Merlin et la vieille Femme" is one of the oldest poems in *Alcools*. The theme finds parallels in another early poem, "La Maison de Cristal," and in the prose story "L'Enchanteur pourrissant." In form and imagery, "Merlin" is related to "Le Larron" and "L'Ermite" and belongs to the same stage of Apollinaire's poetic development. Madame Durry, in an analysis of Apollinaire's religious feelings ([18], pp. 192-233), discusses in detail all three poems.

Merlin, the enchanter who could foretell the future, is a persona of the poet. Morgana is Merlin's memory. Against a background filled with druid magic and faint overtones of Christianity, they enact their drama, the making of poetry. The young Apollinaire attempts to define, in a bookish poem, the creative process and its relationship to sacred and profane love. The poetic language of the Symbolists, the medieval trappings evocative of Breton romances, the role assigned to memory, show an appreciation of tradition which is asserted as late as "Cortège." (An interesting sidelight on the poet who, two weeks after the publication of *Alcools*, composed "L'antitradition-futuriste" in which he dispensed *merde* and roses—*merde* to the past and roses to Apollinaire, his friends and his Futurist acquaintances.)

Lines 5 and 6. The *rose des vents*, "compass" (literally "rose of the winds"), is used as a play on words also in "Clair de Lune." Madame Durry comments that the rose is thornless, not only as an unreal rose, but as a symbol of a pre-Christian world where the crown of thorns has no meaning.

Line 10. *En aval*, "downstream" recalls (as Madame Durry points out) a phrase in *Launcelot* describing Morgana: "Et tant chevalcha amont et aval qu'el trova Merlin."

Line 12. When Merlin cries out "Rival," he is probably addressing the aging body that cages and burdens his soul.

Line 14. *Ce soleil de chair* is, of course, his heart.

Line 15. *Ma semblable* might be better translated "my likeness." Morgana resembles Merlin, because as his memory, she is not only all he has done and been but whatever he is able to do and be, a mirror image of sorts.

Line 52. Memory is love's equal because both abolish time, observes Michel Décaudin.

Line 56. Does Merlin's son walk *le chemin de Rome* as friend or

foe? queries Madame Durry. Perhaps *tout seul* carries the answer: he will find God in his own way.

Line 60. The image of the hawthorn, which occurs also in "La Maison de Cristal" and "L'Enchanteur pourrissant," comes from the *Roman de Merlin*, according to Décaudin.

SALTIMBANQUES, page 100

First published in *Les Argonautes*, no. 9 (February, 1909), with "Crépuscule," and without dedication.

A manuscript published by Jeanine Moulin in *Textes Inédits* [28] suggests that "Saltimbanques" and "Crépuscule," both written in rhyming octosyllables, are derived from a single first draft.

Like "Crépuscule," "Saltimbanques" suggests a mixture of Rhineland memories and of the pictoral themes used by Picasso and other painters. This charming poem contains one of Apollinaire's most musical lines, "Et les enfants s'en vont devant."

LE LARRON, page 102

First published in *La Plume*, no. 343-344 (August 1-15, 1903 [2^e *supplément poétique*]), without indication of dramatis personae.

"Le Larron" was probably written before Apollinaire went to Germany. Like "Merlin" and "L'Ermite," it consists of alexandrines grouped into quatrains and, like "Merlin," it is adorned with *rimes croisées*. A literary poem, "Le Larron" reflects the young poet's reading, particularly his interest in symbolism. Michel Décaudin notes that Apollinaire's Greek seacoast is an imaginary and crowded landscape, "une antiquité de fantaisie" ([14], p. 152), and Madame Durry speaks of the poem's "géographie fabuleuse" ([18], p. 231). The thief himself is a persona of the poet, although to a lesser degree than Merlin the magician or the haunted Hermit. Like Apollinaire in the Paris that existed before the First World War, the thief is a foreigner in an elite society. (However, see Madame Durry's analysis of "Le Larron" [18], pp. 223-233. For her, the poem is an anti-Parnassian statement: one can no longer be a pagan in a world transformed by Christianity. The poet expresses his regret for a classical past, a *paradis terrestre* from which, as member of a somber, bare religion, he is exiled.) By projecting a Christian self into a pagan world, Apollinaire tests the Catholic faith in which he has been brought up, and its monastic ideals, against

the more humanistic "Greek way" that he has encountered in literature. His conclusion, as early as 1903, seems to be that neither creed nourishes both body and soul.

Stanzas 1-7. The poem begins with a dialogue between the thief, the old man, and the choros (of islanders?) who have discovered him stealing fruit in their orchard.

Stanza 1. He is *malheureux* and *malhabile*, "unlucky" and "awkward," because he plays the role of pirate instead of asking for hospitality. *Voleur* in "Zone" becomes an epithet of Christ. The thief is not only an *étranger*, a "stranger" to the region, but *barbare*, "barbarian," which to an ancient Greek meant simply someone who was not Greek— a foreigner. Their guess that he is in exile implies political exile.

Stanza 3. With unconscious irony the choros compares the thief to the goddess of love. The phrase *gestes socratiques* means, in context, amorous caresses, but it also suggests the series of questions which makes up a large part of the poem.

Stanza 4. "Ton père fut un sphinx et ta mère une nuit" is claimed by Apollinaire scholars as a reference to the poet's unmarried mother and to his father whose identity, though supposedly ascertained by Marcel Adéma [5], still teases Apollinaire's latest biographer Francis Steegmuller [39]. One translator has even expressed "ta mère une nuit" as "your mother was a one-night stand."

The verse suggests the thief's mixed parentage, comparable to Apollinaire's own (his mother was Polish, his father probably Italian). For although the choros might think of Night as a Greek goddess, the sphinx was indubitably a foreigner, of Egyptian or Chaldean origin.

The verse suggests also the divine or semidivine origin of the thief who, like Apollinaire, is of mysterious but noble lineage. In "L'Ignorance" ([1], p. 344), Icarus describes the sun's mother as night: "la nuit, ta mère incestueuse, / . . . stellaire et somptueuse, / La nuit cette inconnue parmi les inconnus." According to Greek myth, Night laid an egg (the moon) out of which hatched the sun. Thus the thief, who becomes a Christ-figure by the end of the poem, is given a vague set of solar, lunar, and stellar associations.

The image of the sphinx-father is puzzling since the sphinx is usually considered to be both a female and a monster—consisting of a woman's head and bust set upon the winged body of a lion (or dog) and frequently ending in a serpent's tail. The Thebans, for example, portrayed their moon goddess as a sphinx. Perhaps Apollinaire refers jokingly either to the mystery shrouding his own father or to the story

(invented by himself) that his father was a Roman Catholic cardinal. A sphinx-father is appropriate to the Christian thief because the sphinx can represent both the enigma of death waiting to trap men and the source of true knowledge (as it does in a later poem, "Le Brasier").

Zacinthe might be a deformation of *jacinthe* which means both "hyacinth," "that sanguine flower inscribed with woe," and "jacinth," the precious stone, and thus evokes a fusion of images—a jewel-flower (like the jewel-buds in stanza 17) or a flowering isle. A minor association, adding to the general mythological ornateness and confusion of the poem's background, is the fate of the charming boy Hyacinthus who was loved by Apollo and killed by a jealous zephyr.

Feint continues the theme of disguise and pretense announced by *simuler* and *gestes*. The speakers are, throughout the poem, aware of themselves as actors in a verse drama (*cf.*, for example, the effect of *masques* in stanza 9 and of *feignaient* in stanza 10).

Stanza 5. *Ta voix ligure* contains a pun on "Ligurian," or North Italian, and "ligure," a precious stone mentioned in Exodus, probably the ancient jacinth (or blue sapphire). The jewel image returns later, in the description of a magic wood. The *nénie*, or "lament," of the thief's mother is, strictly speaking, a Greek or Roman funeral song.

"Puisqu'ils n'eurent . . . / De prétexte . . ." that is, the thief's mother and father could only meet by night. Or these two lines could mean "their only excuse was that they loved each other nightly." It has been conjectured that Apollinaire refers indirectly to his own family situation. "La pubère et l'adulte" would then describe the disparity in age between his parents. Certainly the thief is having to defend his family honor.

Stanza 6. This stanza and the one following contain exquisite imagery. The Punic knife suggests the opposition between Carthaginian religion and Greek; the former had a distinctly Oriental flavor and, unlike the Greek, retained certain barbarous rites, including that of human sacrifice. At the same time, the knife may suggest the sacrificial nature of Christianity.

Stanza 7. In "Les Fiançailles," hearts hang among the lemon trees. Here the lemons are described in terms of opposites: oil and water.

Stanzas 8-14. The Actor describes the thief's entrance into the banquet hall where he is questioned by the guests.

Stanza 11. The Actor mocks the asceticism of the Pythagoreans who were not allowed to eat beans.

Stanza 13. The thief's "lyric" eyes establish him as a poet. Later the choros will address him as "poète barbare." This stanza contains a number of beasts and birds that suggest antiquity. The Pythagorean peacock, as Michel Décaudin observes, was supposedly the original location of Pythagoras' soul before it lodged in the Trojan hero Euphorbus, in Homer, and finally in Pythagoras himself. Madame Durry notes the dolphin who saved the poet Arion and others, and the bull of Mithras.

Stanzas 15-21. The choros intervene to tell of all those who have passed by their town and then repeat the woman's question to the thief, "Who are you?"

Stanza 15. The stammering man is Moses (whom Michelangelo portrayed with horns instead of flames). The naked sea is the Red Sea that retreated when the Hebrews passed through it. A similar image occurs in "La Chanson du Mal-Aimé": "Onde ouverte de la mer Rouge."

Stanza 17. The phrase "oiseaux gemmipares" contains a double meaning. *Gemmipares*, "reproducing by buds," and *gemme*, "precious stone," come from the same Latin root. Thus the birds bud like trees and lay jewels instead of eggs. The forest's epithet *précieuse* contributes to the image of precious stones. So too does the ripening of toads, enveloped by azure sky and water, like a pearl in an oyster.

Stanza 18. The triumph passing under a rainbow rather than under a triumphal arch evokes Roman history, as do the sacred geese whose cackling once saved Rome from the Gauls.

Stanza 19. According to Madame Durry, the widows, dressed in black, think themselves still comely; the *grappes* are bunches of grapes, or they are rosaries; the triangle, and perhaps the cope too (which can mean triangle in heraldry), suggest Pythagoras, Greek geometry, and Athena, goddess of reason; the triangle may also be an erotic symbol ([3], p. 194). Michel Décaudin thinks that the hymn to the "black but comely," which echoes the Song of Songs, is directed to the black goddess Cybele; she is celebrated by the grape clusters and set in opposition to Pallas ([14], p. 153). This interpretation seems substantiated by the choros' final criticism of Christianity as a male religion. However, the mention of bishops suggests also the Virgin Mary, the darkness of whose complexion is debated at the end of "Rhénane d'automne," and even non-Christian cults of the moon goddess which flourished in the Near East in the first century. It is only logical that black bishops should do reverence to a black Virgin.

Stanza 20. *Des baisers florentins*—Apollinaire used this same punning phrase in a later poem, "La Chanson du Mal-Aimé," and in what is probably an earlier one, "Adieux" ([1], p. 332). According to Michel Décaudin, the tossing of *alcancies*, clay spheres stuffed with cinders, flowers or perfume, is a Moorish game.

Stanza 21. The choros, as they address a barbarian, offer him a choice of barbarian religions. Madame Durry notes that Belphégor, worshipped by some of Israel's neighbors, can be identified with Priapus, that the sun god may be Baal, and silence, Harpocrates, that the dog may be the one that guarded Europa or the one that Helen lost when she fled with Paris. But Harpocrates, god of silence, is simply a Greek misinterpretation of Horus, the Egyptian sun god, who is often represented as a boy with a finger on his mouth. Thus, "le soleil le silence" is probably a learned joke, of the kind that occurs in "La Chanson du Mal-Aimé," where the poet expresses the same meaning in two ways. As for the dog, if a barbarian symbol, he can hardly belong to Greek myth. Perhaps he is an Egyptian god and wears a beast's head, like Seth, god of evil, or a dog's head, like Thoth, god of wisdom and magic. Perhaps he is the corn spirit, conceived of as a wolf or a dog. This conception, according to Frazer, was common in France, Germany, and Slavic countries, notably in northeastern France (*The Golden Bough*, XLVIII, 2). Apollinaire might have come across folk tales about the corn spirit in Stavelot. Whatever he is, the dog represents not only a non-Greek deity but some aspect of sexuality.

Stanzas 22-31. When they learn the thief is Christian, the choros jeer at his faith, lament his loss to the pagan world and drive him forth.

Stanza 22. "Contre le feu l'ombre prévaut"—Perhaps the choros mean that the shadow of the mortal body prevails against the fire of one's spiritual beliefs and that he who puts his faith in the next world is doomed to die eternally in this one. Thus, the thief on the left, who is damned, will laugh at the thief on the right, because the latter naïvely expects to go to Paradise. The image of the shadow suggests mortality also in "La Chanson du Mal-Aimé" (stanzas 36 and 37) while, in "Le Brasier," the fire image expresses, among other things, an intense activity of the spirit. For Madame Durry, the shadow suggests Christianity, and the fire suggests the choros' solar poetry. In any case, there is a Manichean opposition between the powers of light and those of darkness.

Stanza 24. The play on words contained in *sinistre* is the same in

French as in English. The *tache grise* may suggest death and thoughts of death. Like *ombre*, it is in opposition to fire and to the sun.

Stanza 25. The choros make fun of the Immaculate Conception.

Stanza 26. "Humides fleurs morales"—these flowers, like Mallarmean ones, may be "emblems," not "virtuous." That is, they may be symbols of fertility and of the female, the choros' way of attacking the doctrine of the Immaculate Conception (preceding stanza) and the Christian exaltation of celibate life which, to pagans, seems an impoverished life (subsequent line). As Madame Durry has pointed out, the poem, like "Merlin," reflects philosophical preoccupations of the poet as a young man.

"Va-t'en mais dénudé," "Go but denuded," is an ambiguous phrase. Literally, the thief is poor and the choros, prosperous. Spiritually, his belief (in their eyes) is a bleak one and theirs, fruitful. For Madame Durry he is "privé des fruits" of classical culture; the one who can put only a stealthy hand on the fruits of happiness is the poet ([18], p. 230).

Stanza 27. "L'ombre équivoque," "the equivocal shadow," is another punning phrase. Shadows are equivocal because they can be interpreted either as meaningless or as messengers from another world; the word *ombre* is equivocal because it has two meanings, "shadow" and "shade," or "ghost."

Twilight's "lueurs légères," "gentle glimmers," may recall to the minds of the choros their words about the thief's mother, the night "Qui charma de ses lueurs," the islands of the Cyclades.

Stanza 28. *Briller*, "to shine," and *attirer*, "to attract," suggest that *pantaure* is a glittering magnet. Scott Bates' surmise that *pantaure* is a deformation of *pantasbe*, the magnetic stone discovered by Apollonius of Tyana which attracted gold, has been confirmed by a notebook of Apollinaire's that contains a memorandum about the "pantaure or pantasbe" [15]. Certainly Apollinaire mentions Apollonius elsewhere, in "Zone" and in *L'Hérésiarque et Cie*; and there are other examples of deformed words, coinages, portmanteaus, in his work, such as "chibriape" in "La Chanson du Mal-Aimé."

This stanza pays compliments to the thief in terms of Greek myth. He is compared not only to a magic stone but to the poet Orpheus. In addition, women would have flocked to him like heifers; that is, he is likened to the bull Pasiphaë was enamored of.

Stanza 29. "Il était pâle il était beau comme un roi ladre"—Apollinaire probably used *ladre*, with its double meaning, "stingy" or "lep-

rous," instead of *lépreux*, for reasons of rhyme and meter. Also the thief may be considered stingy by the choros because he refuses to return their amorous overtures. But why is he a leprous king? Perhaps the choros think of Christianity as a sickness comparable to death in life. Perhaps the thief's physical pallor suggests to them this farfetched simile. True leprosy was not known to Europe till the first century B.C. The Greek word λέπρα describes the "white" disease, vitiligo, which is characterized by milky patches on the skin and is curable. Thus, the milk-colored or silvery king would counterbalance the golden *pantasbe*.

If taken as a classical reference, the leprous king might suggest Orestes, prince of Thebes, who was threatened with leprosy by Apollo (although the giving and curing of leprosy was commonly attributed to the moon). A more general European reference might be to the divine king who is killed at the end of a fixed term. Perhaps royalty and skin disease are linked in the popular mind because of the old idea of the king as a scapegoat. Certainly scrofula was known in England as the King's Evil, and it was one of the diseases he could heal with his touch. There are Christian associations, too, with the leprous or ailing king— Christ healing the lepers, Jehovah afflicting the king with leprosy (II Kings 15:5), and even the handsome, though probably impotent, Graal king with his poisoned wound. Apollinaire has assigned to the choros an ambivalent image whose primary function is to surprise and mystify. A secondary effect of the verse is to suggest that the (Hellenistic?) choros are as decadent as some of Apollinaire's immediate Symbolist forebears.

"The sad reed and the funereal load" refer, as Michel Décaudin observes, to the reed the soldiers placed in Christ's hand, instead of a scepter, and to the Cross.

Stanza 31. For a later elaboration of oblong vision, see "Cortège," lines 17 and 18, and appended note. See also "Fiançailles," the passage on the senses (Poem VI). The choros consign the thief to the company of his shadow—and imply that he lives in a world of dreams, insubstantial and morbid. The triad is the Holy Trinity which is seemingly opposed to some form of worship of the Great Mother.

LE VENT NOCTURNE, page 112

First published in *Le Voile de Pourpre*, no. 2 (May, 1909), in *Poèmes rhénans*.

These early alexandrines evoke a Rhenish landscape whose woods and river are haunted by the cries of elves and of the South Wind. To Annie Playden (as reported by Professor Breunig [7]) "Le Vent nocturne" suggested the view of woods and villages Apollinaire could see from his bedroom window at Neu-Glück.

Line 5. When the Phrygian reveler Attis died, his companion, the goddess Cybele, prayed to Zeus to save him, and the ruler of the gods allowed Attis' spirit to pass into a pine tree.

Line 8. Michel Décaudin finds the comparison of woods to an army reminiscent of the woods in the prophecy the witches made to Macbeth.

Line 11. Maids meditate on what may happen, old men on what already has occurred, poets on what cannot be.

LUL DE FALTENIN, page 114

First published in *La Phalange*, no. 17 (November 15, 1907), with "La Tzigane" and "Les Colchiques."

This poem rests obscure, in spite of various interpretations which have been suggested—that the images are primarily erotic (Louis Rene), that the narrator is a sailor, lured by the sirens (Scott Bates), that he is the sun who dies daily, yearning for starry space (Professor Breunig). The form is the same as that of "La Chanson du Mal-Aimé" and the first part of "Le Brasier"—octosyllabic quintains with a rhyme scheme based on *rimes croisées*, marked by occasional assonance instead of rhyme. The similarities between "Lul de Faltenin" and "Les Sept Épées" are striking, and include not only erotic imagery, but "Lul de Faltenin," which is the name of the third sword. This mysterious name supposedly conceals at least two plays on words: *Lul* may be Flemish patois for the phallus; *Faltenin* is a proper name in which Apollinaire may have seen a play on the phrase *phallum tenens*. Michel Décaudin observes that on the page of *La Phalange* following the one which contains the poem (dedicated formally in the first version "A M. Louis de Gonzague Frick") appears a poem by Louis de Gonzague Frick, dedicated to Apollinaire.

The controlling image of the descent into the sirens' grotto reminds Michel Décaudin of a line from Nerval's "El Desdichado":

J'ai rêvé dans la grotte où nage la sirène.

English and American readers will be reminded rather of T. S. Eliot's lines, at the end of "The Love Song of J. Alfred Prufrock":

> I have heard the mermaids singing, each to each
>
> I do not think that they will sing to me.
>
> I have seen them riding seaward on the waves
> Combing the white hair of the waves blown back
> When the wind blows the water white and black.
>
> We have lingered in the chambers of the sea
> By sea-girls wreathed with seaweed red and brown
> Till human voices wake us, and we drown.

Common to both poems are the mermaids dancing among the waves, the descent into the grotto, the final destruction. The two poets approach similar problems (of love, of art) from almost opposite points of view; but whether one embraces life or rejects it, the result seems to be the same. As Michel Décaudin observes, Apollinaire is concerned, in "Lul de Faltenin," as in "Le Brasier" and "Les Fiançailles," with spiritual and artistic aspirations and failures.

Stanza 3. "Le sang jaillit de mes otelles"—*otelles* refers to the point of a lance, or to heraldic emblems resembling a lance head. At the murderer's approach, the victim's wounds bleed.

"Le meurtre de mon double orgueil"—In a manuscript version of the poem published by Professor Breunig [11], a variant reads "Mon assassinat de la veille," "My murder the evening before," a line which suggests to both Professor Breunig and Michel Décaudin, sunset over the water, with the poet as the sun.

Stanza 4. The manuscript reading for *lèvres*, "lips," is *récifs*, "reefs."

Stanza 5. "Car c'est moi seul nuit qui t'étoile"—Apollinaire's removal of punctuation from the text sometimes causes problems. These three lines can be read two ways. However, the original punctuation of the poem (as established by Décaudin in *Le Dossier d'Alcools* [14]) indicates that the above interpretation is correct.

Stanza 6. The sirens become dwarves. A comparable image, though with a different meaning, occurs in "Les Sept Épées," where the third sword, Lul, is carried by "L'Hermès devenu nain."

Stanza 7. I changed the order of the second and third lines. A more

literal translation of the first three lines would read "In her who is skilled and watchful / I saw our forests slowly leaf / And sea and sun gargle." The change, suggested to me by Professor Warren Ramsey, seems justified by a variant reading of line 2: "En qui feuillole nos forêts," which supports the impression that *attentive* and *apprise* describe the sea, not a woman.

Stanza 9. "Les otelles nous ensanglantent"—literally, "the *otelles* cover us with blood." In the last stanza, Professor Breunig has pointed out the wordplay on *otelles* and *étoiles*, "as if the poet wanted to establish a correspondence between them," which is especially marked in the manuscript version.

LA TZIGANE, page 118

First published in *La Phalange*, no. 17 (November 15, 1907), with "Les Colchiques" and "Lul de Faltenin."

The form—octosyllabic quatrains—is also that of "Crépuscule," two of the *Rhénanes*, "Les Cloches" and "Schinderhannes," and the opening and closing lines of "A la Santé." The *rimes embrassées* suggest thoughts that circle and return upon themselves. The image of a bear and of gypsies is found in another Rhineland poem, "Mai," and in "Saltimbanques."

Lines 3-4. In the original there is a pun on *puis*, "then," and *puits*, "well" (for water). Hope crawls, as from a well, from the "then" or "O well" with which the lovers dismiss the gypsy's prophecy. The meaning seems to be one of several: The gypsy's prophecy was most favorable and becomes a well of hope for the lovers; or to the contrary, her words were discouraging; but although an unpleasant future appears unavoidable, hope rises within them as from a well. Or hope rises within them, despite the inner *gouffre* that both lovers (or one) are aware of. If only one of the two is aware of an inner void the gypsy has caused an obstacle to rise between the lovers (perhaps announced by *nos deux vies*), and this is what they think about at the end of the poem. Another possibility is that the gypsy spoke like the Sibyl: and so, when the lovers leave her they consign her puzzling predictions with a mental "O well" to temporary oblivion—but in vain, because everything that happens afterwards makes them wonder if they are fulfilling her prophecy.

Lines 5 and 6. I have omitted the image contained in *dansa debout*,

"danced upright or on its hind legs." One meaning might be, especially if the poem is about Annie, that passion was mastered and so, in the poet's opinion, hope was lost. Madame Durry has pointed out that *privé* means, not only "tamed," but "deprived" or "frustrated" [20].

L'ERMITE, page 120

First published in *La Revue Blanche*, no. 228 (December 1, 1902), without dedication.

"L'Ermite," like "Merlin et la vieille Femme" and "Le Larron," is an early poem. The hermit, monk, or friar who contemplates a skull is a familiar theme in painting, from medieval times on. Apollinaire seems to have borrowed the theme of the temptation of the holy man, his wavering between love of God and dreams of fleshly love, from Gustave Flaubert's *La Tentation de Saint Antoine* and Anatole France's *Thaïs*. The resemblances between the last-named and "L'Ermite" have been expounded in detail by Madame Durry ([18], pp. 194-204). The theme of "Alas poor Yorick" which appears at the beginning of the poem and in two stanzas now omitted, was popular among Symbolists: Laforgue has Hamlet speak in comparably facetious tones to Yorick's skull. According to André Salmon, "L'Ermite" was dedicated to Félix Fénéon in gratitude for his having introduced Apollinaire to *La Revue Blanche*.

Stanza 4. The original contains a pun: "l'amour la mourre." *La mourre*, "mora," is an Italian game perhaps remembered by Apollinaire from his early childhood in Italy.

Stanza 13. *Aémères* describes saints for whom there is no feast day assigned on the calendar. Other esoteric words that sound more like a Symbolist's vocabulary than a hermit's are *isochrones; l'hématidrose*, "the bloody sweat"; *clavaires*. The image of the "pains sans levain," "unleavened bread" recalls, in "Le Larron," the choros' offer of "le pain de froment," "leavened bread."

Stanza 14. One finds scattered through "L'Ermite" phrases and images that appear in other early verse of Apollinaire and in some of his prose: Lilith howls in "La Maison de Cristal" and in "Lecture," *Le Poète assassiné* and in *L'Enchanteur pourrissant*. The eyes that widen sadly suggest not only Lilith and the stars, but the gaze of owls (see stanzas 16 and 17).

Stanza 15. The queen who hangs (herself?) from a star evokes Jocasta and also Phèdre, whose fate, as Madame Durry points out, is related in *Thaïs*: "Elle . . . se pendit par sa ceinture d'or à une cheville d'ivoire." The image of the black woods, with green hope dying above them like the sunset, comes directly from "La Maison de Cristal": "La nuit, les bois sont noirs et se meurt l'espoir vert / avec le jour . . ."

Stanzas 16-17. The image of the owls nailed to the ceiling returns in a later poem, a quatrain in *Le Bestiaire*, entitled "Le Hibou":

> Mon pauvre cœur est un hibou
> Qu'on cloue, qu'on décloue, qu'on recloue.
> De sang, d'ardeur, il est à bout.
> Tous ceux qui m'aiment, je les loue.
>
> (*Œuvres*, p. 30)

The owls in "L'Ermite," like the poet's heart in "Le Hibou," are sad, gentle creatures, living in darkness and tormented by men. Their plight is in some ways comparable to that of the hermit.

Stanza 18. This stanza is constructed from passages in two poems, "Fagnes de Wallonie" ([1], p. 370) and "O mon cœur . . ." ([1] p. 521), and owes to them its rhymes, *plenières* / *sapinières* and *poupins* / *sapins*, the siesta in the pine grove, the skeleton fingers of the pines.

Stanza 21. The effect of the names *Zélotide, Lorie, Louise, Diamante* is at once exotic and lacking in local color—how different from the effect of names in the Rhineland poems. Michel Décaudin quotes a 1906 book review where Apollinaire speaks of eighteenth-century novelists who seek names "like Zélotide, Olinde, Damon, Dorval, so as to locate their novels as little as possible."

Stanza 23. *Fornarines* is a coinage. Margarita, or La Fornarina (so named because her father was a baker), was Raphael's model. Apollinaire turns her into a whole tribe of beauties.

AUTOMNE, page 128

First published in *La Plume*, no. 374 (June 15, 1905).

The poem evokes a misty autumn landscape in the country, suggestive of the Rhineland (E. R. Wolf) or of Stavelot (Michel

Décaudin). Like "Les Colchiques," "Automne" is composed of alexandrines that, through repetition and imagery, suggest a circle. Phrases from the first two lines—"Dans le brouillard," "s'en aller," "paysan," "automne"—weave in and out of the poem, and create an ending like a refrain. The song itself, like the ring, has a circular shape, and suggests (this device is used more outspokenly in "Les Colchiques") that everything returns upon itself, over and over—love, the seasons, the poet's song.

Lines 4-6. The song that is sung in the second stanza may, according to Wolf, allude to Eichendorff's *Zerbrochene Ringlein.* I did not carry over into English the ambiguity in line 6: "Qui parle d'une bague et d'un cœur que l'on brise," "That tells of a ring and of a heart that one breaks." It is probably not only the heart that breaks but the ring too.

L'ÉMIGRANT DE LANDOR ROAD, page 130

First published in *Vers et Prose,* IV (December, 1905–February, 1906), with "Salomé," "Les Cloches," "Mai," and without dedication.

The title of this balladlike poem, written mainly in alexandrines, with a rather casual rhyme scheme, is a reference to Annie's address at 75 Landor Road, London, and the theme, her departure for America in 1904, after Apollinaire's second trip to see her. In the poet's mind, however, it is he who departs. America may be, as Michel Décaudin suggests, a symbol of separation and distance. But also the change of roles expresses the Apollinairean temperament (which must always imagine itself as the wandering, lone, and unloved one), and the poet's wistfulness that it isn't he who is leaving. (The same daydream of going to America appears in "Annie.")

Stanza 1. According to Décaudin, Apollinaire may well have seen headless dummies in store windows. The image of the well-dressed mannequins who become alive occurs again in "La Maison des Morts."

Stanza 2. The personification of fragments of the human personality as shadows and hands (or the gestures of hands), appears in poems of Pierre Reverdy. An early poem, "Matin," published in *Les Ardoises de Toit* (1918), describes a waiting crowd in terms of personified voices, heads, and words:

Les murs limitaient la profondeur de la foule
Et le vent dispersa les têtes qui parlaient
Les voix sont restées à peu près pareilles
Les mots sont posés à mes deux oreilles
Et le moindre cri les fait s'envoler

Stanza 3. "Guider mon ombre aveugle," "To guide my blind shadow," suggests the image of the shadow-wife which occurs in "La Chanson du Mal-Aimé" and in "Signe." (All three poems may have been written in 1904, and probably concern Annie.) There are faint classical allusions to Orpheus leading Eurydice's shade, Antigone leading the blind Oedipus, the boy leading Tiresias.

Stanzas 3 and 4. Are the prairies lyric because Apollinaire imagines them covered with cowboys who sing ballads? These two stanzas suggest both a dream of the Far West (streets, gamblers, a fine funeral, a lonely grave) and Kipling's poems and stories about "Tommy" (the soldier's return from India, the *crachats*, a slang expression meaning literally "spittle," figuratively "medals"). Décaudin points out a resemblance between line 13 and "Mandalay."

Habillé de neuf is slightly ambiguous: does the emigrant think of the new clothes he wishes to buy for his trip or of others he will wear as a corpse? The theme of death recurs throughout the poem. It does not, as in poems by Baudelaire and Mallarmé about journeys, announce a final catastrophe, hated yet longed for. In "L'Émigrant," and also in "La Chanson," images of death express primarily the melancholy mood of the rejected lover, in a world of loveless shadows— "des ombres sans amour."

Stanza 7. "Funereal Fridays" suggests the Friday before Easter. The phrase "la femme du diable a battu son amant" is coined by a temporarily misogynist poet on an expression meaning both rain and sunshine together—*le diable bat sa femme et marie sa fille*, literally "the devil beats his wife and marries his daughter." The English equivalent is "the devil is beating his grandmother." This stanza belonged originally in "Adieux" ([1], p. 332), which furnished lines also to "La Chanson" and to "Vendémiaire."

Stanza 8. The image of hands like leaves appears in other poems, notably in "Rhénane d'Automne." Apollinaire was also fond of the coined verb *feuilloler* which appears again in "Les Fiançailles."

Stanza 10. The image of children's boats on the ocean recalls "Le Bateau Ivre." On the other hand, the tiny bouquet that covers the huge ocean with its petals anticipates the dreamlike images of the Surrealists.

Stanza 12. The second line contains a tongue-twister, "ces tisseuses têtues," which is not carried over into translation. The "sirène moderne" without a husband (because she scorns one?) may be Annie.

Stanza 13. The last stanza is lifted from an early poem, "Le Printemps" ([1], p. 556), which provides lines also for "Les Fiançailles," "Le Brasier," "Mai," and "La Chanson du Mal-Aimé."

ROSEMONDE, page 134

First published in *Les Soirées de Paris*, no. 6 (July, 1912), with "Marie-Sybille" and "Clotilde," without dedication.

These three octosyllabic quintains with their alternate rhymes possibly reflect an adventure in Holland which Apollinaire has described in "Zone," although the mood of the two poems is entirely different. The poet made several trips to Holland between 1905 and 1908. In the first two stanzas the unusual number of perfect rhymes, *de / deux, dame / Amsterdam, vit / vie,* prepare the way for a bilingual pun on *Rosemonde* which suggested to Apollinaire the German for "rosy mouth" and *la rose du monde,* "the rose of the world." The name *Rosemonde* already belonged to Apollinaire's poetic vocabulary (see note to "Palais"). Since the play on words does not come across into English, I have added a line in French to the last stanza. One of the charms of the poem is that it offers an example of a word that suggests meanings it does not have. *Rosamund* is a Germanic name which combines *rose* not with *mund,* "mouth," but with a common suffix meaning "hand" or "protection" (as in *Raymond, Siegmund*). There is irony and worldly charm in the contrast between the girl's name, seemingly so appropriate, and the evocation of the Rose of the World which suggests the mystical Rose or Rose of Heaven, the Madonna.

LE BRASIER, page 136

First published in "Gil Blas," no. 10417 (May 4, 1908), with the title "Le Pyrée," and without dedication.

Apollinaire was particularly fond of "Le Brasier," "Les Fiançailles," and "Vendémiaire." The first two were probably composed at nearly the same time, 1907-1908, and mark a change in the poet's attitude toward his art. He puts behind him the sentimental irony and nostalgia of his poems to Annie and turns to an experimental poetry which, in "Le Brasier" and "Les Fiançailles," transcribes an almost mystical experience of life. The dedication to Paul-Napoléon Roinard first appears in *L'Heure qui sonne* (January, 1913) in a special number honoring that poet.

"Le Brasier" is divided into three parts that describe three different aspects of a glowing passion for a life, a new vision, that consumes the poet. The original title "Pyrée" is lifted from the Latin *pyra* or Greek πυρά, meaning "funeral pyre." The final title *brasier* is a relatively common word, meaning a clear, glowing fire or a source of great heat (originally, and still in English, a pan to hold burning coals). It can be used figuratively as well as literally: *son cœur était un brasier*, "his heart was on fire."

J'ai jeté dans le noble feu, stanzas 1-5. Using one of his favorite forms, octosyllabic quintains that evoke "La Chanson du Mal-Aimé" and "Rosemonde," the poet renounces the past and his former dreams. His renunciation becomes a source of vision. Once freed from illusion, his spirit can contemplate reality. The image of hands, in the first stanza, recalls "les mains coupées," "the severed hands," of the ghosts in "Rhénane d'automne" and the hands of the lonely crowd waving farewell in "L'Émigrant de Landor Road." The heads of the dead recall the headless dummies in "L'Émigrant" and even the beautifully dressed dead in "La Maison des Morts." The states of mind described in those earlier poems, the memories, yearnings, and separations, are now rejected by the poet.

Stanza 4. A recurrent image in Apollinaire's verse, a memory of Italy and the Riviera, is that of lemon trees fruiting and flowering simultaneously and almost continually (see "Les Fiançailles," Poem IV, lines 5-7, p. 172). In "Zone" the poet remembers the shore of the Mediterranean "Sous les citronniers qui sont en fleur toute l'année" and in an early poem, "Le Larron,"

> Les citrons couleur d'huile et à saveur d'eau froide
> Pendaient parmi les fleurs des citronniers tordus.

The image of hearts hanging among the lemons, only hinted at in "Le Brasier," becomes explicit in "Les Fiançailles."

Stanza 5. Amphion and his brother built the walls of Thebes. When Amphion played his harp to the stones, they were drawn into their places on the wall by his music. The strophe contains the image of a town protected by a river and perhaps by walls, the town of Paris or Thebes, which merges with the poet himself. Amphion is a symbol for the power of poetry within the poet that quickens his soul as he lays aside the past, although he continues to be imprisoned by space and time and city landscape, like the lovers on Mirabeau bridge.

Je flambe dans le brasier . . . In enigmatic, and sometimes awkward, free verse that talks around an experience instead of commenting directly on it, this section describes the poet plunging into his "renewed life," freed from the past.

Stanza 1. The bird image suggests to Madame Durry, King Solomon or an Egyptian pharaoh sheltered by birds' wings from the sun. The fire that feeds on itself eternally suggests an apotheosis of poet into star.

Stanza 2. *O Mémoire*—Apollinaire uses the traditional invocation of memory or Mnemosyne, mother of the muses, ironically. He rejects memories of a personal past and forges a new relationship with Europe's literary past.

The Tyndarides, that is, the Dioscuri, Castor and Pollux, whom the poet seems to claim as ancestors, were good fighters, and not very interested in women. They help sailors in distress, and appear to them in the form of St. Elmo's fire. Between them they share death and immortality alternately. Their world of adventure and cameraderie is also Apollinaire's, when he is not under a woman's spell, as poems in *Calligrammes* testify. *Forlignent*, "decline" or "degenerate," is perhaps ironic: the poet establishes his own divinity as equal to that of the Dioscuri. The "vipères ardentes" suggest the flames that feed on the poet and also the twin gods who are sometimes portrayed as snakes.

The *serpents* are again the flames. Their association with the necks of swans may be a learned joke. The poet thinks of the old tale that Zeus came to Leda in the guise of a swan. (From the rafters of a Spartan temple hung the very egg from which the Dioscuri were hatched.) Zeus, of course, would be an immortal swan, and since swans sing only when they die, a songless one. The image of immortal, songless swans disparages the old gods and flatters the songful poet.

The final image of ships and ocean recalls the twin gods who protect sailors; it suggests the theme of life as a voyage and the image of the steamer that appear in "Le Voyageur"; it suggests also the healing quality of water, a theme which recurs at the end of the poem.

Descendant des hauteurs où pense la lumière. The poet turns to the future. Purified by his voluntary exposure to a super-reality, he becomes prophet and seer. The free-verse lines include occasional alexandrines and tend to rhyme, except at the beginning and the end of this section. The image of a descent from heights of light occurs also in "Cortège" and "Signe." The gardens suggest a terrestrial paradise; they are probably that world beyond anything we can see for which the poet yearns. In moments of vision he sees a deified future, a green Paradise, a new temple of Jerusalem. Compare Rilke's "tall steps up to the dreamed-of temple of what is to come." The worm Zamir who built the temple of Jerusalem without tools, according to Jewish legend, is commented on by Madame Durry [17]; she considers him to be a symbol of the creative imagination. As in "La Chanson du Mal-Aimé," *Désirade* suggests at once an island and desire. In the punctuated version published in *Gil Blas,* line 6 of Part III is a question; the ambiguity of the final version was impossible to preserve in translation. What seems to be a scene from Apollinaire's own past, a Riviera town, remote in time and space, juxtaposes memory with vision and thus suggests fresh distinctions between outer and inner reality. (The same stanza, with minor variations, appears in the early poem "Le Printemps" [1] p. 556).

The flock of sphinxes are an intermediary between man and the vision of eternal light. Like the father-sphinx in "Le Larron," they present puzzles. *Sphingerie* is a coinage and introduces a momentary fantasy. The shepherd is at once some lonely shepherd in the Mediterranean hills and the Good Shepherd whose song is not to be forgotten. The five-pointed star suggests the magic symbol of the pentacle and also the celestial rose described by Dante which is like a theater where the blessed sit adoring that light which is God:

> sì, soprastando al lume intorno intorno,
> vidi specchiarsi in più di mille soglie
> quanto di noi là su fatto ha ritorno.
> E se l'infimo grado in sè raccoglie
> sì grande lume, quanta è la larghezza
> di questa rosa nell' estreme foglie!

"I saw, rising above the light all round in more than a thousand tiers, as many of us as have returned there above. And if the lowest rank encloses within it so great a light, what is the expanse of this rose in its farthest petals?" (*Par.*, XXX, 112-117, trans. Sinclair).

The image of the poet in flames, central to "Le Brasier," finds its counterpart in the thirty-first canto of the *Il Paradiso* where the worshipping angels are described: "Le facce tutte avean di fiamma viva," "Their faces were all of living flame" (XXXI, 13).

Like the masked future, the "acteurs inhumains" may be part of that "divine mascarade" which, in a manuscript version published by Jeanine Moulin, is described as too dazzling to gaze upon. They may be sphinxes or angels or animals, higher or lower than man on the chain of being, it hardly matters. They are the new order, hidden in future time, the inheritors of the earth and, thus, the masters of mankind.

O Déchirée echoes *la Désirade* and suggests an ironical second meaning, "O desired earth." The poet, like the earth, has been rent by his youth and is now healed by rivers of forgetfulness and of life. He will be devoured by the sphinxes one day when he cannot answer the riddle they set him, but prefers this kind of fighting death, man's natural lot, to a compromised survival. (Compare the ending of an early poem, "Le Mendiant" [1], p. 565: "J'attends que passent Thanatos et son troupeau.")

RHÉNANES, page 142

Apollinaire originally planned to write a book of poems entitled *Le Vent du Rhin*. Instead, in his Rhenish suite, he has given us a series of landscapes and tiny dramas that evoke a mood, an emotion, an atmosphere and whose cumulative effect is comparable to that of a long poem. There are nine *Rhénanes*, or Rhenish songs, followed in *Alcools* by the date *septembre 1901–mai 1902*, and all, except "Schinderhannes," were first published with the date and place of their composition indicated. Apollinaire spent from August 1901 to August 1902 as tutor in the household of the Vicomtesse de Milhau in her villa at Honnef on the Rhine (where "Nuit rhénane," "Rhénane d'automne," and "Les Femmes" were composed) and her manor at Oberpleis across the river from Bonn (where "Les Cloches" and "Les Sapins" were written). There he fell in love with the English governess in the household, Miss Annie Playden, whose

image haunts many of the poems written at that time, and for several years after, including some of the most beautiful poems in *Alcools*. Other poems of Rhenish inspiration in *Alcools* include "Les Colchiques," "Marizibill," "Le Vent nocturne," "La Tzigane," "Automne," and "Automne malade." A trip to Munich in the spring of 1902 inspired "La Maison des Morts." Of possible German inspiration are "Crépuscule" and "Saltimbanques." Poems that grew out of the year in Germany and Apollinaire's unhappy love affair are "La Chanson du Mal-Aimé," "L'Émigrant de Landor Road," "Un Soir," "Signe," and "Annie." (I have followed Professor Breunig's suggested chronology in "The Chronology of Apollinaire's *Alcools*" [9].)

NUIT RHÉNANE, page 142

First published in *Anthologie critique des Poètes contemporains* (Florian-Parmentier, 1911) with "Les Colchiques," "Le Vent nocturne," "La Tzigane," and "Le Signe de l'Automne." The poem is dated *Honnef, mai 1902.*

This little poem with its clusters of alexandrines seems to rise from a glass of wine, as does Mallarmé's "Salut," and swell till the boatman and his song, the green-haired girls, circling dancers and demure fräuleins, the gold-flecked Rhine are finally dispelled by a breaking glass. The first line's incantatory quality is enhanced by inner rhyme and assonance: *verre / trembleur, plein / d'un / vin, comme / flamme.* The image in the last line has a magical quality (appropriate to a poem about supernatural beings) created by the literal and figurative meanings of *éclat*, "splinter of glass," and *éclat*, "peal of laughter."

The legend of the seven Rhine maidens, as Décaudin points out, belongs to the Rhenish town of Oberwesel. The blonde girls "Au regard immobile aux nattes repliées" form a contrast, not only to the green-haired witches, but also to the Lorelei—with her strange eyes (like Annie's) and her wind-blown hair—who appears later in the sequence of poems. Thus, "Nuit rhénane" introduces us to a world where the natural and the supernatural can exist together.

MAI, page 142

First published in *Vers et Prose*, IV (December, 1905–February, 1906), with "L'Émigrant de Landor Road," "Salomé," and "Les

Cloches." The poem is dated *Leutesdorf, mai 1902.*

The second "Rhénane" describes the Rhine by day, in contrast to the preceding vision of a river haunted by night. Like "Nuit rhénane," "Mai" is composed of alexandrines usually grouped in quatrains, but the rhymes are *embrassées* (ABBA), instead of *croisées* (ABAB), creating a circular effect. The shores in "Mai" keep moving by, suggesting the passing of time. The same sort of thing happens in "Le Voyageur" and "Zone." The likening of a landscape to a woman occurs again in "Les Fiançailles" in a line very similar to line 8 of "Mai":

> Les village lointains sont comme leurs paupières

Both "Les Fiançailles" and "Mai" (as well as "L'Émigrant de Landor Road," "Le Brasier," "La Chanson du Mal-Aimé) are related to "Le Printemps," a poem dated 1902 in *Le Guetteur mélancolique,* which contains the same personification of trees and towns:

> Les pétales tombés des pêchers qui fleurissent
> Sont les ongles cruels des tendres bien-aimées
> Les cerisiers défleuriront au mois de mai
> Leurs fleurs sont des bourgs qui là-bas se rapetissent

> . . .

> Les villages au vent deviennent des paupières
> Voyez voyez cligner des yeux les cerisiers
>
> (*Œuvres,* p. 557)

The description of the wandering gypsies recalls "Saltimbanques." There is a feeling of melancholy, a longing for Annie, expressed by the boat that will not stop, the weeping willows, the fingernails (which, in "Le Printemps," are cruel), the fading martial music, the ruins covered with new foliage.

LA SYNAGOGUE, page 144

First published in *Le Festin d'Ésope,* no. 3 (January, 1904), with "Les Femmes." The poem is dated *Unkel, septembre 1901.*

The dream-like characters evoked momentarily in "Nuit rhénane,"

the figures seen on the distant shores in "Mai," give place to a series of dramatic situations observed close-up. The poet, in fact, becomes an invisible witness to quarrels, laments, and conversations among people, some of whom are legendary, others realistic, some dead, some living.

"La Synagogue" describes two Orthodox Jews, Ottomar and Abraham, the bond between them, and their bone of contention. Almost immediately Apollinaire's lines slip out of the mold of the alexandrine, with comical and onomatopoeic effect, as though, not only their shouts, but Ottomar and Abraham themselves were untranslatable. A comparable metrical transformation takes place in Claudel's "La Vierge à Midi" (*Poemes de Guerre 1914-1916* [1922]) where the alexandrines are progressively charged with emotion, till they burst their limits and turn into *versets*. The meter of "La Synagogue" has been discussed by Madame Durry ([18], pp. 251-254), who notes that it precedes the majority of Claudel's poems written in *versets*.

Professor Breunig has clarified the references to Jewish ritual and their poetic role [10]. Helpful also are the comments of Michel Décaudin ([14], pp. 180-181). The following discussion is based upon theirs. The time in the poem is autumn, the first morning of the Feast of the Tabernacle, which celebrates the vintage season and the Flight from Egypt. A "cabane" of boughs is built in each house, and at the synagogue there is a parade where people carry *loulabim*, "palm branches." *Le matin du sabbat* is, of course, the Sabbath day, part of whose ritual allows one to embrace the Torah, or Law, a roll containing the sacred books of the Pentateuch. The final line of the poem is Apollinaire's grammatically correct misquotation combining a phrase from Psalm 149 and one that occurs throughout the Bible: "He who wields vengeance among the nations, punishments among the races." It seems that Ottomar and Abraham reconcile their differences when they think of the retribution that will one day be handed out to cigar-smoking Christians. As Professor Breunig has pointed out, the Rhine changes character within the poem: at first a Teutonic river, he mocks the Jews; but then, becoming a Hebrew river, he cradles that Leviathan which only the faithful will have a right to partake of on the Day of Judgment.

There remains the question of Lia who seems a little pregnant. If so, who is the father, Ottomar or Abraham? Or neither?

LES CLOCHES, page 146

First published in *Vers et Prose*, IV (December, 1905–February, 1906), with "L'Émigrant de Landor Road," "Salomé," and "Mai." The poem is dated *Oberpleis, mai 1902*.

Four octosyllabic quatrains with *rimes croisées* and a short last line tell in monologue form the story of a love betrayed. The image of the bell towers that spy on the lovers—Décaudin remarks that the steeple of Oberpleis towers above the surrounding countryside—the homely list of Germanic names, lighten the situation. At the end of the poem the tone is ambiguous—perhaps pathetic, more likely, I think, playful.

LA LORELEY, page 148

First published in *Le Festin d'Ésope*, no. 4 (February, 1904), without dedication. The poem is dated *Bacharach, mai 1902*.

Apollinaire owes the legend of the Lorelei to versions of the tale by Brentano and Heine. Like Annie, the Lorelei has blue eyes that lead men astray (for the Playden men's disapproval of Annie's eyes, see Professor Breunig, "Apollinaire and Annie Playden," [7]), and like Apollinaire, the Lorelei is poorly loved. In other poems concerning Annie, there are personae who, like the Lorelei, fuse aspects of both Apollinaire and the woman he loves and so symbolize the love itself, as if it were separate from the poet—for example, "L'Émigrant de Landor Road," "Annie," and "La Chanson du Mal-Aimé." As in "La Synagogue," the lines vary in length and use assonance as well as rhyme. The poem is dedicated to Jean Sève, a prosperous young friend who, according to André Salmon, may have contributed money to Apollinaire's little magazine *Le Festin d'Ésope* (which lasted a year).

Couplets 5-6. The poem contains several kinds of plays on words. In lines 9-11, *flammes* alternates figurative and concrete senses. In addition, the assonance *flamme* / *flambe* is punlike in effect. The troubadour preciosity of these lines stems partly from the verbal play of the courtly bishop and partly from the image of the lady's destructive eye (which reoccurs, with similar effect, in "Les Colchiques"). From the beginning to the end of the poem the Lorelei is associated with images and adjectives of light and fire; besides her flaming gaze in these stanzas, she is blonde (couplet 1), she has eyes like jewels

(couplet 3) and like stars (couplet 13); her hair is like the sun (couplet 19).

Couplet 7. The internal rhyme contained in the antithesis "riez Priez" by linking the two contrasting words "laugh" and "pray" underlines the disparity between the Lorelei's beautiful face and stricken soul, between the men she snares and the one man who has left her, between the power of magic and the ineffectualness of the Church to rescue her. The literal translation of the second line in this couplet is "Order my death and may God protect you."

Couplet 15. Alliteration binds together the contrasting *vierges*, "virgins," and *veuves*, "widows."

Couplet 19. In the final line of the poem an internal rhyme links "ses yeux" with "ses cheveux" and the Rhine with the sun. The opposition between river and sunlight underlines that between water and fire and that between the Lorelei and her fate. A water spirit, she is described throughout in terms of fire and light. Her eyes, which are first compared to jewels, flames, stars, are finally compared to the river that mirrors her dazzling reflection and in which she drowns.

SCHINDERHANNES, page 150

First published in *Le Festin d'Ésope*, no. 7 (June, 1904).

Schinderhannes and his band, Benzel, Jacob Born, Schulz and Julia Blaesius, were executed in 1803. Apollinaire may have come across them, as Michel Décaudin notes, in various sources—folk songs, stories, collections of texts. He alludes to Schinderhannes elsewhere, in *Le Poète assassiné* and in an article about forgers, *Des Faux*, in which a German forger plays his guitar and sings old German songs about Kaetchen de Heilbronn or Schinderhannes when the day's work is done (*La Revue blanche* [April,1903], quoted in Décaudin [14], p. 186). André Salmon describes Apollinaire reciting "Schinderhannes" at the *soirées* of *La Plume*, lingering with relish over the word *pète* and shouting the last line at the top of his voice—and receiving great applause for his performance. The octosyllabic quatrains, like those of "Les Cloches," suggest a ballad or folk song.

Stanza 7. "La fleur de mai c'est le florin"—"The flower of May is the florin." Originally a Florentine coin with a lily on it, "florin" comes from *fiore*, "flower." The play on words reinforces a general contrast between coin and flower that is part of a general contrast between the bandits' greed and their sentimentality.

RHÉNANE D'AUTOMNE, page 154

First published in *Le Voile de Pourpre*, no. 2 (May, 1909), with "Vent nocturne," "Crépuscule, "Les Sapins," with the title "Le Jour des Morts," and without dedication. The poem is dated *Honnef, novembre 1901.*

"Rhénane d'automne" describes a German graveyard on All Soul's Day. Details evoke Germany: the children's names, the cock's crowing *kikiriki* (French roosters cry *cocorico*), the phrase *et de toutes leurs âmes*, "and of all their souls" (a Germanism, according to Michel Décaudin). The beggars drink beer; the mayors are called not *maires* but *bourgmestres*. The *bateliers* suggest the commerce of a great river; the *conseillers de régence* evoke a multitude of little kingdoms. Finally, one of the main actors is the Rhine wind who plays a role also in "Mai," "La Loreley," "Les Sapins," and "Les Femmes."

The form is free verse. The lines vary in length from four to fourteen syllables. Some lines dispense with rhyme, some rhyme, some use assonance instead. The style varies between that of a prose story for children and of a song for adults; its melancholy fantasy is tempered with irony and occasional mischief.

Lines 1-17. A stanza presents the children playing (ll. 1-5), an answering stanza presents the grieving old women (ll. 6-10), a third, like an epode, describes the ritual of All Souls' Day (ll. 11-17).

Lines 1-5. There is a hidden, ironic logic in the first two lines. Where would children play except near their parents? A similar spirit enlivens later details. The names of the children, the sound (or absence of sound) of a rooster and of donkeys lighten the landscape. The cock's crowing is a symbol of renascent life. He announces the sun. And so he is silent, on a day of death which, appropriately, is sunless.

Lines 6-10. There is an implied comparison between the old women and the donkeys: both are labeled *bon* which, in context, suggests "obedient." However, the poet cannot remain serious for long: the donkeys are not entirely good, but nibble the flowers on the graves.

Lines 11-17. "C'est le jour des morts et de toutes leurs âmes"—literally, "It's the day of the dead and of all their souls." "Allument des bougies et des cierges"—"they light little candles and big ones." Perhaps the children have small candles, the old women, tall tapers like those on the high altar. The image of the flames is reflected by

that of veils, clouds, and goats' beards. The alliterative *voiles des vieilles* and *barbes des biques* stress the comparison. Perhaps the veils and clouds are compared to goats' beards because they are wispy. The incongruous juxtapositions presented in this first part of the poem, between children and roosters, donkeys and flowers, old women and waving goats' beards, softens by its fantasy that grief for the dead which is the central theme of the poem.

Line 18. A line filled with inner assonance and rhyme, *tremble / flammes, air / prière*, evoking motion, brightness, and sound, marks the transition between the description of the living and the invocation of the dead.

Lines 19–25. "Ah! que vous êtes bien dans le beau cimetière" means, literally, "How well off you are in the fair cemetery," and finds a parallel in Valéry's "Le Cimetière marin"; "Les morts cachés sont bien dans cette terre." The song is, in effect, a cradle song to the dead. Beggars, blind men, and children who died praying are grouped together. They are a surprising assortment. At the same time, they have insight, or lack of insight, in common.

Lines 26-31. Once again Apollinaire makes juxtapositions that seem surprising, yet have an underlying logic. The link between *bourg-mestres* and *bateliers*, emphasized by alliteration, is that they are both in charge of something, one of a town, one of a boat. Both councillors and gypsies give advice, and both attempt to foretell the future. Gypsies lack passports in this world; the poet implies they (and all of us) will in the next world too. The last two lines of the stanza contain an alliteration, *pourrit / panse / pousse / pieds*, that binds together in an ironical contrast the words *la vie* and *le croix*, "life" and "the cross." In line 31, the correct reading of the original text should be *nous* and not *vous* ([14], p. 67).

Lines 32-42. The song to the dead is interrupted by the wind that puts out the candles, evokes dead voices, evokes too the fluttering fare-wells of dead hands. The wind, like the poet, plays an ambivalent role, at once mocking and tender. He hoots with the owls that an-nounce that the dead are near (l. 32). He quenches those lights which, relit by the children, symbolize life, renewed from generation to generation (l. 33). He covers the dead with leaves (ll. 34-35).

There is much playing on words that suggest death in this part of the poem. The end sounds, *mortes* and *morts* (ll. 34-35), prepare an assonance in line 36, *morts / mères*. In "Et des mortes parfois voudraient bien revenir"—the verb is peculiarly appropriate: *revenir*, "to return," suggests *revenant*, "ghost." Thus, the dead women's yearning is natural to their condition. The conversation with the dead comes, in major part, from a poem in *Le Guetteur mélancolique*, "La Clef" ([1], p. 553), which furnished also the first versions of "Adieu" and "La Dame." Although it occurs in Symbolist literature, the comparison of hands to leaves is, according to Décaudin, more likely a memory of oak foliage in the countryside around Stavelot, where Apollinaire spent the summer of 1899.

Lines 43-52. The poet follows the mourners homeward from the graveyard. "The sky without sun" forms a contrast to "the cemetery full of flames." This final strophe turns sorrow into fantasy. As chestnut burrs suggest the image of the Madonna's heart, transfixed by seven swords of sorrow, so the color of chestnuts suggests legends of a Black Mary and ancient paintings, like those of Cimabue, of a dark Virgin.

LES SAPINS, page 158

First published in *Le Voile de Pourpre*, no. 2 (May, 1909), with "Rhénane d'automne" and others, and dated *Neu-Glück 1901*.

In this charming series of octosyllabic quintains, with their six-syllable middle line and clever rhymes (AABAB), the Germanic tradition attributing magic powers to fir trees is treated playfully. As in "Rhénane d'automne" the fantasy is based largely on the picturesque appearance of things, Apollinaire's imagination being primarily visual. The play on nasal sounds in the last stanza, "Ils vont offrant leurs bons onguents," impossible to approximate in a language whose nasals are all under the counter, anticipates a line in "Saltimbanques": "Et les enfants s'en vont devant."

LES FEMMES, page 160

First published in *Le Festin d'Ésope*, no. 3 (January, 1904), with "La Synagogue." The poem is dated *Honnef, décembre 1901*.

The final *rhénane*, "Les Femmes," is a conversation-poem which, by its juxtapositions of different trains of thought, anticipates the experi-

mental "Lundi Rue Christine." At the same time it follows certain Symbolist traditions. Everything has meaning—cat, blind nightingale, cypress tree, mailman, frozen vineyard. Dramatic irony is caused by the women's seeming unawareness of the world of signs around them. Their conversation evokes, instead, a feminine world shut off from nature and from men. In addition, they seem unable to communicate with each other directly, only by allusion. The poem is a microcosm encompassing the span of adult life as seen from a feminine point of view: marriage, food and drink, bittersweet love, the final enigma of death. There is a continual and growing menace in the background, stated mainly in terms of sound: the nightingale's silence, the hooting of an owl, the wind's organ music in the trees, the howling dogs, the tolling of the church bell. In contrast, appeals to the reassuring rituals and pursuits of everyday life—sewing, vine-growing, schoolteaching, hunting—are emphasized by the repeated names of Lenchen, Kaethi, Lotte, Leni, Ilsa.

The poem is written in quatrains composed of alexandrines. As in "Mai" and "La Tzigane," the *rimes embrassées* give the impression of a circle suddenly closed. In the former poem, the rhymes underline the image of the voyage; in the latter, they underline the repetitious structure of conversations and of life.

Line 13. "La fête du curé"—means literally, "the parish priest's name day."

Line 23. According to Michel Décaudin [16], "Dieu garde," literally, "God help me!" is spoken by Lotte.

SIGNE, page 164

First published in *Schéhérazade*, no. 6 (March 15, 1911), with the title "Signe de l'Automne."

"Signe" was probably written shortly after Apollinaire's final break with Annie Playden. The form, alexandrines grouped into quatrains, is typical of his early verse. The poem is based on the first two strophes of "L'Automne et l'Écho" ([1], pp. 588-589).

Line 1. This verse becomes ambiguous in translation. The object of the verb is *Chef*, not *Signe*.

Line 2. The eighth stanza of "L'Automne et l'Écho" enlarges upon the statement: "Je déteste les fleurs parce qu'elle sont femmes." In the first stanza, the poet voices an attitude comparable to Elinor

Wylie's "I'm a poor lover but a good friend."

Line 4. That is, the nut tree has been harvested, and the poet, poorly loved.

Line 5. Apollinaire's "saison mentale" recalls Jules Laforgue's "couleur locale."

Line 6. *Amantes* refers to women in love. The comparison of hands to leaves appears in "Rhénane d'automne," in "L'Émigrant de Landor Road," and, together with the verb *joncher*, "strew" or "scatter," in "Marie." There is a comparable suggestion of (feminine) faithlessness in the latter.

Line 7. *Une épouse* means "a wife," but somehow in English became too ambiguous. The image of the shadow-wife occurs also in "La Chanson du Mal-Aimé."

Line 8. These doves seem kin both to the weary doves in "Le Brasier" and to the maidenly ones in "Les Fiançailles."

UN SOIR, page 166

First published in *Schéhérazade*, no. 6 (March 15, 1911).

The fusion of earthly and heavenly love, a traditional theme in poetry, is curiously handled by Apollinaire in "Un Soir." To evoke the city, he has used a mixture of images—metal, birds, fungus—that is not entirely successful. The same dubious use of incongruities is seen in the changing role of the girl to whom he speaks. She is seen first as an intervener, as the Madonna or as a patron saint (l. 2), then she is addressed (wistfully?) as "O vêtue," "with your clothes on" (l. 12), finally her image becomes fused with that of Christ or of a conqueror, or both.

After the first stanza, the poet uses the familiar *tu* instead of the formal *vous*, "you." The metallic city, the lights, and the trolley cars with their "feux pâlis" suggest, to Michel Décaudin, a stanze near the end of "La Chanson du Mal-Aimé." The blue eyes, of course, suggest Annie.

In the fouth stanza, the first line, as Décaudin notes, occurs in "Le Mendiant" ([1], p. 565), but with a changed context. The latter seems to be hate-poem. A beggar curses an uncharitable woman as a lover might curse his cruel fair one: she denies the existence of "positive sorrow" (of which he has an abundance); herself a creature who wears tinsel and a false smile, she is drawn by the false and shallow actor

who mocks his feminine admirers. In "Un Soir" the line is one of
three concerned with what Bruce Morrissette has called *persuasive se-
duction*. By a real or pretended mockery the actor who seems so attrac-
tive betrays the watching women and thus damns himself; the ghost
and Judas (their images suggest the hanged man in "Crépuscule")
damn themselves by self-betrayal; surrounded by these reminders that
all kinds of belief are subject to disillusion, why not take chances with
our love? The argument is comparable to that presented in "La
Tzigane": one hopes for love along the way to a foreseen damnation.

LA DAME, page 168

A first version was published in *Le Festin d'Ésope*, no. 2 (December
1903), with "L'Adieu." The final version appeared in *Vers et Prose*,
XXXI (October-December, 1912), with "Le Larron," "Dans le Palais
de Rosemonde ["Palais"],," "La Porte," "Marie," and "L'Adieu."

"La Dame," like "L'Adieu," is based on a passage from "La Clef"
([1], p. 553), and like "L'Adieu," consisted originally of five octosyl-
lables, rhyming ABAAB. According to the editors of the Pléiade, Apol-
linaire changed the title and the last line from those that appear in
the first published version, "au profit de la surprise" ([1], p. 1066).
If one compares the two, one sees that the poet's final thoughts are not
only more surprising but more suggestive, although his new last line is
probably a renovated cliché:

Le Retour

Toc, toc . . . "Il a fermé sa porte.

Les lys du jardin sont flétris . . .
Quel est donc ce mort qu'on emporte?"
—"Tu viens de touquer à sa porte."
—"Et je suis veuve, aux pieds meurtris."

<div style="text-align: right">(Œuvres, p. 1066)</div>

La Dame

Toc toc Il a fermé sa porte
Les lys du jardin sont flétris
Quel est donc ce mort qu'on emporte

> Tu viens de toquer à sa porte
> Et trotte trotte
> Trotte la petite souris

<div align="right">(Œuvres, p. 127)</div>

The suppression of punctuation gets rid of changes in point of view that are distracting in such a brief poem. The new title gives a new direction to the poem as a whole. Most significant is the change in the last line because it indicates one of the kinds of effects Apollinaire was after—techniques that his successors affected too. The new version does not attempt to wind up a story. To the contrary, it deepens the mystery, and does so by suggesting a nursery rhyme and what is probably a verbal play on the expression *on entendrait trotter une souris*, "You could hear a pin drop." The line is not the climax to the poem, but harmonizes with what goes before. It is broken up onomatopoeically, and is linked to the lines that precede it by the assonance between *toquer* and *trotter*, by the suggestion of silence that follows a knocking at the dead man's door, and by an implied comparison between the lady, as she steals away or runs about distractedly, and a mouse. Or perhaps it is her feet, appearing and disappearing beneath her long skirts, that make the poet think of a mouse.

Michel Décaudin comments, on the changes made in the poem, "les ressorts de la suprise—à laquelle Apollinaire attribue des vertus lyriques inexplorées—auront été multipliés en quelque vers" (*Dossier*, p. 200). He hazards the guess that the last line may be based on a reminiscence of Verlaine:

> Dame souris trotte,
> Noire dans le gris du soir,
> Dame souris trotte
> Grise dans le soir.

<div align="right">("Impression fausse," Parallèlement)</div>

LES FIANÇAILLES, page 170

First published in *Pan*, no. 6 (November–December, 1908), with the title "Fiançailles," and without dedication.

"Les Fiançailles," a confession and an ars poetica, is appropriately

dedicated to Apollinaire's friend Picasso "dont j'admire l'art sublime" (letter to Madeline [3], p. 74). At the end of *Le Poète assassiné*, a later work in which Apollinaire's ideas concerning the poet's destiny have been modified by his own experience of the war, Picasso, who has played a considerable role in the tale, carves in air a bust of the dead poet, "un profonde statue en rien comme la poésie et comme la gloire." According to Professor Breunig [12], "Les Fiançailles" reveals the kinship between Apollinaire and Picasso, for the poem is concerned with those artists who must find in themselves totally new forms of expression; "dans sa meilleure poésie Apollinaire partageait avec Picasso et les meilleurs cubistes l'esprit héroïque et l'inquiétude terrible dont cette peinture est impregnée."

Like "La Chanson du Mal-Aimé," as Michel Décaudin notes, "Les Fiançailles" is composed of various fragments (called, for convenience, Poems I-IX). The first three groups of lines (labeled Poem I below) come from an early poem, Poems II-V exist in a manuscript version entitled "Les paroles étoiles," Poem VIII exists in a manuscript version entitled "Le Pyrée." Like "Le Brasier," "Les Fiançailles" marks a change in Apollinaire's attitude toward the writing of poetry: he will cease to write of love and instead will transcribe, in a new kind of verse, the poet's almost mystical experience of life.

Poem I. The first section is from "Le Printemps" (*Poèmes divers* [1], p. 556), and originally consisted of three quatrains composed of alexandrines. In a notebook of Apollinaire's, a version of the opening lines is found near references to his stay in the Rhineland. The juxtaposition suggests to Michel Décaudin [15], an allusion to Annie and a relationship to those poems written in May, 1902. As at the beginning of "Le Brasier," Apollinaire evokes past loves—faithless, hopeless, full of illusion. The poem opens on an idyllic spring landscape whose inhabitants have all been made unhappy or restless through love. Already in the first line a play on words, *errer*, "to wander" and "to be mistaken," creates an ambiguous atmosphere: do the foresworn lovers wander together or separately? is their mistake one of betrayal or one of an attempted reconciliation?

Line 2. *Feuilloler*, a coinage, occurs again in "Le Printemps" in the phrase "les feux qui feuillolent," "the fires that leaf." The reader is startled not only by the coinage but by the comparison of feathers to leaves and by the image of leaves falling from a leafless evergreen.

Line 3. The bluebird that sheds its feathers appears also in "La

Tzigane": "Et l'oiseau bleu perdit ses plumes." A symbol of happiness, the bluebird is associated by Apollinaire with love that is menaced or that has come to an end. The cypress and, in line 8, the lemon trees suggest a landscape in the south of France. In this context cypress trees also suggest a graveyard.

Line 4. In "Le Printemps" *Madone* was not capitalized or placed at the beginning of the line, although at the end of that poem Our Lady borders the roads with roses. The change the line underwent before its inclusion in "Les Fiançailles" emphasizes a fusion of heavenly and earthly loves that is more successful in "Les Fiançailles" than in another poem where religious and erotic images are mingled, "Un Soir." *Madone* suggests not only the Virgin but Beatrice and Laura in the love poems of Dante and Petrarch. One of Petrarch's *canzoni*, "Chiare, fresche e dolci acque," describes Laura appearing like a vision of spring on a bank of flowers. In "Les Fiançailles" "Madonna" is primarily a spring deity who has in her care flowers and doves (or girls), though she is also both the beloved and the Virgin (whose image returns later in Poem VIII). I have translated *une Madone* simply as "Madonna," to suggest the Italian poets.

Line 7. In "Le Printemps" this line reads

Au pigeons qui le soir semblent des Paraclets

By changing *pigeons* to *pigeon*, *le* to *ce*, and present tense to past, Apollinaire has made the image at once more precise and more mysterious.

Lines 8-9. Apollinaire has changed the original "filles éperdues," "distracted girls" of "Le Printemps" to the less limiting "dernières venues," "last comers," which may describe women or—as I took it, because the phrase suggests motion—the doves mentioned in the preceding stanza. The returning theme of love, presented in these two lines by three different words, *s'énamourèrent, amour, aimons*, has (necessarily, in my opinion) been rendered in English by the one word "love." The meaning seems to be that those who were the last to arrive at the orchard or the last to encounter love have fallen in love with love itself much as we (i.e., the poet) did.

Lines 10-11. In "Mai," flower petals remind the poet of a woman's face and hands; the passage, like this one, comes from "Le Printemps." Both the image of faraway villages like women's eyelids and that of the hearts hidden among the lemons in the orchard suggest anamorphotic drawings of landscapes where faces or human figures are concealed and, thus, indicate one of Apollinaire's links with the Surrealists.

The juxtaposition of hearts with lemons evokes a love that is bitter-sweet, evokes too the hanging of votive offerings to a rural deity.

Poem II. The poet awakes from his dreams of love, from illusions concerning his art and his faith, to find himself in an ugly world. If Poem I describes a dream, Poem II presents an actuality. The style, in contrast to the opening lines, indicates a casual attitude toward meter and rhyme. "Les paroles étoiles," a manuscript version conserved in the Doucet collection and published by Michel Décaudin, clarifies some of the obscurities in Poems II-V.

Line 1. The poet's friends scorn the verse he has written.

Line 2. The stars may be hopes, ambition, or more probably those poems dreamed of and not written which remain the poet's pride, even in defeat. Compare "Les paroles étoiles":

J'ai l'orgueil de me souvenir de mes souhaits glorieux
[J'ai rêvé] des poèmes si grandioses que j'ai dû les laisser inachevés

The image of drinking, which suggests at once life and poetry, returns in "Vendémiaire," where the poet drinks the universe, and in the general title to the collection, *Alcools.*

Lines 3-6. The poet has become disillusioned with the promises of religion, with happy endings, with the myths contained in his own poetry. His faith in these has disappeared while he slept. The lines immediately following in the manuscript version read as follows:

Puis après la fuite et la mort de mes vérités poétiques
Je m'éveillai au bout de cinq ans [et suivit] une nuit citadine

He has awakened after five years—a period Décaudin suggests we may link with his literary preoccupation with Annie (and with the themes of heartbreak and loneliness), which lasted from the end of 1901 to the end of 1906 ([14], p. 207).

Lines 7 and 8. *L'éveil,* "awakening," suggests, in the phrase "Étoiles de l'éveil," morning stars and also, and more significantly, stars "qui donnent l'éveil," "that raise the alarm," or give warning. The stars are cruel because, knowing our future, they conceal it. The poet has been in danger while he slept; his awakening from false dreams is a warning both concerning dreams and the real world. There is an ironic contrast between the stars, traditionally a literary image, and the unmannerly gas lamps.

Lines 9-12. The city (especially at night) plays a major role in several of Apollinaire's poems: "Zone," "La Chanson du Mal-Aimé," "Le Voyageur," "Un Soir," "Vendémiaire." In the city of "Les Fiançailles," death lacks dignity, love has become sordid, and birth, a masquerade.

Line 13. *Cette nuit,* "that night," contrasts with *ce soir,* "this evening" (l. 7, Poem I). As the manuscript version makes clear (see quotations in note to ll. 3-6), it is after the poet's awakening that he wanders through the city at night. The ugly women remind one of those in "Zone," and are, perhaps, in both poems symbolic of the poet's (temporary) reaction against his own unhappy love affairs.

Poem III, lines 1 and 2. Although "Les Fiançailles" was published six months later than "Le Brasier," it may, in this passage, record an earlier state of mind. Having rejected the past, the poet does not, as in "Le Brasier," immediately feel liberated but, at first, bankrupt, incapable of achieving his new poetry. The middle section (Poems III–VIII) is written in free verse.

Line 3. As in line 13, the stars symbolize elusive poems.

Lines 4 and 5. Icarus heads a list of famous flyers in "Zone" who circle about Christ, the original airplane. Here, two Icaruses are drawn toward the poet who has been deified and transformed into a celestial body. In "Le Brasier," he becomes a star; in "Les Fiançailles," he becomes a solar system (centered about a double sun), a constellation or an entire universe.

Line 6. The theological beasts of the mind are probably allegories of cardinal sins. They may be the leopard, or lust, the lion, or pride, and the wolf, or covetousness, that Dante meets in the dark wood and which are based on the same three beasts in Jeremiah. Or Apollinaire may be thinking of a bestiary; his own was to be published in March 1911. They may even be the signs of the zodiac which in the medieval imagination played an important role in determining character.

Line 7. Among the poems written about Germany are two that concern the poet's relations with the dead, "Rhénane d'automne" and "La Maison des Morts." In the latter the dead gather around the poet affectionately. The poet may, in "Les Fiançailles," be looking back at a period when he had, among other illusions, that of free entry into the world of spirits. After this line there occurs one in the manuscript version, "Les paroles étoiles," that Apollinaire deleted later, "Car ma vie avait le pouvoir de faire renaître tout l'univers": it suggests that

the dead were drawn to the poet as a source of life in the same way that the two Icaruses were drawn to him as a source of light.

Lines 8 and 9. The poet recalls that he was formerly a seer. Now he is aware only of his own mortality.

Poem IV. In both poems renouncing the past, "Le Brasier" (especially in Part I) and "Les Fiançailles," the imagery evoking past loves and past days reveals that Apollinaire, like Eliot when he turns from "the broad-backed beauty dressed in blue and green," still loves what he puts from him.

Line 2. Days are personified also in "L'Émigrant de Landor Road."

Lines 5 and 6. The image of the lemon grove, by recalling the one at the beginning of the poem, indicates that the whole first part of "Les Fiançailles" describes a mood or event now beyond recall. There is an ironic contrast between the dead days and where they are found—in churches, in lemon orchards that bloom all year round.

Lines 9 and 10. The ardent bouquets are witty conversations, perhaps, or poems or laughter or avowals of love. The mulatto girl is Marie Laurencin, who may have been of creole origin ([5], p. 96). At all events she looked like a Creole, with tightly curling hair which Apollinaire describes in "Marie" as "Crépus comme mer qui moutonne."

Poem V, lines 1-6. At this point, the mood changes, becomes more confident. To whom does the poet speak? perhaps to his friends who are mentioned in line 1, Poem II, and were, in the original version of the line, addressed directly:

Mes amis, ne craignez pas de m'avouer votre mépris

Perhaps he addresses God: the passage originally opened with a line later crossed out, consisting of the one word *Seigneur*. The looser style of "Les paroles étoiles" clarifies several ambiguities. The poet seems to ask forgiveness, but not for the ignorance in which he dreamed false dreams for five years. Originally Apollinaire wrote, "Pardonnez-moi d'avoir reconquis l'ignorance," "Forgive me for regaining ignorance," that is, for beginning all over again. He is proud of his attempt to start anew and does not apologize for it at all. His newly acquired ignorance is equated with a rejection of traditional techniques of poetry:

autrefois
J'ai fait des poemes selon des règles que j'ai oubliées
Aujourd'hui je ne sais plus rien [faire]

Like Rimbaud, he cultivates a vision that remains essentially ineffable; unlike Rimbaud he is not the divine inventor of what he sees but the beholder who shares in the divinity he contemplates:

> Mais les fleurs si je les regarde deviennent des flammes
> et réciproquement
> [Et] Cardinales, me paupières me découvrent à volonté
> tous les mythes
> [Et] Silencieux je médite divinement

Lines 7-9. The shadow which at last becomes solid was originally "l'ombre de ma substance," "the shadow of my essence or of my body." If the words are ambiguous, the general sense is clear: the poet looks to a time when he will have the power to communicate his visions. The shadow may be actual poems or the workings of the poet's imagination. These last lines use concepts and vocabulary belonging to metaphysics—in particular, to ontology, to describe artistic creation.

Poem VI. What sources of knowledge may the poet exploit? The senses are monsters, that is, they appertain to the body and not the spirit. Apollinaire's point of view in this poem is just opposite to his attitude in "Cortège," where the poet's imagination, like a detective's, is stimulated by sights, smells, taste, touch, sounds.

Line 2. *Paresse*, "idleness," may be that seeming idleness which is fruitful to the artist. Again, it may be a mocking comment on *le repos du dimanche* (l. 1).

Lines 3-5. The phrasing is paradoxical but the meaning, I think, is clear: "How to avoid being fooled by the senses which interrupt my meditations with false reports from the real world?"

Lines 6-11. I have always found this passage ambiguous. Does *l'un* mean any, that is, every one of the senses? Or a sixth sense? Or sight, since it is likened to things the poet looks upon? But it is beheaded. Perhaps, then, it is desire, ranging from the sexual to the artistic urge. "Je voudrais encompasser une ardeur infinie" might then mean that the ardor described in lines 6-10 was not enough—was still finite. However, *ardeur* can also be placed in opposition to the whole passage, suggesting the fiery state of the poetic-stellar-angelic being described in "Le Brasier." And the one who is beheaded may, as an image, comment on the blind irrational nature of conclusions based solely on the senses.

Lines 12-14. The monsters are presented not as creatures who per-

ceive, but as sources of perception. Thus, hearing is not a monster who listens, but one who roars. In addition, the senses tend to be described visually. "Le tonnerre te sert de chevelure" suggests lightning. "Et tes griffes répètent le chant des oiseaux" fuses the visual and the auditory.

Line 15. The verb *empoisonner* may be a criticism of all the senses—they poison by falsifying reality and by expending the poet's energies.

Lines 16 and 17. My eyes swim far away because what I behold is far away—in contrast to what I touch, which is near to me. The farthest objects of my vision are the stars. They are inviolate because I see but cannot touch them; they are my unproven masters because I cannot know if they really govern my life as astrologers believe.

Line 18. The monster of smell, with his head in flower, suggests a fruit tree.

Lines 19 and 20. Taste, laurel, and women are associated in Apollinaire's mind. In "Cortège," right after a misogynous observation about women, the poet discusses taste and uses the same image of laurel as here: "Il me suffit de goûter la saveur du laurier qu'on cultive pour que j'aime ou que je bafoue." In *Le Poète assassiné*, the faithless Tristouse Ballerinette (Marie Laurencin) has, in the opinion of the *oiseau de Bénin* (Picasso), the taste of laurel: "Et elle doit avoir la saveur de la feuille du laurier." The play on the words *laurier / Laurencin*, is an obvious key to Tristouse's identity. In "Anvers" ([1], p. 590), the last two lines link the poet with Marie or (according to the editors of the Pléiade [1], p. 1138) Lou:

> Des noms le mien et celui qui
> A la saveur du laurier femme

Why is the monster who tastes of laurel, the most beautiful, and why is he unhappy? It seems to me there is a connection in Apollinaire's mind between the taste of laurel and the unhappy side to sensuality or passion or love—past loves he has rejected, new loves he has embarked upon or that await him (he met Marie in 1907). This association may be underlined by memories of Petrarch's verse. Laura is a green laurel ("Rotta è l'alta Colonna e'l verde lauro"), described not in terms of taste but of smell: "ove l'aura [pun] si sente / d'un fresco ed odorifero laureto," "where the breeze [or Laura] smells of a fresh fragrant laurel grove." In addition, laurel as the loved woman and laurel as (poetic) fame are linked by Petrarch, as by Apollinaire: "Qual vaghezza di lauro?" "Such desire for laurel?"

Poem VII. In the final passages of the poem the poet no longer expresses misgivings or talks around his subject. As in the last part of "Le Brasier," only more smoothly and with humorous touches, he attempts to transpose directly into language new attitudes and gestures of the spirit.

Line 1. *Les mensonges*, "lies," may refer to the five senses (Poem VI), the old game of poetry (Poem V), the past (Poem IV), and its allusions (Poems I-II).

Line 2. This and the preceding line may be examples of lies or illusion: the moon only looks like an egg, drops of water only look like jewels. Both images juxtapose the enduring and the transient. "Ce collier de gouttes d'eau" is comparable to Valéry's "Maint diamant d'imperceptible écume." Apollinaire may have had in mind the drowned Ophelia (herself a victim of illusions) whom he describes briefly in "Poème lu au mariage d'André Salmon."

Lines 4 and 5. The identical description of passionflowers occurs, as Michel Décaudin notes, in two poems from *Le Guetteur mélancolique*, including "Le Printemps" and "L'Ermite," and concludes with a comparable image: "la sainte cruauté des pasiflores." *Passion* is a play on meanings, suggesting sufferings in both body and spirit, the sufferings of Christ and those of the poorly loved poet. The two verses may constitute yet another "lie"—those consolations of religion which Apollinaire seems to reject in Poem II.

Line 6. "La pluie de naguère"—*Naguère* is an adverb belonging to poetic language, and means "a short while ago." The image suggests that the world surrounding the poet has undergone purification or baptism.

Line 7. Domestic angels, in "La Blanche Neige," evoke Germanic fairy tale. These angels who work for Apollinaire at home recall stories of the angelic substitute who does the job much better than one could oneself, as in Browning's "The Boy and the Angel." Of course, they also suggest the helpmate. Probably Valéry thinks of his wife when he writes, in "Palme":

> Un ange met sur ma table
> Le pain tendre, le lait plat.

Perhaps Apollinaire thinks of Marie, though it seems doubtful.

Line 8. *La lune* and *la tristesse* recall the moon and the drowned girl in lines 2 and 3.

Lines 9 and 10. Apollinaire puns on the familiar expression *Toute la sainte journée* in which *sainte* means "damned" rather than "holy." In conjunction with the passionflowers, the full moon, and the angels, these lines suggest Easter.

Lines 11 and 12. In the last two lines, through the eyes of a woman, the poet watches himself withdraw into the distance and listens to his song grow fainter.

Poem VIII, line 3 and 4. In these two quatrains the poet hovers between free verse and a fixed-verse form "J'ai tout donné au soleil / Tout sauf mon ombre," "I have given all to the sun but my shadow" that is, I have given everything. Or, I have given all but what cannot be given, at least to the sun, which lends shadows substance. Or, my shadow exists only in that it belongs to me and thus cannot be given away. Or, my shadow is something too precious to part with: in "Clotilde," the loved one ("Cette belle ombre que tu veux"); in "La Chanson du Mal-Aimé," a reminder of mortality or a part of the self; in "Les Fiançailles" (Poem V), the works of the imagination. The opposition between sun and shadow, the verbal play on *ombre*, "shadow," and *ombre*, "shade," occur in both "La Chanson" (stanza 37) and in "Clotilde" (ll. 5-8). The idea of parting with one's last possession, one's shadow (instead of one's soul?), on any terms, occurs in "La Chanson" where those "pauvres fameux" would sell their shadows for Annie's love. The sun, like the fire that Apollinaire stokes with his memories in "Le Brasier," suggests the intensity proper to a poet's existence. Thus, I have given everything to life—except my death, my poverty, the unconscious levels of my being, and perhaps my poems.

Line 5. The bizarre juxtaposition of modern and mythical images occurs also in "Zone." Are the dragnets for the drowned, for the fish, or for the half-dead sirens? *Ballots* suggest bales or boxes of cargo piled on a pier. Sirens are used for a humorous effect, also, in "Zone" where they sing beautifully. In "Lul de Faltenin," they, or their grottoes, have a sexual implication. In "Vendémiaire," like past time, they have slipped forever into the sea. Here they may be half dead because netted and gasping, or because they are part of the traditional imagery that Apollinaire thinks of himself as abandoning.

Line 6. The ship in the distance suggests the poet in the distance (Poem VII, l. 12). There is a more definite fusion of poet and ship in "Le Voyageur":

Tu regardais un banc de nuages descendre
Avec le paquebot vers les fièvres futures

Lines 7 and 8. Apollinaire plays on *anémones*, "anemones" or wind-flowers," and the Greek "ἄνεμος," "wind." These two lines occur also with a minor variation in "Le Printemps," where "O vierge signe pur . . ." immediately follows a verse about the Madonna. The virgin is not only the Madonna; she is Virgo, a constellation and sign of the zodiac, the third sign of summer (as Madame Durry notes), beginning around August 22. Madame Durry also notes the verbal play on *pur*: naturally Virgo is a pure sign; in addition, as Madonna, she purifies. However, for the poet, I think the virgin has also a more personal meaning. Apollinaire's birthday is August 26. In a poem about his awakening into a new life, his own sign Virgo shines like a promise of achievement. At the same time, in conjunction with the homophone *mois*, "month," / *moi*, "me," the obscure reference to the poet's own birthday becomes humorous: "O virgin pure sign of the third me."

Poem IX. The final verses (including the last stanza which was published in *Pan* as a separate section) return to the form of Poem I. They are constructed about the image of the sixty-seven Templars who, after their trial in May, 1310, were burned at the stake. As in "Le Brasier," fire represents inspiration and fertility as well as purification and death. There is also, in "Les Fiançailles," the theme of the artist's persecution (cf. Croniamental, in *Le Poète assassiné*, who is torn to pieces by a mob). The poet burns no longer like a star in "Le Brasier," but like a martyr.

Line 1. *Flamboyants* may have several meanings, referring not only to the death by fire of the Templars but to their behavior and apparel during the later years of the order. The Templars were famed for their gallantry, their knightly valor and (at first, anyway) for their upright lives; in a poem about purification, they might well seem to the poet a fitting symbol of the chaste life and the ordeal by fire. If the Dioscuri, who appear in "Le Brasier," were known for their brotherly devotion, the Templars became known for their homosexual practices, and thus evoke, equally with the twins, a world of men in which women have no part.

Line 2. "Prophétisons ensemble." Although the Templars were persecuted for the sake of their property, they were accused of heresies that may have appealed to Apollinaire. Gnosticism, for example, seems

hinted at in lines 8 and 9, Poem V. Comparable to the swan song mentioned in "Le Brasier" is the power to prophesy, ascribed to the dying.

Lines 2 and 3. That is, my spirit is as ardent as the flame that destroyed you.

Line 4. The girandole suggests gyrating fireworks: the burning martyrs become celestial bodies, or the bonfires that consume them become mimic suns. It suggests also Easter and Midsummer Day fires and the burning of effigies. Apollinaire may have read accounts of such customs—or may even have seen them in Northern France or in Rhenish villages, where a huge straw-covered wheel was rolled flaming downhill into the Moselle (Frazer, *The Golden Bough*, LXII, 5).

Lines 5 and 6. *Liens* means "bonds"; that is, the fetters that bind the victims and also their flesh. *Une libre flamme*, "a free flame," describes both the fire that burns them and their proud spirit. "Ardeur que mon souffle éteindra" can be interpreted in several ways: my ardor or yours (the Templars') or the flame's, which my breath, my poem, my death will extinguish. "O Morts à quarantaine" invokes the Templars once more and can be taken, in the context, as prophesying the poet's early death: "You Templars who died at forty (as perhaps I shall) . . ." Apollinaire was interested in writing prophetic verse, as were some of his confreres; compare Max Jacob's assertion that some of the poems in *Le Cornet à Dès* foretell the First World War.

Lines 7 and 8. "Je mire de ma mort la gloire . . ." may also mean "I take aim at my death's glory . . ." I have not rendered exactly *mirer*, "to take a bead on," and *viser*, "to aim at." There is an implied comparison, in these lines, of poet to Templars: "I take aim with my death at suffering and renown (as you did), as if I (like you) had practiced at the quintain." Michel Décaudin cites, apropos of the reference to the quintain, Apollinaire's introduction to selections from Aretino, where in the process of explaining the word, he attributes to it a sexual meaning: "l'homme fait de la femme une quintaine" ([14], p. 208).

Line 9. Uncertainty, the bird (of the quintain), represents to some extent the snares of flirtatious women, or the state of being poorly loved by them—that five years' slumber from which the poet has awakened. There is a verbal play on *feint*, "faked," *fin*, "end" (i.e., the object at which the jouster aims), and *fin*, "clever."

Line 10. That is, it became spring once more. According to Madame Durry, the image of love and of the sun dancing is related to "Merlin" (l. 18) and "L'Ermite" (l. 14).

Lines 11 and 12. To whom does *tes* refer? To uncertainty who is called *vous* in line 9? To the sun or to love or to the village? Perhaps Apollinaire addresses the Grand Master once more, describing his spiritual descendants or the Templars themselves—gallant, in their fine or wretched clothes. In any case, those who build the poet's pyre are those who set him an example of courage by their death.

CLAIR DE LUNE, page 180

First published in *La Grande France*, no. 19 (September, 1901), with the title "Lunaire."

This little poem, published in *La Grande France* with two other early efforts that Apollinaire did not choose to put in *Alcools*, marked the poet's first appearance in print. A superficial parody of Symbolist images (and of qualities which Apollinaire's verse possessed at that time), it has little excuse for being included in *Alcools*. The style mixes the colloquial and the precious in such a way that one cancels the other out, instead of the two creating an ironic contrast. The comparisons between moonlight and honey, stars and bees, towns and gluttons are drawn out and repetitious without, I think, being funny.

Line 5. The translation reverses the order of this, and the following, line. A play on words is contained in the expression *tout doux*, "gently," literally "all sweet."

Line 7. Another play on *doux* occurs in the phrase "la très douce aventure" which is given an additional meaning by its literary overtones. Lines 7-10 were printed in *La Grande France* as a second strophe. The spacing and the punctuation of that version indicate beyond any doubt that *or caché* means "now hidden" and not "hidden gold."

Line 10. The play on words—*rose des vents*, "compass," literally "rose of the winds"—which I have indicated by adding the word "compass," occurs also in "Merlin." There was an eleventh line, printed as a stanza by itself, in *La Grande France*. In contrast to the rest of the poem, it contains that poetic virtue of surprise which Apollinaire was to exploit later:

O rose à peine rose en des livres savants. . . .

1909, page 182

First published in *Alcools*.

Time is personified also in "L'Émigrant de Landor Road" and "Les Fiançailles." Michel Décaudin finds in "1909" echoes of Baudelaire's "Recueillement" and of earlier poems of Apollinaire, an *inédit* and a few verses of "L'Anguille" ([1], pp. 855, 356). The tone of voice in this free-verse poem reminds me of an American poet who was writing at the same time—Vachel Lindsay.

The poet turns from 1909, a beautiful and well-dressed lady, to evoke the women of the people whom he likens, in a Futuristic comparison, to the race of machines. Michel Décaudin notes that the final passage is taken from a manuscript version of "Vendémiaire," and he concludes that "1909" is a definition of poetic inspiration.

A LA SANTÉ, page 186

First published in *Alcools*, followed by the date *Septembre 1911*.

The title contains a pun on *santé*, "health" (*à votre santé*, "here's to you") and *Santé* the name of a prison where Apollinaire was held from September 7 to 11, 1911, in connection with the disappearance of "La Gioconda" from the Louvre on August 21. When the picture was stolen (by an Italian, it later turned out), a former secretary of Apollinaire's, Géry Pieret, who had stolen several statuettes from the museum, took one of them to the *Paris-Journal*, hoping to make a little money. The paper gave the affair great publicity. Apollinaire and Picasso became worried because Picasso had in his studio two of the stolen statuettes; they took the two pieces of sculpture to the *Paris-Journal* to be returned anonymously. But Apollinaire's identity became known, and he was accused of concealing the thief and abetting the crime. The police had decided Pieret was a member of an international gang intent on robbing France of her art treasures. In a few days Apollinaire was liberated, and thanks to the efforts of his friends, he was soon legally exonerated. But the memory remained painful (see "Zone," ll. 113-114). His distress makes these six poems with their echoes of Verlaine and Villon among his most moving.

The translations do not keep the musical quality of the poems, created, not only by varied rhyme and meter, but also by intense use of assonance. In Part III, line 8, "On y fait couler la fontaine" means

literally "They turn on the running water." The last line of Part VI contains a pun: *clarté* means both physical "light" and mental "clarity."

AUTOMNE MALADE, page 192

First published in *Alcools*.

There is manuscript evidence that this free-verse poem with occasional rhyme may have been written in Munich, in the spring of 1902. It was certainly conceived as part of the Rhenish group: in the manuscript "La vie / S'écoule" is written in over "Le Rhin / Qui coule."

The poet links a mood to a season and turns a nineteenth-century theme, the death of the year, into a humorous, if nostalgic, evocation of the Rhineland. Are the nixies and dwarves, who have never loved, a comment on Annie? Both nixies and a version of the final lines occur in another *rhénane*, "Un Soir d'été ([1], p. 529), more obvious in its treatment of emotion.

HÔTELS, page 194

First published in *Alcools*.

For Professor Breunig, the first two stanzas evoke the pension at Stavelot, which Apollinaire and his brother left without paying their bill, and the rest of the poem, a Paris hotel on the Rue de Constantin where they lived subsequently. But according to Michel Décaudin, the poem is about hotels or furnished apartments, not about a pension, thus not about Stavelot at all. The translation does not attempt to imitate the clever rhymes or the beat of the four-syllable lines.

Lines 19-20. "Savons la langue / Comme à Babel," "we know language as they did at Babel," that is, we each speak a different language.

CORS DE CHASSE, page 196

First published in *Les Soirées de Paris*, no. 8 (September, 1912), with "Le Voyageur" and "Fanny" ("Annie").

As in "Marie," the melancholy memory of an old love surfaces momentarily. Lines 6-8 (ll. 6 and 7 appear in a manuscript version of "La Chanson du Mal-Aimé") suggest that Apollinaire has not forgotten Annie. Michel Décaudin observes that lines 9 and 10 express a theme

common also to "Le Pont Mirabeau" and "Marie": time goes by in spite of man's sense of permanence. The poem commemorates the end of the poet's affair with Marie Laurencin, as do "Le Pont Mirabeau," "Marie," and, indirectly, "Zone" ([3], p. 70).

These octosyllables, bound by a recurring nasal rhyme, present the images of stage and of masked actors (compare "Le Larron"). Our love, says the poet, was not dependent on chance or on magic, it was a tragedy, fated from the start, like the tragedy of De Quincey who fell in love with a streetwalker he could never find again. Her memory was a poison as sweet and chaste as the opium he was addicted to. To live is to walk across the stage; to remember is to look back. Memories are like hunting horns, offstage, that call to you, and their echoing and repeated notes suggest the past, and especially memories, in poems of Vigny, Baudelaire, Laforgue. The literary image of the horn, the persona of De Quincey, the references to ancient tragedy make of this poem based on personal experience a symbolic drama in miniature.

VENDÉMIAIRE, page 198

First published in *Les Soirées de Paris*, no. 10 (November, 1912).

"Vendémiaire" was published the month before "Zone" and in the same review, but may have been composed two or three years before. The form, loosely rhyming free verse, is comparable to that of "Zone." The title contains the name of the first month in the republican calendar, September 22 to October 21. In Professor Breunig's opinion, the theme and techniques of the poem suggest 1912 as the date of composition. According to Michel Décaudin, the title, the use of unanimist ideas, and various internal references indicate that the poem was written in 1909 or 1910.

The central image is that of the vintage. At first, the stars that predict the future are harvested by the poet who will become famous. Then, in the main sections of the poem, those cities of Europe that have played a role in French history (or that Apollinaire is fond of) are harvested by the city of Paris. Finally, the poet, who sees himself as the gullet of Paris, harvests not only Europe but the universe and thus becomes a gigantic figure, fusing microcosm with macrocosm.

The wine offered by the cities has religious connotations. Brittany, Lyons, Provence offer their Christian martyrdoms and myths, and Rome, its "two-thousand-year-old wine." The cities of the North,

Sicily, Coblenz speak in mythical and religious terms. The image of wine links the Christian religion to ancient cults celebrating the death and revival of vegetation and of love. The fusion of wine with blood recalls Attis and particularly Adonis who bleeds to death in autumn (or spring, or summer) and soaks with his blood the soil from which living things will grow. On the historical level, the poet evokes European wars of religion and the remission of sins that is granted the true believer through the shedding of blood. The kings that die and will be reborn are linked with Christ, as He is with more ancient divine victims. All acts of sacrifice and of libation become one, fused in the image of the poet who quaffs the wine, or blood, of the universe and is thus renewed. In "Le Brasier" and "Les Fiançailles," instead of being the one who accepts the sacrifice, he becomes the divine victim.

Lines 1-4. The poet speaks for his epoch and for his own poetry to those who will live after him. The death of kings may refer to the assassinations of King Carlos of Portugal and of King Humbert, and to the attempt against the life of the Prince of Wales at Brussels ([14], p. 224). As in "Crépuscule" and "La Chanson du Mal-Aimé," Apollinaire plays on the meaning of *trismégiste*, literally "three times great." In the other two poems, "great" is contrasted with "dwarf." In "Vendémiaire," it is linked with "courageous" (in the face of death) and so suggests greatness on a figurative level: the kings undergo a kind of apotheosis. It suggests also that their shadows swell, now that they are shades.

Lines 24-30. Recurring through the poem, and most striking in this passage, is the fusion of humans with landscape. Such imagery suggests the paintings of Dali or Tchelitchew's "Cache cache."

Lines 31-38. Rennes and the cities of Brittany offer Paris an ethic, a systematic "mystery," that comprehends both the code of courtly love and the quest of the Graal. "Double raison" has two meanings: the twofold allegiance to woman and to a religious symbol, and a reason more precious than *la raison*. The two words, *raison*, "reason," and *raisin*, "grape," are used almost interchangeably to describe the wine offered to Paris. In these lines *raison* suggests *raisin*; in Sicily's song (ll. 68, 75), the process is reversed.

Lines 40-44. The industrial cities of the North speak jokingly. "Les métalliques saints de nos saintes usines" (l. 42) plays on the word *saint* which, as an adjective, can mean at once "blessed" and "damned." (Compare "Les Fiançailles," ll. 86 and 87.) The Priapean image of

Ixion is ambiguous. Apollinaire may think of him in Hades, revolving forever on his flaming (and smoking) wheel. Or, more likely, the verse refers to Nephele, a cloud, by whom Ixion became father to the Centaurs. Both here and later (ll. 44, 73), Ixion, who is described as the one who makes things, is a persona of the poet.

Lines 50-53. Apollinaire thinks of the great pilgrimage church at Lyons, Notre Dame of Fourvière, of Lyons' silk industry, and of the city's location at the juncture of the Saône and the Rhone.

Lines 54-58. These lines suggest not only the sacrificial aspect of the mass but (religious) wars and, lastly, executions. The Protestants seized Lyons in 1562. Their acts of violence in the town were bloodily avenged after the St. Bartholomew massacre. Apollinaire thinks perhaps of the seeming paradox that one of the chief fortresses of France should have been repeatedly a center of religious activity and of religious quarrels (in the thirteenth century, two ecclesiastical councils met at Lyons; in the fourteenth, two popes were crowned there). However, he probably thinks too of the nonreligious killings and scenes of anarchy that have occurred in that city. Cinq Mars and his friend De Thou were executed in Lyons in 1642. There was a massacre of Royalists and Girondists in 1793 and of Terrorists after Robespierre's death (they were drowned in the Rhone). All through the nineteenth century, Lyons was the scene of violent industrial or political disturbances, and at the end of the century, witnessed the assassination of France's President Carnot.

Lines 60-66. The cities of Provence invoke their past. "Noble Paris seule raison" brings to mind the theological Sorbonne of medieval Paris and the absolute supremacy of the North over the South after the suppression of the Albigenses. The images of the Host, of the noble loves and their orphan dance, create, as do the final lines of the song of the Breton cities, a fusion between courtly love and a religious ideal.

Lines 68-76. The Sicilian cities offer to Paris their dead, from battles of Phoenicians, Greeks, Carthaginians, Romans, Saracens, Germans, and in particular, it may be, from the Norman kingdom and from those French armies of Charles d'Anjou that died during the Sicilian Vespers. I have not, in lines 68 and 75, preserved the image of grapes which in the original provides a play on words (*raisin /raison*) and, in line 75, a humorous association: "O grapes and those eyes dull and in family groups."

Line 73. *Oblique créateur* means "indirectly a creator." The refer-

ence is to Ixion's romance with a cloud (whom he mistook for Hera) and to her subsequent progeny which, here, are baby clouds and not Centaurs. *Oblique* also describes the hero in Hades, bent upon his smoking wheel, "creator set at an oblique angle." And, since *oblique* can mean "underhanded" or "crooked," the line evokes Ixion's murder of his father-in-law (in order to save money) by luring him onto a bed of burning coals.

Lines 77-80. Apollinaire places the sirens on Scylla's reef in the Straits of Messina. As in "Zone," he thinks of them as winged. The sirens represent a lost, legendary past and also, as in "Lul de Faltenin," sensuality. The passage may contain the mal-aimé's unflattering conclusion about women, especially in view of lines 85-91, which link the images of swimmers, drowned bodies and stars to evoke desire in much the same manner as does a recurrent stanza (13, 37, 49) in "La Chanson du Mal-Aimé."

Lines 92-93. The poet probably refers to an earthquake that shook Sicily at Christmas in 1908 ([14], p. 224). Night is "covered with open eyes," like the cowherd Argos or like a peacock. The earthquake is the hydra, a poisonous, many-headed snake who lives in fresh water and whose whistling or hissing cries may here represent the noise of steaming or turbulent waters during the quake.

Lines 95-97. Not surprisingly, one of the cities that serenades Paris and poet is Apollinaire's birthplace. A manuscript version reads: "Moi qui t'adore ô Rome ô Rome où je suis né." Rome seems to condemn the poet's evocation of sirens and of desire. The poet may, in these lines as in "Le Brasier," reject his former loves and former ideas about poetry.

Line 98. The worship of the cross as a religious symbol is often linked to some form of nature worship. The cross that puts forth new branches suggests the image, in "Salomé," of John the Baptist's staff that breaks into flower. It suggests, too, Tannhäuser's pilgrimage to Rome, where the Pope tells him "Your sins will never be forgiven until my staff blooms again." After the hero's departure, the papal staff (which probably, like a crosier, contained a cross in the handle) burgeons out.

Line 99. The fleur-de-lis at the Vatican might refer either to Charles d'Anjou's dozen years as senator in Rome, or to the removal of the popes to Avignon.

Lines 101-103. These lines comment on how the Church has fallen

away from primitive Christianity. They indicate also an association between Christian rites and those of non-Christian gods of vegetation. For another occurrence of the phrase *liberté végétale*, see "Poème lu au mariage d'André Salmon," line 5.

Lines 113 and 114. The image in these lines, and in the entire passage about Coblenz, may have been suggested to the poet, not only by the beautiful site of the city, but by its name. Coblenz is situated on the left bank of the Rhine at its confluence with the Moselle. Accordingly, the ancient city was named *Confluentes*, of which Coblenz is a corruption.

Lines 119-125. The love that Coblenz bears Paris brings to mind Paris' love for the cities on the left bank of the Rhine. After the French Revolution, Coblenz was one of the principal meeting places for French émigrés. In 1794 it was taken by the Revolutionary army and remained under French control, as capital of the Rhine and Moselle *départment*, until 1814. In 1822 it became the capital of the Prussian Rhine province. The warlike imagery describing both Coblenz and Paris recalls France's military past and heralds Germany's future. Coblenz is a center of the Moselle and Rhine wine trade, and a transit center for Rhenish railroads and navigation. As such it has suffered terribly in wars. It is also, as the poet suggests (ll. 126-135), a meeting place where discords may be resolved.

Lines 140-160. The poet describes the universal wine in unanimist terms. It consists of all living things (l. 141), of the past (l. 146) and the future (l. 142), of man's conquest over death by faith (l. 143), of his conquest over nature by iron and fire (ll. 144-145). (I did not attempt to preserve the allied sounds in *fer, feu, fier, éclairs*.) Human thought, in its various forms, flavors the wine (ll. 146-150), as do the human games of war (ll. 151 and 152), of love (ll. 152 and 153) and of poetry (ll. 151 and 154); "les bons vers immortels" (l. 151) that will whiten our bones refer at once to *vers*, "verse," and *vers*, "worms." Apollinaire's proclaimed inability to express his vision (ll. 155 and 156) is comparable to passages in "Les Fiançailles" (and to Dante's profession of speechlessness whenever he wants particularly to impress the reader). Lines 154-156 also evoke a passage in "La Jolie Rousse" which concludes *Calligrammes*, as "Vendémiaire" does *Alcools*:

Nous voulons vous donner de vastes et d'étranges domaines
Où le mystère en fleurs s'offre à qui veut le cueillir

Il y a là des feux nouveaux des coulers jamais vues
Milles phantasmes impondérables
Auxquels il faut donner de la réalité

(*Œuvres*, p. 313)

Lines 161-174. The poet exits at sunrise, as he does in "Zone." But how different his mood. He is drunk on a vision. The universal wine becomes increasingly universal: it is composed now of action and of time (l. 161), expressions of desire (l. 162), definitions of being (l. 163). The poet is the link between worlds, the magician who gives a name and a sense to things, the interpreter of the universe, the inspired prophet who will never feel a hangover.

Bibliography

1. APOLLINAIRE, GUILLAUME. *Œuvres poétiques*, Préface par André Billy, text établi et annoté par Marcel Adéma et Michel Décaudin. Bibliothèque de la Pléiade. Paris: Gallimard, 1959.
2. ———. *L'Hérésiarque et Cie.* Paris: Stock, 1910.
3. ———. *Tendre comme le souvenir.* 9th ed. Paris: Gallimard, 1952.
4. ———. *Le Poète assassiné.* Paris: Club du meilleur livre, 1959.

5. ADÉMA, MARCEL. *Guillaume Apollinaire, le mal-aimé.* Paris: Plon, 1952.
6. BATES, SCOTT. "Sur 'Lul de Faltenin,' " *Le Flâneur des Deux Rives* (June, 1955).
7. BREUNIG, LEROY C. "Apollinaire and Annie Playden," *Mercure de France* (April 1, 1952).
8. ———. "Le Roman du Mal-Aimé," *La Table Ronde*, no. 57 (September, 1952).
9. ———. "The Chronology of Apollinaire's *Alcools*," *PMLA* (December, 1952).
10. ———. "La Synagogue," *Le Flâneur des Deux Rives*, no. 4 (December, 1954).
11. ———. "Le Manuscrit de 'Lul de Faltenin,' " *La Revue des Sciences humaines* (October–December, 1956).
12. ———. "Apollinaire et le Cubisme," *La Revue des Lettres modernes* (Autumn, 1962).
13. CHAMPIGNY, ROBERT. "Analyse de 'Rhénane d'Automne,' " *French Review* (December, 1959).
14. DÉCAUDIN, MICHEL. *Le Dossier d'Alcools.* Geneva: Droz, 1960.
15. ———. "Complements à un Dossier," *La Revue des Lettres modernes* (Autumn, 1962).
16. ———. "Carnet critique," *La Revue des Lettres modernes* (Autumn, 1963).

17. DURRY, MARIE-JEANNE. "Apollinaire et le ver Zamir," *La Table Ronde* (April, 1955).

18. ———. *Guillaume Apollinaire: Alcools*. Tome I. Paris: Société d'édition d'enseignement supérieur, 1956.

19. ———. " 'Cors de Chasse,' " *La Revue des Sciences humaines* (October–December, 1957).

20. ———. "Sur 'la Tzigane,' " *La Revue des Lettres modernes* (Autumn, 1963).

21. GUIRAUD, PIERRE. *Index du Vocabulaire du Symbolisme* Vol. I: Index des mots d'*Alcools* du Guillaume Apollinaire. Tome I Paris: Klincksieck, 1953.

22. LAWALL, SALLY NESBITT. "Apollinaire's 'La Maison des Morts,' " *Romanic Review* (April, 1961).

23. LAWLER, JAMES. "Les Sept Épées," *Le Flâneur des Deux Rives* (September, 1954).

24. LÉAUTAUD, PAUL. "La Chanson du Mal-Aimé," *Le Flâneur des Deux Rives* (March, 1954).

25. LOUIS, RENÉ. "Lul de Faltenin," *Le Flâneur des Deux Rives* (June, 1954).

26. ———. "Encore 'Lul de Faltenin,' " *Le Flâneur des Deux Rives* (September, 1954).

27. MARSHALL, T. E. "Composition and Structure of Guillaume Apollinaire's 'Alcools.' " Unpublished Ph.D. dissertation, University of California, Berkeley, 1959.

28. MOULIN, JEANINE. *Guillaume Apollinaire, Textes Inédits*. Geneva: Droz, 1952.

29. ORECCHIONI, PIERRE. "Le Thème du Rhin dans l'Inspiration de Guillaume Apollinaire," *La Revue des Lettres modernes* (1956).

30. PIA, PASCAL. *Apollinaire par lui-même*. Paris: Editions du Seuil, 1960.

31. ———. "A propos de *Zone*," *La Revue des Lettres modernes* (Autumn, 1963).

32. PIRON, MAURICE. "Sur quelques passages de 'la Chanson du Mal-Aimé,' " *La Revue des Lettres modernes* (Autumn, 1963).

33. ROUVEYRE, ANDRÉ. *Apollinaire*. Paris: Gallimard, 1945.

34. ———. *Amour et poésie d'Apollinaire*. Paris: Editions du Seuil, 1955.

35. SALMON, ANDRÉ. *Souvenirs sans fin*, I and II. Paris: Gallimard, 1955-1956.

36. SCHMITS, GEORGES. "Quelques strophes du 'Mal-Aimé,'" Mercure de France (November, 1959).

37. SHATTUCK, ROGER. *Guillaume Apollinaire, Selected Writings*. New York: New Directions, 1950.

38. SOUPAULT, PHILIPPE. *Guillaume Apollinaire ou les Reflets de l'Incendie*. Marseille: Les Cahiers du Sud, 1927.

39. STEEGMULLER, FRANCIS. *Apollinaire, Poet among the Painters*. New York: Farrar, Strauss, 1963.

40. WOLF, E. R. "Apollinaire en Rhénanie et les 'Rhénanes' d' 'Alcools,'" *Mercure de France* (August 1, 1933).

41. ———. "Le Séjour d'Apollinaire en Rhénanie," *Mercure de France* (June 15, 1938).